The Reign of James VI and I

Each volume in the 'Problems in Focus' series is designed to make available to students important new work on key historical problems and periods that they encounter in their courses. Every volume is devoted to a central topic or theme, and the most important aspects of this are dealt with by specially commissioned essays from authorities in the relevant fields. The editorial Introduction reviews the problem or period as a whole, and each essay provides an assessment of the particular aspect, pointing out the areas of development and controversy, and indicating where conclusions can be drawn or where further work is necessary. An annotated bibliography serves as a guide to further reading.

PROBLEMS IN FOCUS SERIES

FURTHER TITLES ARE IN PREPARATION

The Reign of James VI and I

EDITED BY
ALAN G. R. SMITH

First edition 1973
Reprinted 1977, 1979, 1981

Published by
THE MACMILLAN PRESS LTD
London and Basingstoke
Associated companies in Delhi Dublin
Hong Kong Johannesburg Lagos Melbourne
New York Singapore and Tokyo

ISBN 0 333 12162 7

Printed in Hong Kong

Contents

Preface

THERE are obvious omissions in this book of essays on the reign of
James VI and I, most notably, perhaps, articles on the Jacobean Church
of England, on the English economy as a whole, and on foreign policy.
It was originally hoped to secure contributions on each of these subjects,
but it proved impossible to do so within a reasonable time limit. I have
tried to compensate to some extent for the lacunae in my introduction.
A valuable outline of religious policy in James I's reign in England is
given by Dr Nicholas Tyacke in his chapter 'Puritanism, Arminianism
and Counter-Revolution' in Conrad Russell (ed.), *The Origins of the
English Civil War* (1973).

The spelling and punctuation of quotations have been modernised,
though this was done with reluctance in the Scottish chapters, where the
loss of the flavour of the original is much regretted. Place of publication is given for all books cited in the Bibliography. In the References
and Notes the place of publication is London unless otherwise stated.
(This does not apply to periodicals and works issued by historical clubs
and societies, where the place of publication is never given.)

I would like to thank my contributors for their co-operation; it was a
pleasure to work with them. We all hope that our volume will prove
useful to students of history who are interested in the reign of the
monarch who united the Crowns of Scotland and England. Finally I
owe a personal debt to Miss Patricia Ferguson, who typed both the
Introduction and chapter 9 in her usual immaculate way.

University of Glasgow   A.G.R.S.

Introduction

ALAN G. R. SMITH

JAMES VI, one of the most successful of all the rulers of Scotland, was at least a relative failure as James I of England. To ask why is to pose the most obvious general problem of the reign. By the time of his accession to the English throne in 1603 James had already made substantial progress in asserting his authority in Scotland in both the ecclesiastical and secular spheres. As the first two chapters of this book show, he had done so largely by skilful diplomacy. The success of his church policy will be familiar to those who have already read the other works of Professor Donaldson, but Mrs Brown breaks new ground in her discussion of his relations with the nobility, which she sees as the dominant secular issue of the reign in Scotland. The traditional picture of James struggling to suppress the intolerable ambitions and activities of an aristocracy which was one of the most lawless and difficult in Europe[1] is, she argues, a travesty of the truth. James indeed owed his success to cooperation with the magnates; 'he was effective precisely because he had not attempted new and autocratic policies towards his nobility, because he had not tried to undermine their political position' (see below, page 36), and he continued this policy with general success after 1603.

Indeed the years after 1603 saw the creation of what can be regarded as a 'new monarchy'[2] in Scotland. James succeeded in strengthening the authority of the Scottish bishops and in making some changes in the worship of the Kirk which were designed to bring it closer to English practice. At the same time he was able to assert his authority in secular affairs to an extent without previous parallel in Scottish history. 'Thus I must say for Scotland,' he boasted to his English Parliament in 1607, '... here I sit and govern it with my pen: I write and it is done: and by a clerk of the Council I govern Scotland now, which others could not do by the sword.'[3] James was never a man to underestimate his own achievements and on this occasion he certainly exaggerated the extent of his authority—he had for example only limited success in bringing the Highlands under his control—but it was pardonable hyperbole. Despite some decline in the sureness of his touch in both Church and State in

For Notes to the Introduction, see pp. 226–8.

the last years of his life, his general success in Scotland is not seriously in question. His own skill and the advantages which his accession to the English throne in 1603 gave him in his dealings with Scotland go far in explaining the extent of that success, but it is also worth noting that the period 1600–1620, arguably the high-water mark of his Scottish reign, was also a time of generally good harvests in Scotland.[4] Clearly a relatively stable and satisfactory food supply must have been of considerable help to James in his efforts to secure that 'delectable time of peace' which, contemporaries assured him, marked his 'happy reign and most excellent government' in Scotland.[5]

Why was James less successful in England? It can be argued that there was a general deterioration in the king's character and abilities during his later years, and that whereas this came at a time when his worst problems in Scotland were over, it coincided with the crisis of his reign—the years after 1618—in England. Again it can be suggested that not only were the problems which he faced in England considerable but also that some of them posed the kind of difficulties for which his experiences in Scotland had not really prepared him. Finally, while admitting that he certainly *was* less succesful in England, it can be argued that some of his failures there have been exaggerated or misunderstood.

James's personality was an extraordinary combination of strengths and weaknesses. He had some admirable traits. He was warm-hearted, affectionate and generous, and had a genuine love of peace and dislike of violence which can be seen not only in his foreign policy but also in his determined efforts to put a stop to duelling in England.[6] He had considerable intellectual abilities and he could be shrewd in his judgement of men and events, witness his verdict on William Laud and his perceptive estimate of the implications of the conduct of the House of Commons in 1621. (See below, pages 12, 175–6.) In some ways he was in advance of his times. His desire for a 'perfect union' between England and Scotland after his accession to the English throne in 1603 is a striking example of this, and he was extremely sceptical about the traditional practice of touching for the 'king's evil' by which English monarchs attempted to cure those of their subjects who suffered from scrofula by laying their hands upon the afflicted parts. He was eventually persuaded to conform to the practice of his predecessors, but only took part in what he clearly regarded as a superstitious ceremony with extreme reluctance. A foreign observer in 1613 noted that the whole business was 'very distasteful' to the king.[7] Again his denunciation of smoking, published in 1604 in his *Counterblast to Tobacco*, would certainly win the approbation of modern physicians. James's scepticism about witchcraft, which, as Dr Larner emphasises in chapter 4 of this book, developed during his later years, also put him in advance of much contemporary opinion.

It is unfortunate that the good traits in the king's character were matched by serious defects. James was probably disappointed in his family life. His queen, Anne of Denmark, whom he married in 1589, was a stupid woman, clearly not a suitable bride for a man of James's intellectual tastes. When his initial ardour for her cooled there was little to hold them together and in the later years of the queen's life they were virtually estranged. He dearly loved his daughter Elizabeth, but she left his side in 1613 when she married the Elector Palatine. His elder son Henry died in 1612, and his younger son Charles was too shy and withdrawn to respond to his father's need for affection. In this situation James fell under the domination of male favourites, especially Robert Carr, created earl of Somerset, and George Villiers, who was eventually made duke of Buckingham. James showed the warmth of his feelings for them by showering them with money and grants of office. This was a commentary both on the generosity of his nature and on the way that generosity could be perverted. The largesse which he bestowed upon them helped to ruin his finances, create trouble with his Parliaments and spread corruption at Court.

There is no agreement among scholars about the precise nature of James's relationships with Somerset and Buckingham. It is generally agreed that the king had homosexual tendencies, but there are differences of opinion as to whether or not he put his inclinations into practice. Judgements in a matter where the evidence admits of no certain conclusion are likely to reflect historians' overall assessments of the king. Professor Willson, who paints a generally unfavourable picture of James, accepts the view that when he 'pawed his favourites so fondly in public, he was not likely to restrain himself in private', whereas Professor Donaldson, who sees him in a much more sympathetic light, concludes that 'the mere fact that the king made so much of his favourites in public suggests that nothing to be ashamed of took place in private.'[8] Whatever the final verdict on this matter, there can be no doubt that James's virtually complete dependence on Buckingham by the 1620s had a most unfortunate effect upon his personality, colouring and limiting his judgement of anybody who opposed the favourite's will.

The king's hatred of violence also reflected some unfortunate aspects of his personality. It was to some extent an aspect of his personal timidity, which unfriendly critics called cowardice, and it was obvious that he hated to appear among crowds of his subjects, as Queen Elizabeth had delighted to do. In 1607 the Venetian ambassador noted that, as a result, he was 'despised and almost hated' by the common people.[9] He was much more at home among scholars and divines, but his love of theological debate was vitiated by a desire to parade his learning. The clergymen whom he liked to gather around him at dinner were there to admire his displays of erudition rather than to act as partners in a genuine discussion. In his written works however James did not hesitate to appropriate the ideas of these divines and the labours of other literary assistants to an extent which was incompatible with even the comparatively lax scholarly standards of the seventeenth century. His books certainly contained a good deal less of his own work than he wished the world to believe and his accounts of how they were produced have been described—fairly enough—as 'utterly untrustworthy'.[10] His own ideas, as we have seen, were sometimes ahead of his time, but his stress on 'divine right' which has attracted so much attention in textbooks, was essentially commonplace. There was a general belief at this time in the divine right of all duly constituted authority, and it is difficult to see the doctrine of divine right as a cause of the distrust which developed between the Crown and the House of Commons in James's reign—members believed in it just as much as the king himself.[11]

James's determination to leave to others the donkey work involved in his writings illustrates one of the most serious weaknesses in his character: laziness. He quickly became bored with administrative details, which he left to subordinates while he himself went off hunting. In the years between 1603 and 1612 his deficiencies in administration were concealed to some extent by the labours of Robert Cecil, earl of Salisbury, but after the latter's death they became glaringly obvious. Moreover James's incurable self-conceit fed on the initial warmth of his reception in England. 'Shall it ever be blotted out of my mind,' he stated gleefully in 1604, 'how at my first entry into this kingdom, the people of all sorts rid and ran, nay rather flew to meet me; their eyes flaming nothing but sparkles of affection, their mouths and tongues uttering nothing but sounds of joy, their hands, feet and all the rest of their members in their gestures discovering a passionate longing and earnestness to meet and embrace their new sovereign.'[12] He was oblivious to the fact that even before he spoke these words the initial euphoria had subsided; already in 1604 he was regarded with suspicion by many of his new subjects. In later years the obsequiousness of English courtiers shielded him from much of the harsh reality of his unpopularity, but by the end of his reign James certainly knew that many members of the House of Commons mistrusted him. He put this down to the malice and stupidity of individual M.P.s; it never entered his head that he himself might in any way be to blame.

With James's conceit went unprepossessing manners and an undignified appearance, which made a very bad impression on people who had been used to the charm and majesty of Queen Elizabeth. One modern authority concluded that, if a single epithet had to be selected to characterise James, it might well be 'unkingly'.[13] Many contemporaries would have agreed, but that is certainly a harsh and partial verdict. A more balanced assessment was written in the eighteenth century by David Hume.

> Many virtues . . . it must be owned, he was possessed of, but no one of them pure, or free from the contagion of the neighbouring vices. His generosity bordered on profusion, his learning on pedantry, his pacific disposition on pusillanimity, his wisdom on cunning, his friendship on light fancy and boyish fondness. . . . His capacity was considerable, but fitter to discourse on general maxims than to conduct any intricate business. . . . Awkward in his person and ungainly in his manners, he was ill qualified to command respect; partial and undiscerning in his affections, he was little fitted to acquire general love.[14]

It does seem clear that James's character deteriorated and that his abilities declined during the later years of his reign in England. All serious students of the period, whatever their general verdict on the king, accept this, but it is difficult to date the decline precisely and there is no agreement as to its extent. Professor Willson sees the deterioration really gathering pace after 1616, and as affecting 'not only . . . his physical powers but also . . . his strength of will and . . . character. . . . Slowly the British Solomon sank into physical decay and into premature senility.' The date suggested is probably as good as any—the decline certainly became obvious during the second decade of James's rule in England—but Willson may exaggerate the extent of the king's deterioration. His picture of James in the 1620s, 'a broken, debauched and repulsive old man . . . in his dotage', is something of a caricature.[15] Recent work on the Parliaments of 1621 and 1624 for example[16] has presented the king in a much more favourable light, and it is probably best to accept a more moderate view of his decline, perhaps that of Pro-

fessor Donaldson, who sees him in the 1620s as 'past his prime . . .
[with] vigour of mind and body ebbing away'.[17]

In any event a decline certainly took place and although there has
not yet been any fully satisfactory account of its causes, recent discussion
of James's medical history may provide important clues. There is no
doubt that for much of his life the king suffered from a painful illness.
Our information about this comes from extensive notes left by his doc-
tor, Sir Theodore de Mayerne, one of the outstanding physicians of the
day, and includes a comprehensive medical profile, written two years
before James's death. It reveals that he had long suffered from recurrent
attacks of abdominal colic accompanied by nausea, fast and sometimes
irregular pulse, and weakness and spasms of his limbs. He suffered fits
of unconsciousness and his urine turned red, 'like Alicante wine'. He
was often very seriously ill during these attacks, which became more
severe and frequent after 1610. 'In 1619,' Mayerne records, 'the attack
was accompanied by arthritic and nephritic pains, he lost consciousness,
breathing was laboured, great fearfulness and dejection, intermittent
pulse, and his life was in danger for eight days. It was the most dangerous illness the King ever had. In 1623 an attack lasted only two or three
days, but was very severe. It was followed by arthritis and he could
not walk for months.' Mayerne also kept daily notes on James's ill-
nesses which describe the 'ferocity' of the pain which the king often
suffered and how, at the height of an attack, he might suddenly become
delirious.

It has recently been suggested that James's illness may have been
porphyria, a rare metabolic disorder which is characterised by a dis-
coloration of the urine, which turns purplish or dark red. It causes attacks of varying degrees of severity and is notable for the damage which
it can cause to the nervous system, with a consequent weakening of the
patient's physical and mental capacities.[18] Whether James did suffer
from porphyria or from some other illness—and medical experts are
still divided on the matter—the severity of his attacks could explain
much of the decline in his abilities during the last decade or so of his
life. It was certainly most unfortunate for James and for the country
that the attacks were at their height during the period after 1618, the
most difficult time of his reign in England. These years, following the
outbreak of the Thirty Years War in Germany, saw the collapse of his
foreign policy, founded upon peace and friendship with Spain, and also
parliamentary and economic crises at home. The ailing king was not
able to deal adequately with these serious problems, though it should be

said that his conduct of affairs may not have been quite as incompetent as has sometimes been suggested. (See below, pages 160, 240 note 2.) [19]

Another line of argument which may help to explain James's failures in England is to point out that the difficulties which faced him in his new kingdom in 1603 were serious and that some of them were not the kind of problems which could be adequately dealt with on the basis of his Scottish experiences. In his anxiety to secure his peaceful accession to the English throne he had, during the last years of his rule in Scotland, set out to woo both the English Catholics and the Puritans. As a result both expected concessions from him in 1603, although any significant efforts to ease the lot of the Catholics would be opposed by the Puritans and the English bishops. The bishops were also extremely apprehensive of a possible agreement with the Puritans. It was a situation in which even the most skilful monarch might offend powerful sections of religious opinion. In English secular politics the 1590s had witnessed the growth of corruption in court circles. One of the main reasons for this had been the cost of the war with Spain which had caused the never very generous Elizabeth to limit even more than usual her grants to ministers and courtiers. There was inevitably a great struggle for such favours as remained, with members of the rival Essex and Cecil factions resorting, on occasion, to outright bribery to gain their ends. James therefore inherited a tradition of growing political corruption, and his open-handed efforts to satisfy the desire of his new subjects and his Scottish favourites for titles and profits led to financial difficulties for the Crown, to a further growth of corruption and to trouble with his Parliaments.

It was clear for other reasons too that James could expect difficulties in his dealings with Parliament. Elizabeth had had serious trouble in the monopolies debate of 1601, and when James met his first Parliament in 1604 a powerful section of opinion in the Commons informed him that members had only put up with some of the queen's actions because of her age and because they expected a better deal from him. These were ominous words: increasingly well-educated and articulate M.P.s were clearly determined to have their own way with a new sovereign who was also a foreigner.

In the field of foreign affairs James initially had less difficulties. There was widespread support for his determination to bring the expensive and indecisive Spanish war, which had begun in 1585, to an end. When that had been done in 1604 however the king had to make difficult decisions about the whole future course of English policy in a Europe in which dynastic and religious rivalries were still serious.

Much of James's experience in Scotland hindered rather than helped in the solution of these problems. His ecclesiastical policies in England have recently undergone important reassessments (see pages 10–13 below), and it is difficult at this moment to be sure whether his conflicts with Scottish Presbyterianism helped or hindered him in his dealings with the English Puritans. There can be little doubt however that the long years which he spent in poverty-stricken Scotland gave him delusions about the wealth of England, or at least about his ability to exploit that wealth for his own purposes: as we have seen, his reckless generosity to favourites, courtiers and officials soon excited adverse comments in the House of Commons. James, used to a Scottish Parliament which was almost wholly under the control of the Crown, took these in ill part. In his early years in England he clearly had difficulty in grasping just how sophisticated the English Parliament was, and this was doubly unfortunate at a time when the House of Commons was determined to extend its influence in the state. English M.P.s moreover, while they might oppose the king's policies in ways which baffled and infuriated James, always treated him with the greatest formal respect. He found this and the obsequiousness of English courtiers a welcome change after the outspoken bluntness of many of his Scottish nobles, but the combination of deference and determined opposition was not one to which he had been accustomed in Scotland, and it took him some time to get used to it.

The great objective of James's policy in Scotland was to secure the English throne, and he thought that the best way of doing so was to try and stay on good terms with all foreign powers. He put the success of this policy down to his own skill, although the main reason was that Scotland was a poor and unimportant kingdom, well out of the mainstream of European politics: foreign rulers were pleased enough to accept James's friendship and goodwill, but this was a mark of their indifference to Scotland's attitude rather than, as James saw it, a tribute to his own importance. His assumption that the same policy of general friendship would automatically work when he ruled the much more important kingdom of England, the leading Protestant power in Europe, was clearly fallacious. Nevertheless he clung to his ideas to the end. It seems clear therefore that the foreign policy disasters of 1618–24 had their roots in James's Scottish experience.

It is easy to list the problems which James inherited from Elizabeth and to point out that his previous rule in Scotland made some of these difficulties more serious than they might have been for a native-born Englishman, but, as has recently been pointed out, 'listing his difficulties cannot justify the way he handled them'.[20] It is necessary now to examine a number of areas of James's rule in England and ask in general terms how far he succeeded or failed in each.

James's policy towards his Catholic subjects alternated between relative leniency and severity. He himself was inclined to be tolerant, provided they were prepared to reject the deposing power of the pope, and in the later years of the reign his determination to secure a Spanish marriage for Prince Charles reinforced this inclination. On the other hand his Parliaments constantly demanded the full enforcement of the recusancy laws and on occasion still harsher measures against Catholics. The king had to take their views into account, and sometimes, as in the aftermath of the Gunpowder Plot of 1605, he supported them. The Gunpowder Plot however marks the end of an era in English Catholic history. In the Elizabethan period Catholics had been heavily engaged in political plots and intrigues. After 1605, as Dr Bossy shows in chapter 5, they tended to lapse into political quietism, and perhaps the most interesting development in the Catholic community in James's reign is the growth in its size. The number of priests rose from about 250 in 1603 to about 750 in 1640 and of the laity from perhaps 35,000 in 1603 to perhaps 60,000 in 1640. Much of this increase certainly took place in James's reign, and although most Englishmen condemned the general leniency of the king's attitude it can be argued that his overall policy was fairly successful. He permitted enough practical toleration to prevent his Catholic subjects from resorting to a series of desperate plots against him (the Gunpowder Plot was a quite untypical incident) but not enough to allow an intolerably large number of conversions. The 50,000 or so Catholics of 1625 were hardly an obvious threat to the integrity of the English State or to the authority of the established Church.

It is a commonplace of course that the Church played a role of overwhelming significance in the life of the nation. Virtually all Englishmen in James's reign, with the exception of the small minority of Catholics and a handful of separatists, regarded themselves as members. Moreover the illiterate mass of the population depended on the weekly sermons which they heard in church for 'political' information of the most general kind; news of what was going on in England and in the wider European world. Control of the pulpit clearly gave the clergy immense influence, as the Puritans, with their stress on a preaching ministry, were quick to grasp.[21] Among the educated, the habit of reading was comparatively widespread by this time and it is significant that nearly half the books published in James's reign dealt with religious topics.[22]

It is tempting to examine the Jacobean Church in the light of our knowledge of the later developments of the 1630s, the age of Laud and Neile, the Arminian archbishops of Canterbury and York who did so much to make the Church an object of hatred to even moderate Puritans. It is however a false perspective to see that later situation as inherent in the reign and policies of James.

The king was intensely interested in theological controversy and when he arrived in England he was immediately given an opportunity to display his interest in and knowledge of ecclesiastical matters. On his journey south Puritan ministers presented him with the 'Millenary Petition' in which they set out their grievances against the established Church and asked for reformation. James, much to the dismay of his bishops, agreed to hold the Hampton Court Conference of 1604 to discuss their complaints. It is not possible to examine here the details of the Puritans' demands,[23] but it seems clear that the Petition was a moderate document asking for changes which would make both the government and worship of the Church more acceptable to Puritans but not suggesting any drastic limitation of the powers of the bishops or revolutionary changes in the Prayer Book.[24]

It used to be thought that at Hampton Court James and the bishops united to reject the demands of the Puritans and that the conference accomplished little of consequence except for its authorisation of a new translation of the Bible. This interpretation, which goes back to the work of S. R. Gardiner and R. G. Usher, is no longer tenable. Twelve years ago Professor Mark Curtis showed beyond reasonable doubt that the conference was a three-party rather than a two-party affair.[25] James was by no means in the pocket of his bishops. He had firm views of his own and took a stand independent of both Puritans and hierarchy, deciding some of the matters at issue in favour of one side, some in favour of the other. The conference produced a fairly long list of reforms affecting both the government and the worship of the Church and Curtis argues that 'a conference whose final report contained so many important decisions and recommendations cannot be called a total failure.' This seems a fair comment and it is clear that the real failure of the conference lay not in its lack of decisions but in James's inability to see that they were carried out. As usual the king believed that executive details could be left to lesser persons, and the bishops, who dominated the committees which were set up to put the decisions into practice, saw to it that many of them were not put into effect.

Among the decisions which were carried out were a number of changes in the Book of Common Prayer. These were incorporated in a revised version of the Book issued in 1604, and in the same year Convocation issued a series of Canons,[26] which contained a systematic statement of opinions which could not be held by members of the Church of England. In addition Article 36 of the Canons required the subscription of the clergy to the Royal Supremacy, the Thirty-Nine Articles and and the Prayer Book as revised in 1604. In December 1604 Richard Bancroft, who had succeeded John Whitgift as archbishop of Canterbury, began a campaign against nonconforming ministers. Clergymen who refused to accept the provisions of Article 36 of the Canons were deprived of their benefices. Not more than ninety all told seem to have been deposed:[27] a comparatively small number. (However one defines Puritan there were certainly far more than ninety Puritan ministers.) We can therefore say that the great majority of the Puritan clergy were not *so* dissastified with the Hampton Court Conference and the other ecclesiastical measures of 1604 that they were prepared to give up their livings.

Moreover, as Professor Collinson has emphasised,[28] the modest accommodations granted to the Puritans at Hampton Court should be seen in the wider context of James's ecclesiastical policy as it unfolded in the years after the conference. During the late Elizabethan period new theological trends had developed in the Church. In 1589 in *A Sermon Preached at Paul's Cross* Richard Bancroft came near to advancing if he did not actually state the view that the Anglican episcopate did not depend for its authority on the civil magistrate but existed by divine right, and after James came to the throne this theory of episcopal divine right was developed by other ecclesiastics, such as William Barlow and George Carleton. By the 1590s a group of Anglican divines were also expressing doubts about the doctrine of predestination, the idea that all men were foredoomed by God to eternal damnation or salvation irrespective of their conduct on earth. This idea, one of the key testing points of Calvinist orthodoxy, produced much clerical thought and discussion during James's reign, and by 1625 a growing number of ecclesiastics, including Richard Montague, who became bishop of Chichester under Charles I, were laying more and more stress on man's freedom to work out his own salvation by his actions in this world.[29]

These ideas about divine right episcopacy and free will have often been lumped together under the general title of 'Arminianism', after the Dutch theologian Jacobus Arminius, whose teachings on free will were condemned by the orthodox Calvinists of the Netherlands at the Synod of Dort of 1618–19. It is misleading however to imply that the English Arminians were a closely integrated group holding identical views: some Jacobean clerics who believed in divine right episcopacy, such as Carleton, held orthodox Calvinist views on predestination,[30] and it is right to stress that there was a wide spectrum of opinion among the Arminians, just as there was among their Puritan opponents.

Anyway James was very suspicious of both the new theological trends in the Church of England and was not disposed to favour their supporters. He nominated one Calvinist to succeed another in the archdiocese of York in 1606 when Toby Matthew, who held the see until 1628, succeeded Matthew Hutton. Then in 1611 he appointed as Bancroft's successor at Canterbury not the man generally expected to get the job, Lancelot Andrewes, who favoured very exalted ideas of episcopal authority, but George Abbot, an orthodox Calvinist of the old school. James wholeheartedly supported the condemnation of Arminianism at Dort and was most suspicious of the up-and-coming Arminian William Laud, who became a client of Buckingham. When the latter pressed for Laud's advancement James replied, 'He hath a restless spirit and cannot see when matters are well, but loves to toss and change and bring things to a pitch of reformation in his own brain.' Finally in 1621, with a bad grace, he acquiesced in Laud's appointment to the minor Welsh see of St David's. 'Take him to you,' he told Buckingham, 'but on my soul you will repent it.[31] In view of all this it is hardly surprising that Collinson concludes that 'Calvinism was anything but a declining cause in England for as long as James I lived and these were lean years for the English Arminians. Evidently Hampton Court was very far from marking a total repudiation of puritanism in the broader sense'.[32]

James moreover was very well aware of the need to preserve the dignity of the Church as an institution. This could only be done if its higher officials were able to maintain a style of life commensurate with their responsibilities and he reversed Elizabeth's policy of draining the Church of its wealth. This had been instituted by a parliamentary act of 1559 which has been appropriately called an act for 'the plunder of the Church'. It provided that bishops could lease their lands on very favourable terms to the Crown (the 'could' often became 'must' under pressure from the queen) and also made it possible for Elizabeth, during the vacancy of a see, to take any episcopal estates she desired in exchange for much less attractive property in her own hands. James put a stop to these practices by an act of 1604 and even proposed to devote royal impropriated tithes (tithes which had once been held by monasteries but were now in the Crown's hands) to augment the inadequate stipends of ministers. He was only dissuaded from this step by strong pressure from Bancroft.[33]

In assessing James's ecclesiastical policy as a whole it can be argued that he might have been wise to make more substantial concessions to Puritan opinion in 1604 or at the very least to see that the decisions of Hampton Court were carried out in full. This may be true, but it must also be insisted that during his lifetime his policy did bring about a fairly general comprehension in the Church in so far as it drove out only a small minority of the more extreme Puritans and in that it rejected, or at the very least was unsympathetic to the new theological trends which had been making themselves felt in the Church since the 1590s. A 'decisive change' came with the accession of Charles I. By the 1630s his sympathy towards Arminianism meant that 'former doctrinal abnormality became the norm'[34] and that the Church was split into Laudian and Puritan wings with catastrophic consequences for the hierarchy during the Long Parliament.

Under James the apparatus of both central and local government was basically the same as it had been under Elizabeth, including as one of its most important constituent elements the law courts, which at this time, when administration and justice were inextricably intertwined, were of fundamental importance in the government of the country. Parliament was still summoned only when the Crown wanted to raise money or pass laws, but the Commons showed during James's reign that they wanted a much greater say in the determination of policy than the king was prepared to concede. Central government, local government, the law courts and Parliament are considered in chapters 8, 9, 10 and 11 of this book and they need be discussed here only in so far as they provide material for a general assessment of James's achievement during his reign.

There is little to be said for James's conduct of either central or local government. Mrs Prestwich (chapter 8) shows that the great evils at the centre were the king's incurable extravagance and the influence of corrupt vested interests at Court. These were decisive both in making necessary and in ensuring the failure of the two great attempts at administrative and financial reform during the reign, those of Salisbury and Cranfield. In local government Mr Forster (chapter 11) singles out as one of the important themes of the reign a lack of effective control from the centre: 'Paternalism had waned since Elizabeth's time, and with it the scope of local government had narrowed. . . . For much of James's reign directions and sanctions were spasmodic.' This is a familiar picture of the king's lack of interest in administrative details, and the growth of purpose which can be seen in the localities in the 1620s was clearly due to the emergency situation produced by the economic and political crises of these years.

In his study of the law courts Professor Jones (chapter 10) points out that the relationship between the ecclesiastical and other 'prerogative' courts on the one hand and the common law courts on the other has often been misunderstood. The difficulties between them, which centred on the boundaries of their respective jurisdictions, were part of a much wider problem, that of defining the proper jurisdiction of *all* courts. Suggestions that the king 'supported' the prerogative courts against the 'common lawyers' distort a much more subtle and complicated reality; and indeed, as Professor Jones suggests here, it can be argued that James 'placed too much reliance upon common lawyers and the common law'. There was however one court, the High Court of Parliament, with which James did have constant trouble during his reign. This was not due to any fundamental conflict in constitutional theory between Crown and Commons but, as is argued in chapter 9, to practical difficulties which arose from James's errors in his dealings with the Lower House, and from the growing political maturity of the Commons themselves.

Overall James's conduct of government was clearly unsuccessful and he personally must take most of the blame for the failures in central and local administration: his extravagance and laziness were the major reasons for the decline in administrative efficiency which marked his reign. On the other hand his relationships with the law courts and his attitude to the common law have often been oversimplified or misrepresented, and although he did make serious mistakes in his dealings with Parliament it can be argued that it was the aggressiveness of the Commons which was primarily responsible for the conflicts of the reign.

Some historians who have found little favourable to say for James's conduct of internal government have discovered even less to defend in his foreign policy. Professor Willson for example presents a very hostile picture. He concludes that James's foreign policy 'proved the most shameful failure of his reign' and sees him as the dupe of Sarmiento, count of Gondomar, the man who, with a brief interval, served as Spanish ambassador to England from 1613 to 1622. The wily Gondomar, argued Willson, soon gained an almost complete ascendancy over the king, which he used to subserve Spanish interests: 'James's weaker nature quailed before that of the fiery Spaniard.'[35]

Later work, especially that of Professor C. H. Carter,[36] has been much more favourable to James, denying forcibly that the king was in any sense under Gondomar's control and arguing that in the middle years of the reign the two men worked closely together to achieve a goal in which both sincerely believed, peace and friendship between their two countries founded on a marriage alliance between Prince Charles and a Spanish infanta. Carter also stresses the irresponsibility of the parliamentary critics of James's foreign policy, pointing out that they would not supply him with enough money to ensure that he would have no pressing need for a Spanish dowry and also that they were very ignorant about the details of the European situation.

There is certainly something to be said for Carter's interpretation. It seems reasonably certain that his picture of the relationship between James and Gondomar is a good deal nearer the truth than the old legend of the dominant ambassador and the subject king. There is no doubt too that James's parliamentary opponents often showed alarming ignorance of the realities of the European situation, as for example in 1621 when they demanded the recovery of the Palatinate—which involved the defeat of Habsburg armies in central Europe—but were only prepared to vote supplies for a sea war with Spain. On the other hand Parliament's implacable hostility to Spain certainly represented the feelings of the country at large,[37] and it was James who was being unrealistic when he thought that he could ignore with impunity the strongly held views of the vast majority of his subjects. It was a mistake which Elizabeth would never have made.

James's sincere, idealistic love of peace throughout his life is not in doubt and his aims in foreign policy, after he had concluded what is generally held to be a sensible and honourable settlement with Spain in 1604, were to remain on terms of friendship with all foreign powers and to make England (and himself) the peacemaker and arbiter of Europe. These ambitions were reflected in his attempts to forge ties with both European Protestantism and Catholicism through marriage alliances between his children and foreign princes of both religious persuasions. Negotiations for such marriages began very soon after his accession to the English throne and culminated in the wedding of his daughter Elizabeth to the young Elector Palatine, one of the leading

Protestant princes in Germany, in 1613, and in the negotiations for a Spanish marriage for his son Charles, which dominated much of the second decade of his reign.

This policy of general peace and goodwill, however admirable in the abstract, had serious practical weaknesses, especially as James tended to forget that the course of foreign events was determined more by the actions of other powers than by his own honourable intentions. In the early years of his reign, up to the death of Henry IV of France in 1610, the hostility between France and Spain enabled James to pursue his policy of friendship with both with a fair measure of success—neither wanted to risk incurring his hostility—but, it has been argued that he would have been much better employed during these years in trying to achieve a solid understanding with France which would have been strong enough to endure in the period after 1610 when French policy towards Spain became much less hostile. Failure to reach such an agreement, Professor Lee contends, was largely responsible for the disasters which overtook James's policy after the outbreak of the Thirty Years War in 1618.[38] With the benefit of hindsight we can see the force of this argument, but it is much less obvious that James should have had a prevision, in the early years of his reign, of the outbreak of a general European war towards its end.

A more serious criticism is that, once the Thirty Years War *had* broken out, James failed to appreciate the significance of the changed international situation. The invasion of the hereditary dominions of his son-in-law, the Elector Palatine, by Spanish forces, in the autumn of 1620 should have indicated beyond all doubt that he must choose between the Spanish match and supporting Protestantism and, granted his position as the leading Protestant prince in Europe, it should have been clear to him where the choice must lie. James however, failed to see the obvious. Ageing, ill and terrified at the prospect of war, he tried to convince himself that his influence in Spain would soon restore the situation. That influence however was minimal in the aggressive Spain of the 1620s and James's efforts were doomed to failure. By the time of his death, war with Spain, still undeclared, had become virtually inevitable.

Any general judgement of James's foreign policy must recognise the idealism which prompted it, and there is perhaps something to be said for it in practical terms during the earlier years of the reign. It did however contain a basic contradiction. James's desire to be a universal peacemaker, all things to all men, was bound to break down when serious conflict began in early seventeenth-century Europe, where political and religious rivalries were still acute. His failure to see this brought him great unpopularity in England and did not in the end keep the country out of the war which it had been his greatest ambition to avoid.

James was certainly not one of the more successful rulers of England. His personality was always uninspiring; his health and abilities declined sharply during the later years of his life, the testing time of his reign in England; and his successes in Scotland did little if anything to help him in facing the difficulties which he encountered south of the Border. On the other hand, while it is difficult to defend his conduct of English central or local administration, his conflicts with Parliament were only partly and perhaps not primarily of his own making, his foreign policy has more to be said for it than was once allowed, if not as much as the revisionists would have us believe, and his ecclesiastical policies were a good deal more successful than has often been supposed. Mrs Prestwich wisely reminds us that, despite the difficulties which James inherited from Elizabeth, it is wrong to see the failures of his English reign as inherent in the situation of 1603. Similarly it is necessary to insist that Charles I's errors in both Church and State could hardly have been predicted on the basis of his inheritance of 1625. James may have weakened the monarchy but it was very far from collapse at the time of his death: collapse only came as a result of his son's disastrous policies.

The problems with which we have been dealing so far have involved an assessment of James personally and a discussion of policies which turned essentially on his relationships with the political and religious elites in England, Scotland and Europe. But what of the mass of the people? One of the great problems of the Jacobean period, when there were no exact statistics, is to try to discover how ordinary Englishmen and Scotsmen fared. This involves consideration of Jacobean Britain's economic situation, which was determined by the condition of trade, industry and agriculture.

James's reign saw the establishment of the first permanent English colonies overseas, with settlements at Jamestown in Virginia and at Plymouth in New England. Chapter 7, by Dr Wright, is devoted to these colonial ventures, which had such great long-term significance for England's economic expansion. In the narrower context of James's reign however the American settlements had a quite insignificant effect on English trade; they did not begin to make a sizeable contribution until the middle of the century.[39] Indeed, despite considerable expansion in commerce with the east during the Jacobean period, English overseas trade, as Dr Dietz shows in chapter 6, was still overwhelmingly intra-European in 1625, just as it had been in 1603. London dominated the export trade which continued to be based on the sale of woollen cloth, though the period did see a decline in the importance of the 'old draperies,' the heavy woollens exported mainly to northern European, and an increase in the significance of the 'new draperies', lighter cloths which went primarily to the southern part of the Continent. In fact a shifting of trade and investment from northern to southern Europe was probably the single most significant change in the pattern of English trade during James's reign, which also witnessed, after the end—in 1614 —of a post-war boom, slumps and depressions which had most unfortunate effects on the domestic situation, producing 'unemployment, credit difficulties . . . and widespread discontent'.[40]

Historians have naturally tended to concentrate their attention on England's international trade for which considerable, relatively easily handled evidence is available. It is much more difficult to be precise about internal trade, which was certainly more considerable in volume and often involved the movement of goods over only a few miles. In Professor Supple's words, 'it is easier to intimate the importance of domestic commerce than to measure it',[41] but any account of the period should certainly recognise its significance.

It is generally agreed that the early seventeenth century did not see 'revolutionary' developments in English trade, but one distinguished authority, Professor J. U. Nef, has argued that James's reign was one of the most important periods in an early English 'industrial revolution' which occupied the years 1540 to 1640.[42] He bases his arguments on the growth of new 'capitalistically owned' enterprises during this period, laying particular stress on the progress of the coal industry, and sees crucial importance in the introduction of technical changes, which, he argued, played a significant role in reducing the cost of industrial relative to agricultural products. Other historians have united to reject his conclusions. It has been shown that many of his claims are based on isolated and quite untypical examples, and although it is true that the coal industry showed a fourteen-fold increase in production between 1550 and 1690 it must be remembered that it started from a basic output of only a little over 200,000 tons a year in the mid-sixteenth century; naturally rates of increase seem large when the original, absolute amount is small. Also such significant technical advances as did take place in the late sixteenth and early seventeenth centuries were made in the country's lesser industries, such as mining and metallurgy. The major industries of the period, for example the leather, and most important of all, the textile industries, were hardly, if at all, affected by technical devolopments. The relative fall in the cost of industrial compared with agricultural products was almost certainly due primarily to the generally low standard of living of the poorer sections of the community who had to spend a very large proportion of their income on the most basic necessity of life: food. They had little money with which to purchase industrial goods and demand for these remained relatively low at a time when the competition of a growing population for too little agricultural produce was rapidly pushing up the price of basic foodstuffs.[43] This is not of course to deny that the period did see an overall growth in English industry, but it is a long way from recognising this to admitting the validity of a late sixteenth and early seventeeth century 'industrial revolution'.

In Scotland James's reign as a whole seems to have been an era of economic expansion; and Professor Lythe, in his chapter on 'the Economy of Scotland', devotes considerable attention to the growth which took place in trade and industry and brought significant benefits to the Scottish economy. All developments in industry and trade however, both in Scotland and in England, are overshadowed by the fundamental importance of agriculture in the life of Jacobean Britain.

The great mass of the population lived in the countryside. As Professor Lythe points out, 'not more than one Scotsman in five or six lived in surroundings which could, even by the widest definition, be called urban; and it is certain that a great many of these townsmen maintained close rural connexions and strong agricultural interests.' For most Scots of the time 'the supply of daily bread remained the insistent rural concern.'[44] The situation in England, as Professor Hoskins has so forcibly reminded us, was broadly similar. In this situation the annual harvest was the fundamental fact of economic life for the workers of both countryside and towns, and the weather, which in the short term largely determined the supply of agricultural produce, was an even more perennial subject of conversation than it is today.

The second half of the sixteenth century was overall a bad period for harvests in Scotland, and twenty-four years out of the fifty were marked by unusually high food prices. The first twenty years of the seventeenth century were however, as we have already noted, much better, and in England too there was a spell of good harvests at this time, fifteen out of the eighteen between 1603 and 1620 being better than average. But in the early 1620s there were bad harvests accompanied by famine in both Scotland and England [45] and the poorer sections of the community suffered appalling hardships. In Scotland men were reduced to mixing the blood of cattle with their oatmeal in order to sustain their strength, as well as to other even less pleasant extremities. In England the situation was no better. In 1623 men on the Lincolnshire wolds were eating dog's flesh and old horse-meat and in the same year in the parish of Greystoke in Cumberland, people died, 'for very want of food and maintenance to live'.[46]

The fact that men could starve to death in late Jacobean Britain is a salutory reminder that life was still extremely precarious for the poorer classes, and it is important to ask whether their general standard of living was improving or declining at this time. With regard to Scotland the paucity of evidence makes any firm conclusions unwise, especially as the information which we do have does not all point in the same direction. Those who favour a pessimistic view can draw attention to an overall growth in population during James's reign which does not seem to have been accompanied by an equivalent rise in agricultural productivity and which produced a labour surplus with widespread unemployment and numerous complaints about the growing number of beggars. Moreover, while the purchasing power of the wages of skilled workers in the towns probably remained relatively stable during James's reign, that of the unskilled seems to have deteriorated considerably.[47] Against this gloomy picture optimists can point to the good harvests and the growth in political stability which marked the years 1600–20. These developments, in the words of Professor Lythe, 'ensured a more reliable and stable level of domestic food production' [48] and this must surely have benefited some of the poorer members of the community.

In England there is little doubt that James's reign saw an increasing polarisation in society, with the wealthier becoming relatively more prosperous and the less wealthy becoming still poorer. It was a good time for landowners who benefited from increasing rents, which had been rising steadily since the later years of Elizabeth's reign. Much of this increase was passed on to the community as a whole by those of their tenants who farmed on a large enough scale to be able to sell surplus agricultural produce, which fetched a high price on the open market.[49] The prosperity of these upper ranks of rural society and of the wealthier citizens of the towns took concrete form in the great burst of housebuilding and rebuilding which went on throughout the country during the years 1570–1640, probably reaching its peak in the Jacobean period. All ranks of the more prosperous section of the community took part, from the great nobility with their vast 'prodigy houses' such as Audley End and Hatfield, through the gentry, merchants and yeomen, down to and including the wealthier husbandmen.[50]

Meanwhile those who relied wholly or to a significant extent on wages to buy food—that is to say, workmen in the towns and a very substantial part, perhaps between a third and a quarter, of the agricultural population[51]—found that their standard of living, already low, was declining still further. The basic reason was the rapid population increase of the Tudor period which seems to have continued unchecked for most of James's reign[52] but which was not accompanied by any equivalent increase in agricultural productivity or job opportunities.[53] In this situation wages, though they did rise in monetary terms, failed to keep pace with prices and the numbers of the poor and of vagrants rose. The situation seems to have been at its worst in the second decade of James's reign when the purchasing power of the wages of agricultural labourers and building craftsmen was the lowest in the whole of recorded English history.[54] The extent of poverty in one Jacobean town at this time is indicated by a census of the Sheffield poor, compiled in January 1616. The population of the town was 2207, of whom 725 were 'not able to live without the charity of their neighbours. These are all begging poor.' There were 100 householders, 'which relieve others. These (though the best sort) are but poor artificers.' Then there were 160 householders 'not able to relieve others. These are such (though they beg not) as are not able to abide the storm of one fortnight's sickness but would be thereby driven to beggary.' Finally there were 1222 'children and servants of the said householders; the greatest part of which are such as live of small wages, and are constrained to work sore to provide them necessaries.' [55]

That is a grim picture and, although we must not assume that Sheffield was typical of the country as a whole, it does seem clear that, whatever the problems of the English and Scottish elites under James VI and I, the major problem for the 'lower orders' was how to obtain enough food to keep body and soul together.

1 Scottish Politics 1567-1625

JENNIFER M. BROWN

IN 1599 seven copies of *Basilikon Doron*, James VI's account of kingship, were privately printed and given to his wife and son and to 'some of my trustiest servants', who included, at first sight surprisingly, the earls of Huntly, Erroll and Angus, those earls who had had a long run of defiance of the Crown in the late 1580s and early 1590s. What they thought, if they read it, of James's condemnation of the Scottish nobility's 'natural sickness, that I have perceived . . . a feckless arrogant conceit of their greatness and power'[1] can only be guessed at. What is certain is that this judgement of them has been subsequently endorsed by historians of James's reign. James himself has been given credit for bringing to an end, before he left Scotland in 1603, the long struggle for control by the monarchy over a nobility which had for at least two centuries enjoyed too much power. He had, it is claimed, succeeded in curbing their political dominance, thereby ensuring the authority of the Crown; and apparently to give theoretical justification for his position, he had introduced, when he wrote the *Trew Law of Free Monarchies* and *Basilikon Doron* in the late 1590s, a concept of monarchy which was totally new to Scotland, based on the theory that kings were answerable to God alone and not to their people. In terms of secular politics therefore the major issue of the reign is the place of the magnates in Scottish political life and their relationship with the Crown.

The 'natural sickness' James had certainly had opportunity to observe. His minority began in 1567 in unusually difficult conditions, because his mother was still alive and a real political threat; indeed James survived the Civil War of 1568–73 as king largely because of Mary's political blunder in escaping to England, leaving the extensive group of her supporters leaderless. After 1573, when Mary had become an embarrassment rather than a threat, the minority proceeded on lines similar to earlier minorities, with power in the hands of one faction which was eventually challenged by another. In this case the man in control, the efficient and ruthless earl of Morton who had become regent in 1572, succeeded in restoring a degree of order, but in 1578 this was again threatened when James was used as a figurehead in a temporarily successful attempt by a dissident group of magnates led by the earls of Atholl and Argyll to bring the regent down. And in 1582, a year after Morton's final fall from power and subsequent execution, and just at the point when the king, under the influence of the French adventurer Esmé Stuart, duke of Lennox, was beginning to assume control, he was kidnapped by William Ruthven, earl of Gowrie, and other extreme Presbyterian lords. If their motives were not unreasonable in so far as their attack was directed against Lennox, who was suspected of French and Catholic leanings, and who certainly had too much control over the king, their methods were outrageous.

This episode, 'more Scottico' as one historian describes it,[2] gives colour to the familiar Scottish theme of a magnate-dominated society in which the king as he grew up had to struggle to free himself from whatever faction was in power and gain some measure of control over all; to be a 'universal king' as James said after his escape from the Ruthven Raiders in 1583.[3] But the problem in the 1580s was not merely the assumption of control after a minority. This would not in itself, as the experience of James's predecessors shows, have presented any real difficulty. And more generally it is too simple an interpretation of Scottish political life to regard it as a long power struggle between Crown and magnates. Certainly there were individuals who qualified for the description of overmighty subject. But under previous Stewart rulers there had been a reasonable degree of balance between royal authority and magnate power, a balance maintained not by formal sanctions, which the monarchy did not possess, but by co-operation based on respect for the Crown on the one hand, and an understanding by the Crown on the other that it depended on a nobility strong enough to exercise control and maintain royal policy in the localities. Respect for the Crown is demonstrated by the very survival of the Stewart line in the exceedingly difficult circumstances of the fifteenth and sixteenth centuries. Indeed had it not been for the long minorities which put great strain on royal government and inevitably brought the magnates into more than usual prominence, the theme of the overmighty Scottish nobility might never have gained such credence. Moreover far from the king being a depressed poor relation, kept in his place by an arrogant aristocracy, there are signs that by the end of his reign James V had departed from the traditional policy of maintaining good relations with his nobility, and was acting in as autocratic and, for some, as terrifying a manner as ever did Henry VIII.[4] Had James lived longer and left an heir old enough to take over government, the Scottish monarchy would probably have developed towards an increasing degree of absolutism on lines similar to those of England and France. But this development was stunted because for forty years after James's death in 1542 there was no effective royal government, apart from the brief interlude of Mary's six-year rule which ended in humiliating failure. The difficulties of this situation, bad enough in themselves, were increased by the fact that these were the crucial years of the Reformation, which involved not only religious change but a major upset in foreign relations and a heightening of political faction in internal affairs; and in the absence of a monarch capable of giving a lead in any of these things, the influence of the magnates was inevitably enhanced. It is not therefore surprising to find that in the late sixteenth century English observers regarded the Scottish nobility as having an excessive degree of power. By English standards, they did. But this was not because they were a unique group of ungovernable barbarians bred on a tradition of defiance of the Crown—as a social animal, the Scottish magnate was no more touchy, arrogant and ready to indulge in feuding and brawling than his English counterpart[5]—but because in this period the running of the country had devolved on them, giving them an even more unusual position in political life than a minority alone would have done.

From James VI's point of view therefore relations with his magnates were not merely a crude struggle for authority with nobles anxious to withhold it from him. On the contrary great care had been taken to train him for kingship. Like other sixteenth-century royal children he was put through a formidable education, in which his principal tutor was the distinguished but unpleasant George Buchanan; and from Buchanan he learned a political theory of elective monarchy answerable to 'the people'. This interpretation of kingship was particularly useful in justifying the enforced abdication of Mary; and much history was invented to support it. But although Buchanan's immediate motives were political, nevertheless what his theory came to in practice was the long-accepted idea of co-operation between the monarch and the great men of his kingdom, an idea to which no alternative in Scotland had as yet been able to emerge.

Because James was that unusual phenomenon, a king who wrote books, his adult views are well known. At first sight he appears to have taken up a position diametrically opposed to that of Buchanan: that the king was ordained by and answerable only to God, which was the major theme of both the *Trew Law of Free Monarchies* and *Basilikon Doron*. It is important however to put James's concept into perspective. In political terms he had the old problems of a king who has to find a means of governing and maintaining law and order without any of the controls of a modern state. But as Professor Donaldson shows, in his chapter in this book, he also had the new problem of a well-organised minority group within the Kirk, the extreme Presbyterians, who claimed that there were 'Two Kingdoms', Church and State, and who denied the king any authority over the ecclesiastical kingdom while having no scruple about interfering in the affairs of the temporal. In theory attacking the very basis of James's position, in practice complicating secular politics, there is no doubt that they represented, to James, the greatest of his Scottish problems. Thus, while incidentally James was rejecting the theory he had learned as a child, the real purpose of divine right was to counteract the claim put forward by Andrew Melville for the Kirk; and where the Kirk was concerned, James's theory was put into practice.

The situation on the political side was very different. The logical fulfilment of divine right would have produced what one historian has called a 'Stewart Despotism'.[6] It would have undermined, if not destroyed, the place of the magnates in the State, for while they might retain their position as the Crown's most powerful servants, they would lose their jealously guarded right to be its chief counsellors; and in Scotland, where the nobles were accustomed to treat their king with a great deal of familiarity, where the art of flattery which was to make James's move to the English Court such a soothing experience had not been developed, it would have been a very bold step indeed.

There is however no evidence that James attempted, or even contemplated taking such a step. One of the chief points of interest about *Basilikon Doron* is that while James's advice to his son on dealing with the extremists in the Kirk is entirely consistent with the major theme of the book, his approach becomes very traditional indeed when he turns to political issues. Nowhere in the book perhaps does James show to better advantage than in the section on government, on the choice of servants—or of a wife—which is full of sound, moderate common sense. Certainly he had harsh criticisms to make. His description of the 'feckless arrogant conceit' opens one of the most quoted passages of the book, in which, in memorable prose, he condemned those magnates who 'bang it out bravely, he and all his kin, against him and all his'. Feuding by the nobles was an evil which the king must 'root out', as later in

England he was to take strong measures against the newer and less socially devastating practice of duelling. And 'for remedy', he counselled his son, 'teach your nobility to keep your laws as precisely as the meanest', which is admittedly one of the less realistic of his ideas.

If this is a major criticism of the magnates, however, the credit side far outweighs the debit. Whatever their vices, these were the great men of the kingdom. Their place must be recognised, for they were vitally necessary to the Crown: 'consider that virtue followeth oftest noble blood . . . the more frequently that your court can be garnished with them, think it the more your honour . . . since it is, they must be your arms and executors of your laws.'[7] When choosing his servants, to whom should the king look? To men of ability, certainly; to 'mean men' for financial matters—and here there is an echo of the occasion in 1596 when James, appointing the group of people known as the Octavians to manage his finances, was 'very merry, saying that he would no more use Chancellor or other great men in those his causes but such as he might convict and were hangable'.[8] But in general it was the magnates who were most worthy to serve the king, and who made his government illustrious: 'delight to be served with men of the noblest blood that may be had; for besides that their service shall breed you great good-will and least envy, contrary to that of start-ups, ye shall oft find virtue follow noble races, as I have said before speaking of the nobility.'[9] And finally, as if to underline the difference between the theoretical implications of divine right and the practical relationship which James wanted, 'eschew the other extremity, in lightlying [slighting] and contemning your nobility. Remember how that error broke the King my grandfather's heart' (James V).[10] In other words, when writing about the practical business of running his kingdom, James made no departure at all from traditional ideas, and was indeed saying exactly what his predecessors would have done had they written books on the subject.

If then James had a consistent policy towards the magnates, it was the long-established one of acknowledging their pre-eminent place, working with them as far as possible, and handling them tactfully; in effect believing the best until the worst happened, as he himself said succinctly, when writing to Elizabeth in 1583, 'neither mind we to control nor remove any of our nobility or others who had faithfully given their dependence on us heretofore, nor prejudge them in their honour, lives or livings in any sort, except they give us special occasion hereafter to the contrary.'[11]

This letter, written after he had escaped from the Ruthven Raiders, makes it clear that James was not inclined to pursue a policy of repression against the nobles as a class because of the alarming behaviour of one faction. His treatment of the only other noble faction which caused serious trouble, the northern Catholic earls of Huntly, Erroll and Angus, shows this idea taken to a further stage, for in this case James was remarkably reluctant to repress even the rebellious earls themselves, in spite of his avowed hatred of the feuding they were engaged in, and in spite of pressure amounting to bullying from Elizabeth and from the Kirk. This crisis might seem to demonstrate the weakness of the monarchy as compared with the power of the nobility; for these earls entered into treasonable negotiations with Spain, and at the same time were involved in violent internal unrest in the north-east which culminated in the famous murder of the earl of Moray at Donibristle in 1592 and the defeat of a royalist army led by the earl of Argyll in 1594. But James's reluctance to act did not arise from inability caused by lack of resources. When he wanted, he could perfectly well put an army into the field. Indeed one of the most interesting aspects of this affair is that when he did so in person, the earls capitulated rather than do battle with the king. There were limits to defiance of the Crown. His policy was dictated by very different considerations. He hated fighting, and wasting money on fighting; he much preferred some other kind of settlement. Much more important, he was far more in sympathy with the attitudes and ambitions of his magnates than is sometimes thought. He understood well enough what their motives were; and these motives were not concerned with a direct attack against him. He himself, as Professor Donaldson shows when discussing his dealings with the Presbyterians, was sufficiently a man of his times to use division and faction to his own ends. In politics too, where one faction was apparently working against him, his attitude was not that of an autocratic king concerned only to crush dissident magnates but rather that of a man with a balanced and sensible approach. Thus while he used the Kirk to extort at least a nominal rejection of Catholicism from the northern earls, he was shrewd enough to appreciate that in their dealings with Spain 'their enemy was the Queen of England, not the King of Scots who might well profit from their plottings';[12] indeed in 1592 he himself was considering the possibility of seeking Spanish help against England, an idea which fortunately went no further than a memorandum setting out the advantages and disadvantages. Similarly he was probably well aware that the major reason for trouble in the north was that Moray had deliberately challenged Huntly's long-established supremacy, built up over the previous 150 years by royal support—for it had been part of crown policy since the mid-fifteenth century to encourage the rise of the earls of Huntly and use them as its lieutenants—and by a network of local alliances. Moray's attempts to attract to his own follow-ing families dependent on the house of Huntly was an act of provoca-tion which inevitably created unrest and feuding; and the later romantic legend of the 'bonnie earl of Moray' has done great disservice to the parts played by both Huntly and the king, in obscuring this fact. In short Moray took a gamble and lost. For the king in these circum-stances to have yielded to pressure from the Kirk and attempted to take strong measures against Huntly, who himself in the traditional and well-understood manner offered reparation for the murder to Moray's kin, would have been to turn a difficult local situation into a national crisis. Nothing was to be gained by trying to destroy the power of a family whose record as crown servants had been good, and who might well continue, given the right treatment, to serve the king use-fully. As it was, James's inaction prevented anything more than strong feeling and a great deal of vocal uproar; and by 1599 he was able with justification to include the former rebels, the earl of Huntly and his associates, in the group of 'some of my trustiest servants' to whom he sent his book.

These men were James's friends. He knew them well, he dined, hunted and discussed affairs of state with them. He and they were men of similar interests who shared the same way of life, not two opposing and hostile parties. This is most obviously true of the earl of Huntly, to whom James was personally devoted; and when at the end of the struggle in 1596 James wrote to Huntly telling him that he must submit and satisfy the Kirk or never 'be a Scotsman again', the opening to that letter, which reminded Huntly how the king had 'incurred skaith [hurt] and hazard for your cause, and presently what estate I am in for it',[13] was not the statement of an absolute king, but of a man to whom the obligations of personal friendship overrode the aloofness of monarchy.

The Kirk's interference in politics, which James had to some extent used and to some extent resisted in dealing with the northern earls, was to add to his difficulties in coping with the other two magnate crises of the reign, that caused by James's counterpart to Elizabeth's Essex, the flamboyant and irresponsible Francis Stewart, earl of Bothwell, and the Gowrie Conspiracy of 5 August 1600. Bothwell is a mysterious figure whose motives are far from clear; and it is possible that his melodramatic posturings might have gained little attention had it not been for the fact that he had the support of the more extreme ministers of the Kirk, who saw nothing inconsistent in attempting to browbeat the king into taking action against the Catholic earls while at the same time protecting a far more irresponsible Protestant—or nominally Protestant—one. After a career in which he sometimes supported the northern earls and sometimes appeared as the leading Protestant, but whose one point of consistency was personal defiance of the Crown, he was finally driven into exile in 1595. He had undoubtedly caused James much concern. But he was essentially an individualist, one who represented no party or policy save that of his own curious ambition.[14]

Even more inexplicable is the so-called Gowrie Conspiracy. But while it is no doubt true that only on the Day of Judgement will the whole truth be revealed, it is difficult to believe that there was not a Gowrie plot, probably to kidnap the king. The alternative, that the timorous James risked his person in an elaborate theatrical venture which involved a pretence of strangling, and from which the Ruthvens would conveniently emerge as traitors, is so totally out of character as to be incredible. The one thing that is certain is the masterly way in which James made political capital out of it. The aftermath of the Gowrie Conspiracy was in some ways more dangerous for the king than the events of 5 August themselves, for the extreme Presbyterian ministers made it clear that they suspected the king of a plot against the Ruthvens, who were regarded, with far more reason than Bothwell, as the leading Protestant magnates. The danger lay in the fact that the ministers, with their powerful medium, the pulpit, frequently understood the use of propaganda as a political weapon far better than the monarchy. Both Mary and Charles I failed to take advantage of the counter-weapon, the printed broadsheet, to justify their policies and actions. But James was shrewd enough to appreciate its value; and it was fortunate for the monarchy that this time the Kirk was combated on its own ground, and indeed beaten to it by a king who lost no time in getting his story out.

James had in every case handled these crises with skill and common sense. Above all he was a practical politician. There is nothing in his actions to suggest the doctrinaire approach of a king acting out theories of absolute monarchy. Indeed these episodes are something of an embarrassment to precise theories of magnate-dominated society or of James's success in 'curbing' his nobility. James himself clearly regarded these incidents not as part of a general pattern, but as a small number of nobles causing trouble; and this is much more convincing than a general condemnation of the nobility as a class on the basis of defiance by the earl of Gowrie and his associates in 1582, by his son in 1600, and by Bothwell and the three Catholic earls. Equally it can hardly be argued that in 1582 and again in the 1590s the nobility had still not been brought to heel by the king, but that by 1600 he was in control of all but one unruly family; for the Gowrie Conspiracy was almost certainly as much a plot to kidnap the king as the Ruthven Raid had been. There is a great difference between the two, in that the Ruthven Raid involved a number of people successfully taking action at a time when the king had barely assumed control, whereas the Gowrie Conspiracy was restricted to a few, possibly because of the earl's apparent belief that plots succeeded only if kept secret. But it is a difference of degree, not of kind; and the Ruthvens of 1582 cannot therefore be used to demonstrate a general thesis—that this kind of action was 'more Scottico'—which the Ruthvens of 1600 no longer illustrate. Nor can the earl of Bothwell be regarded as an example of the over-mighty magnate peculiar to Scotland, for his dramatic bursting in on the half-dressed king in his bedchamber at Holyrood has much in common, both in action and intent, with the similar attempt by Essex to overawe Elizabeth; the main difference was that it was arguably less devastating for a king who cared little for personal dignity than for the virgin queen. But Essex's action does not mean that Elizabeth was in general magnate-ridden; and the arrogant defiance of the Crown by James's cousin in Scotland should not be used to support the opposite idea.

Very much the same conclusion can be drawn from the less dramatic aspects of the reign. James, like his predecessors, certainly wanted to govern effectively and to maintain law and order, but there was little in his approach to these problems that was in any way novel. For example he relied on and encouraged personal and local alliances as a means of securing a degree of peace. This operated at various levels. In the same way that the Crown had made use of the earls of Huntly in the north-east, so from the mid-fifteenth century it had used the Campbells, earls of Argyll, in the western Highlands, building them up at the expense of creating tension between them and other less powerful families in the area because of the advantages to be gained from having men in control who were both loyal and strong enough to be effective. James continued this policy, and by working in close co-operation with Argyll achieved a limited measure of success after 1610 by breaking the power of one clan which had long troubled its neighbours and the Government, the clan Gregor. But what had happened was that the king had backed the stronger party—the earl of Argyll, his extensive kindred and those families who gave him service in return for his protection—in a long-standing feud between Campbells and MacGregors; and while such action paid off in cases like this, where one clan became particularly lawless, it was no more than an *ad hoc* policy and not one which provided a real answer to the difficulties of the Government in dealing with a part of the country which was becoming increasingly a separate society, and therefore increasingly misunderstood in Edinburgh. This was the real problem of the Highlands; for in this period the strengthening and greater vitality of their language and literature reflects the fact that Celtic society was becoming more assertive. Thus it was not enough for the Crown to use Argyll, a semi-lowland non-Gaelic magnate, to achieve any real solution.

Sixteenth-century governments had also made use of the well-established Scottish practice of bonding, and had introduced the general band, by which all landlords were made responsible for ensuring the good behaviour of their tenants; and James continued this device, both in the Highlands and in the other area which gave constant trouble, the Borders. This meant relying directly on the clan chiefs, and hoping that their own internal feuds would not take precedence all the time over their obligations to the Government. It was a not entirely unsuccessful method, and it had the advantage of putting responsibility on to local chiefs. But it was subject to the weakness which permeated government policy; it depended on the loyalty of the individual, without ready sanctions to ensure that loyalty.[15]

Lack of sanctions arising from inaccessibility meant that traditional methods had limited effect. In his Highland policy however James did devise two new means of approach, which show both his awareness of the gulf between Highlands and Lowlands, and at the same time lack of understanding, and even indifference to the seriousness of that gulf. In *Basilikon Doron* he had tossed off the problem in a few lines; the Highlanders were, to him, far less of a menace than the Presbyterians. He merely advised his son to make those on the mainland obey his laws, with sublime indifference to the fact that this was precisely the difficulty. For the isles he suggested the plantation of colonies of Lowlanders.[16] This he did implement, sending such a colony to Lewis, but it was completely unsuccessful; and far from influencing the islemen, those who stayed were absorbed into Gaelic society. The second ap-

proach arose out of his increased determination after 1603 to minimise
as far as possible the differences between England and Scotland, and
therefore necessarily the difference between the two cultures in Scotland. Thus, beginning with the Statutes of Iona in 1609, he made a
determined attempt to enforce the learning of English in the Highlands,
and to bring the chiefs into closer contact with the Government and
lowland society by trying to make more efficient the means of citing
them before the council to ensure that they would turn up when summoned.[17]

Again the inability of the Government to enforce this policy and the
lack of appreciation of what Celtic society was like, meant that James
had no more than superficial success; and apart from Kintyre, where
Argyll's control was tight enough to make lowland plantation practicable and to keep the area amenable to royal policy, the highland problem was as unsolved as it had been before his reign. On the Borders on
the other hand much more was achieved, although it was not James
alone who pressed a new policy. The solution to the border problem
was provided by the greater willingness before 1603 of both Scottish
and English Governments to co-operate in coping with it; and this was
of course intensified when the Borders became the 'middle shires' after
1603.

In some ways most traditional of all was James's encouragement of
the personal bond, the bond of manrent. This bond, common in Scotland since the mid-fifteenth century, and akin to the English indenture
of retinue, was normally used to bind the lairds and lesser nobles in
allegiance and service to the magnates. But it also had a place in the
settling of disputes, being used to ensure good relations between parties
in conflict in civil or criminal matters. Since the fifteenth century there
had been a development of law and increasing recourse to the courts.
But there was still in James's reign a strong survival of the older
method of resolving crime and civil dispute, based on dependence on
the kin, or alternatively the lord, to act for the individual. Twice James
ratified this method. In 1585, in a dispute between the commendator
and baillie of the abbey of Holywood and Roger Greirsoun of Lag concerning rights over certain tenants of the abbey, the king ordered that
the commendator should receive their rents, but that the tenants should
be bound in manrent to Roger only and serve him as their predecessors
had done and be defended by him.[18] And in 1592, when William Weir
of Stanebyris gave a bond of manrent to James Weir, laird of Black-
wood, for satisfaction for the murder of James's son, the king secured

parliamentary ratification for it on the grounds that the bond was 'given for a necessary and good cause viz for keeping . . . the parties . . . in perpetual quietness in all time coming'.[19]

James used the magnates then in the traditional manner in the localities, and approved of a practice which depended entirely on good lordship. On the other hand he did make a strong effort to strengthen royal justice. It was in this field that he made his other major criticism of the 'great men' in *Basilikon Doron*, when he complained bitterly about the 'greatest hinderance to the execution of our laws . . . these heritable sheriffdoms and regalities, which being in the hands of the great men, do rack the whole country'.[20] This was not simply a problem of magnate privilege as such; by no means all heritable sheriffs were magnates. But it was a problem of vested interest in the localities, and for this reason impossible for James to deal with successfully. Thus his attempt in 1609 to introduce justices of the peace did not work. James the realist admitted in *Basilikon Doron* the extent of the difficulty, 'For which I know no present remedy, but by taking the sharper account of them in their offices'. And in practice he mixed traditional methods with a certain amount of innovation, retaining the earl of Argyll as hereditary justice general, for example, and occasionally taking 'the sharper account', as when in 1599 he summoned before the Council Douglas of Cavers, Home of Spott, Murray of Fallahill and Lord Hay of Yester, sheriffs of Roxburgh, Berwick, Selkirk and Peebles, for failure in their duty.[21]

There remains the suggestion that he deliberately built up lesser men, the lairds and burgesses, to offset the power of the nobility. It is true that lesser men featured in James's administration, that he made a determined effort in 1587 to induce the lairds to attend Parliament, and that after 1603 those nobles who had dominated Scottish politics in the sixteenth century appeared far less often on the Council. It is also true that James created a new group of minor nobility by erecting temporal lordships out of the church lands; and this policy in particular has been seen as a strong attempt by the king to create a party drawn from lesser men bound to him by gratitude, whom he could use at least to bypass, if not to oppose, the magnates. This idea is a follow-on from the theme of the overmighty nobility, and of the king who believed that his authority would be effective only if their power was curtailed, and who used those means to do it. It has been epitomised in the emphasis given to the most famous of James's lesser servants, Thomas Hamilton, 'Tam o' the Cowgate', created Lord Binning in 1613 and earl of Melrose in 1619. This man had a long and distinguished career under James, serving on the Council and as one of the Octavians, lord advocate, secretary and president of the court of session. He was descended from a younger son of a family of lairds, the Hamiltons of Innerwick, who four generations previously had become an Edinburgh burgess and lawyer. Tam's father, also a lawyer, had been involved in public affairs during James's minority; he and two of Tam's brothers became lords of council and session; and the famous nickname, which may seem to some to suggest a humble origin, acquires a very different perspective when it is appreciated that the house in the Cowgate from which it came was grand enough for the king to stay in when he visited Scotland in 1617.[22]

There was after all nothing new or unusual in using educated lesser men as professional administrators. Every medieval king in Scotland and elsewhere had done so, and indeed few magnates would have wished to give the time or trouble to be resident in the seat of government, placed at Edinburgh from the time of James III, to deal with routine administration. That the Scottish magnates had been more closely involved than most in the long periods when there was no effective king merely underlines the exceptional strains put on Scottish government, and does not mean that the magnates were at all times insistent on their rights to pronounce on the intricacies of royal finance or the fare for the crossing at Queensferry. What brought them to the centre of government was primarily the Court; and after 1603, when there was no longer a court to attract them, and when the king in London was using the Council as the immediate instrument of his rule, it is hardly surprising that the Council was dominated by those who had made their career in professional administration and less frequently attended by the older nobility. In theory and practice James made the traditional division between the role of the magnates and that of lesser men in government. Indeed, by advising his son to use 'mean men' only in financial matters, he was assigning to them an unrealistically restricted part. In practice they were full-time bureaucrats; though how efficient they sometimes were, and how casual and personal Scottish government under James VI could be is shown in an undated letter written by James in a towering fury to the lord clerk register:

I have been Friday, Saturday and this day waiting upon the direction of my affairs, and never man comes. Them of the Exchequer that were ordained to take the accounts, never one. The affairs of the household should have been ended this day, no man comes down. I sent for the advocate both Friday and Saturday—never met no answer. Likewise after the baillies . . . the like answer. I ordained as ye heard a certain number to make a writing for reforming of the Session—no such thing meditated. . . . In short, no tryst or meeting is kept. What is spoken this night is forgot the morn. . . .[23]

Similarly James's attempts to bring the lairds to Parliament, the creation of lordships of erection and the wholesale hand-out of peerages begun in 1599 and accelerated after 1603 to the extent that the number of the peers was doubled, can all be seen in a wider context than the desire to counteract magnate power. It was not James who gave the lairds a new place of importance and influence. During the sixteenth century their wealth and consequently their political importance had been on the increase to such an extent that there was little to distinguish at least some of the lairdly families, the Setons of Fyvie, the Kers of Cessford, Murrays of Tullibardine and Scotts of Buccleugh, who did well in James's reign, from those who held the older earldoms. Lawrence Stone has at least in part defended James's lavish English peerage creations on the grounds that Elizabeth's excessive parsimony had deprived many important and wealthy families of the titles they might justifiably have expected;[24] and the same principle applies to James's Scottish creations after 1603.

Precisely the same common sense recognition of social pressure can be seen in James's lordships of erection. They were given not to build up a party, but to solve a problem which was causing discontent. Monastic lands had fallen into the hands of the nobles and lairds before the Reformation, but with the disadvantage of being possessed on the non-heritable ecclesiastical title of commendator. By creating temporal lordships James removed this anomaly and, as with any other royal grant, gave these lands to those he regarded as loyal and wished to reward. This is very different from the idea that in some way these creations were in a class by themselves, producing a degree of gratitude and service to the Crown not found elsewhere. That they did not is shown by the fact that in 1621, when James was using every possible pressure to push the Five Articles of Perth through Parliament, when his control of Parliament had reached its high point of organisation, when it had been made clear that opposition would be seen as direct denial of royal authority, the king did not get complete support from the lords of erection, nor from his new nobility.[25] For men like Balmerino, the grant his father had received of a lordship of erection meant far less than present opposition to the Articles, and perhaps also resentment over the way in which James had used his father as a scapegoat in negotiations with the pope which had become embarrassing to the king in 1609.[26]

Shortly before the Union of the Crowns the English diplomat Sir Henry Wotton wrote a description of James which was an admirable summing-up:

> He is patient in the work of government, makes no decision without obtaining good counsel and is said to be one of the most secret princes of the world. . . . By his lavish creations of marquises, earls and barons, he does not appear jealous of the great lords. Such creations, far more numerous than in England, he uses to bind his followers to him since he lacks the means to reward them in other ways. . . . He has no guard, either because he cannot afford one or because he relies upon the love of his people which he calls the true guardian of princes.[27]

This shows why James could regard himself as a successful king. His kind of kingship the nobility understood and respected. How far it was from kingship by divine right as practised by his son is made very clear by his writings and actions. He was effective precisely because he had not attempted new and autocratic policies towards his nobility, because he had not tried to undermine their political position—indeed his own words in *Basilikon Doron* that 'the small barons are but an inferior part of the nobility and their estate'[28] suggest that the distinction which some historians have regarded as being an integral part of his policy had never occurred to him—and because above all he was accessible, willing to consult and easy to get on with. Unlike 'the Presbyterians', 'the nobility' was not a threat to James. Rather, as he understood very well, 'the lack of a standing army and the absence of a bureaucratic system of local government . . . did not weaken the monarchy. It was the reverse, for these circumstances preserved the supremacy of the aristocratic society in which the monarchy was embedded and from which it drew its strength.'[29] The king who doubled the peerage was not afraid of magnate power. Indeed what he did was to create a new group of peers who were to cling to the old aristocratic attitudes, and emerge as prominent in the opposition to Charles I.

On the question of the English succession, dramatic and exciting though it was, James again displayed moderation. Before 1603 he never made the mistake his mother had done, of letting his ambition to succeed

Elizabeth dominate his policies or his rule in Scotland. At no time did he dance to Elizabeth's tune, in order to persuade her to name him her heir. He was prepared to disagree with her, and on many occasions did. Far from supporting her when the Armada crisis threatened in 1588, he demanded and was given a pay-off—even if less than he had hoped for —in return for his co-operation. He showed clearly in his dealings with the northern earls that he was not prepared to accept the interference of another monarch in the internal affairs of his kingdom. Only in the matter of Mary's execution is there a case for saying that Elizabeth's goodwill meant more to him than the death of the mother he had not seen since he was a baby, and for whom he knew he could do nothing; and this reaction was both understandable and sensible. There were possible legal arguments against his succession; and he had occasional moments of doubt which led him into uncharacteristically rash ideas about seeking aid from Spain and from Essex, and which no doubt lay behind the promise of support in his claim to the English throne made in a bond drawn up in 1599 by twenty-seven of the Scottish nobility.[30] But he refused to be dominated by Elizabeth, he wrote her letters casual to the point of rudeness, ultimately because he was confident, as Mary had not been, of the succession. He was quite simply the most suitable, if not the only suitable candidate; and his complaint that Elizabeth was lasting as long as the sun and the moon was not the complaint of a man who doubted the future but of one who was impatient for it.

More remarkable, in view of the fact that he was overwhelmed and enraptured by his reception in England, was his continued interest in Scotland. He promised to return every three years but did not do so; he made only one ruinous visit in 1617, mainly to press for the acceptance of his Five Articles. But if this is what is remembered in Scotland, to the English one major difficulty about King James, at least until 1612, was the fact that he was surrounded by Scots who had flocked south with him, 'standing like mountains betwixt the beams of his grace and us',[31] and that he insisted on fighting the causes of his northern kingdom: if not total union of the kingdoms, at least commercial union, and if not that, at least some commercial concessions and dual nationality. His speech to the English Parliament in 1607 arguing the case for union shows a real and sympathetic understanding of what Scotland had lost in 1603; for he forecast very clearly the way in which Scotland would become as the northern shires, remote from the centre of government, 'seldom seen and saluted by their king', and made a plea for a less antagonistic and hostile approach by the English which makes moving reading.[32] And in the first years of his rule in England, for all the criticisms of his laziness, his passion for hunting at the expense of governing, undoubtedly he spent much time on Scotland. The new and admirably efficient postal service which he set up between Edinburgh and London was in constant use.[33] Letters flowed north from king to Council, hectoring and paternalistic in tone, complaining that he had to spell out the details as if they were children, but with long and careful explanations of what he wanted done and how they should do it. The contrast between this approach and the high-handed authoritarianism of Charles I, who thought it enough to dictate his policy without attempting to consider or explain how it might be implemented, is measured by the ends to which father and son came.

The last years of the reign are something of a decline. For the first time James showed signs of becoming truly autocratic and of losing the moderation and understanding of Scottish problems which had done so much to compensate for the difficulties of absentee kingship. The Five Articles of Perth, introduced in 1617 and pushed through the General Assembly in 1618 and Parliament in 1621, were a direct affront to religious feeling. The accompanying threat to the landowners of the 'constant platt', James's scheme to ensure that the teinds (i.e. tithes) went to the Church, created unrest among the nobility and lairds.[34] Faced with widespread opposition, James had the sense to drop all but the Five Articles; resentment died down, and the last four years passed peacefully enough. But it was a foretaste, if a mild one, of what was to happen in the next reign when the new king tried to put divine right into practice. Indeed a strong argument for maintaining that absolute monarchy came not with James VI but with Charles I can be seen in the determination of the opposition to Charles, an opposition which had not existed during most of James's reign, and was only in embryo in the last years of his rule.

In his speech of 1607 James said of himself, 'I am ever for the medium in every thing. Between foolish rashness and extreme length there is a middle way.'[35] Only at the end of his life, when his English experience and the growing opinionatedness of old age made him depart from his moderate approach, did this cease to be true. James VI was outstandingly successful in Scotland not as an example of absolute kingship nor even because he solved all his Scottish problems, but because he understood and acted on a policy of co-operation and practical common sense. He governed his country conscientiously and effectively, using traditional methods to do so, and using them successfully because he was a realist who knew very well both his powers and his limitations. If his theory was new, he was, in terms of Scottish politics, the last and greatest exponent of the old style of Scottish kingship. And this may well explain, at least in part, the paradox that James VI had far less difficulty in governing than James I.

2. The Scottish Church 1567-1625

GORDON DONALDSON

THE political problems of King James's Scottish reign were in the main
the old problems, of curbing the power of the nobility and maintaining
and extending law and order, which had exercised his predecessors for
generations. Even those political questions had taken on a new com-
plexion in the era of the Reformation, when ecclesiastical differences
provided fresh grounds or pretexts for disturbances and when dissension between those who supported the Reformation and the English
alliance and those who stood by Rome and the traditional alliance with
France intensified ancient feuds. Nor was the problem of Church-State
relations in general wholly new, for the claims of the Reformed Church
to independence of the State, and even superiority over the State, re-
called some of the more extravagant pretensions of medieval popes.
Its attitude has indeed been neatly characterised as 'Presbyterian Hilde-
brandism',[1] and the astonishing episode when Andrew Melville, the
Presbyterian leader, plucked his king by the sleeve and called him 'God's
silly vassal',[2] recalls some of the humiliations inflicted by popes on
medieval emperors. There is much good sense, and some sound historical truth, behind the familiar phrase, 'New presbyter is but old priest
writ large' and in King James's own sage remark, 'No bishop, no king.'
But James VI had to face a novel situation, the direct outcome of the
circumstances in which the Scottish Reformation had come about.

The Scottish reformers were not initially of a very different mind
from those of England on the issue of Church-State relations, and it is
an oversimplification to believe that the different courses which events
took in the two countries arose from the fact that a revelation was vouch-
safed to the people north of the Tweed which was denied to their less
fortunate neighbours south of that river. Again and again, from the
earliest times when Scottish Protestants were in a position to proclaim
their views, they appealed to the civil power to accept their programme
and carry through the reform of the Church. But in 1559–60, when the
young Queen Mary was still in France, married to the French king, and
Scotland was ruled by her mother Mary of Guise with the support of a

For Notes to Chapter 2, see pages 229–30; for Bibliography, see page 218.

French army, it became evident that the innovating faction—prompted by both patriotic and religious motives—was not going to attain its aims with the support of the Government. The reformers did not however thereupon lay claims to any intrinsic power of the Church to determine its own polity in disregard of the civil authority. Instead they proceeded to what they called the 'deposition' of Mary of Guise and set up a kind of provisional government, consisting of a 'great council of the realm', composed essentially of the Protestant magnates who were styled 'the lords of the congregation'. This Council commissioned a group of Protestant ministers to draw up their First Book of Discipline, a programme for the reform of polity, endowment and worship, which the reformers craved the civil power to put into effect. The whole outlook of the time is perhaps best exemplified by the fact that the Council not only nominated the first superintendents, who were to exercise most of the administrative functions previously carried out by bishops, but also issued to them their commissions to act, and—most strikingly of all —by the fact that a superintendent, once appointed, professed to exercise his authority 'in the name of God and of the secret council, our present and lawful magistrates'.[3] It would seem that the much-abused term 'Erastian' can be applied to this arrangement as appropriately as it can to anything that was done in England: perhaps the closest parallel is Edward VI's appointment of bishops by letters patent, without any form of election.

This provisional government of what might be called a 'godly council', a substitute for the 'godly prince' whom Scotland did not have, was in control until Mary came back from France in August 1561. The whole question of the relations of the Reformed Church with the Crown had then to be thought out afresh, and the prospect—if it had been one —that the Scottish Reformed Church, like the English, would develop under the supremacy of the secular power, vanished for the time being. Mary was not indeed the intransigent Roman Catholic she is often represented to have been, and was prepared to accept a situation which involved conceding official recognition to the Reformed Church: she several times issued a proclamation forbidding any alteration in the state of religion which had existed on her arrival in the country, and in virtue of this proclamation priests were prosecuted for saying mass; she agreed to an arrangement whereby a third of the ecclesiastical revenues was taken up to augment her own income and to pay stipends to the reformed clergy; and she consented to acts which gave the Protestant ministers the right to the parish manses and which transferred much of the ancient ecclesiastical jurisdiction to a new secular court. Yet despite all those statesmanlike concessions Mary went to mass, and a queen who went to mass could not be supreme head on earth of the Church of Scotland, or even supreme governor of the realm as well in all ecclesiastical things and causes as temporal. The Reformed Church therefore found a substitute for a godly council or a godly prince by adopting as its supreme authority a General Assembly, which seems to have taken shape by a combination of the Protestant 'Council of the Realm' with some of the ministers. The assembly developed into a kind of 'godly parliament', containing the same three estates which at that time formed the Parliament of Scotland—any nobles who cared to attend, burgesses chosen by the town councils and, to form the clerical estate, superintendents, bishops who accepted the Reformation, and a number of selected ministers. While the lay element was clearly important in both theory and practice and sometimes outnumbered the clerics, initiative in the Assembly seems nevertheless to have lain mainly with the clergy, and it was from among them that the moderator, or chairman, was all but invariably chosen.

As long as Mary's personal reign continued, the situation was unstable and the Reformed Church and its General Assembly were in a somewhat uneasy relationship with the Crown, especially after Mary married Darnley by Roman Catholic rites and the prospect was that her son would be brought up as a Roman Catholic. The overthrow of Mary in 1567 was not, at least ostensibly, on religious grounds, but the fact remained that the Reformed Church, which had come into existence not on royal initiative or with royal support, but in defiance of the Crown, owed its final establishment to a second revolution against the Government. Thus, by the time James VI succeeded, a certain tradition of ecclesiastical independence had taken root, and it was not going to be easy to shake it off. However the new king—or rather a nobleman on the infant's behalf—took an oath to defend the Reformed Church, and the regents who conducted the Government in his minority were all sound Protestants. Not only so, but in 1572 an Act of Supremacy exacted from all clergy an oath acknowledging the king as 'supreme governor of the realm, as well in things temporal as in the conservation and purgation of religion'.[4] At the best it was always in men's minds that the king's mother was still alive and might be restored and also that, should James die, the succession was uncertain and civil war a possibility. It was no time to abandon any safeguards for the reformed religion, and the Massacre of St Bartholomew's Eve came in 1572 as a sharp reminder of what might happen under an 'ungodly prince'. Therefore, although there was some debate about the propriety of keeping the General Assembly in existence under a Protestant Government, and the last of James's regents, the earl of Morton, did question the legality of the Assembly, it continued in being.

Meantime problems of ecclesiastical endowment and of administration at regional and local levels had not been solved. The bulk of the church revenues remained in the hands of the men who had been in office in 1560, whether or not they conformed to the new regime, though by an act of 1567 Protestant clergy were to succeed them as vacancies occurred. Only five superintendents had been appointed, partly because they were too expensive for the limited funds available to the Reformed Church and perhaps partly because nominations could hardly be made by Mary as they had been by the godly Council. Three of the bishops who became Protestants had continued to administer their dioceses, and in the areas where there was neither Protestant bishop nor superintendent, the oversight of the local churches was put in the hands of a minister appointed by the General Assembly to act as a 'commissioner' on a part-time basis. The regent Mar remarked in 1571: 'The polity of the Kirk of Scotland is not perfect; nor any solid conference among godly men that are well willed and of judgement, how the same may be helped.'[5] Prospects of a more uniform and stable system were opened in 1572. It was then decided, with the approval of all concerned, that as bishoprics fell vacant they should be filled by ministers who should sit in Parliament, exercise the same functions as superintendents and be subject to the General Assembly in spiritual matters. This was obviously a sensible device to use the endowments of the bishoprics to pay the overseers in the new Church, just as parish endowments were already being used to maintain some ministers. But the scheme, however sound it may have been in principle, was abused in practice, for some of the bishops selected were of poor calibre, nominated by influential nobles, and they continued the practice, which had been going on for a generation, of alienating ecclesiastical property to their patrons and others. Besides, the surviving superintendents continued to function, sometimes in an uneasy relationship with the new bishops, and there still had to be 'commissioners' in dioceses where the pre-Reformation bishop had not been dispossessed but did not serve in the Reformed Church. When in 1574 a contemporary remarked that the Scottish Church had still 'no settled polity'[6] he was not guilty of any exaggeration.

This was the situation when Andrew Melville (1545–1622), who is to be remembered as the real founder of Scottish Presbyterianism, came on the scene. After spending a decade on the Continent, half of it in the Geneva of Beza, he returned to Scotland in 1574 and was almost immediately in influential positions as principal first at the College of Glasgow and then at St Mary's College, St Andrews. Melville wrote little, and never committed his views on ecclesiastical polity and endowment to paper, but contemporaries as well as later historians have been unanimous in seeing him as the architect of a scheme to give the Reformed Church in Scotland a 'settled polity' of a novel type.

Melville, while he had no more notion of tact or diplomacy than Knox had had, would appear to have been a cool and clear thinker, dominated by logic and reason and unwilling to compromise for the sake of expediency. He knew all the answers to the problems which were perplexing the Scots. Neither executive nor legislative power was to be in the hands of individuals, whether bishops or superintendents, but was to be exercised by committees or courts, especially the presbytery, which was to be responsible for an area intermediate between the diocese and the parish. Laymen, in the commonly accepted sense of the term, were to be excluded from ecclesiastical government at every level, but alongside the ministers there were to be elders of a new type—not laymen annually elected to the office, but 'ecclesiastical persons' appointed or ordained as elders for life and possessed of 'a spiritual function' on a par with that of the ministers.[7] Logically this would have meant the domination of a clerical oligarchy, and the exclusion of nobles and burgesses (unless they happened to be elders) from the General Assembly.

Not only were the laity thus to be ousted from their place in the church courts, but the authority of Crown or Parliament over the Church was firmly rejected. Melville taught that Church and State formed 'Two Kingdoms', as if they had co-ordinate jurisdictions, mutually exclusive, and that the sovereign of the State had no more authority in the Church than any other member had. But he did not propose a corresponding exclusion of ministers from power in the State. When he lectured King James to the effect that in Christ's kingdom, the Church, the sovereign was not a king, nor a lord, but only a member,[8] he could not advance as a corollary that in the secular kingdom Christ was only a member: in short, as God was head of both kingdoms, and the ministers were His spokesmen, it was their business to 'teach the magistrate' how to exercise his civil jurisdiction.[9] When the king remarked to Robert Pont, a somewhat milder Presbyterian than Melville, 'I think I have sovereign judgement in all things within this realm,' Pont retorted, 'There is a judgement above yours, and that is God's, put in the hand of the ministry, for we shall judge the angels, saith the Apostle.' [10] There is another succinct expression of the same concept: 'Far otherwise does the king sit in the synods among the pastors than he doth in the throne of the kingdom among the estates: here to make laws for subjects and command, but there to receive laws from God and obey.' [11] This might be called theocracy, but in practice it could mean only the direction of affairs by the majority in the General Assembly. Looked at in a wider context, Melville's challenge revived, or intensified, an existing problem: it has been explained that a habit of resistance, of disobedience to the Crown, had been sown almost from the start of the Reformed Church, and this was reinforced by the teaching of Melville.

Melville had as clear ideas on the subject of endowment as he had on church government and on Church-State relations. The reformers, in the First Book of Discipline, had made sweeping claims to ecclesiastical property, but even in their first flush of success in 1560 they had been realistic enough to concede that the temporalities of the monasteries should remain with the existing holders, who were mainly lay commendators, and subsequently they had acquiesced, though with a bad grace, in the arrangement whereby only a proportion of a third of all ecclesiastical revenues was to be at their disposal—an arrangement in which Knox saw 'two parts freely given to the Devil, and the third must be divided between God and the Devil'.[12] Since 1567 the share of the Reformed Church in the ecclesiastical property had been steadily increasing, but this was not enough for Melville. He claimed for the Reformed Church a prior right to all ecclesiastical revenues, including the monastic temporalities, and denounced as sacrilege the diversion of any of them to laymen.

Melville appears to have converted to his views the majority of the ministers, or at any rate the majority of the ministers who regularly attended the General Assembly. But he did not convert all. Some of the older men, adhering to the beliefs of the reformers, clearly regarded his proposals without enthusiasm and continued to show a preference for an episcopal or quasi-episcopal system. Others, including some younger men, reacted so strongly against Melville that they enunciated a theory of episcopacy by divine right before such a theory had emerged in England. The most notable of this group was Patrick Adamson, who became Archbishop of St Andrews in 1576 and was one of the few among the Scottish clergy who could make some show of competing with Melville in scholarship and acuteness of mind. Adamson asserted that 'the office of a bishop . . . hath the ground of the word of God, and in purity hath continued from the days of the apostles to this time'; and, when the Assembly condemned as 'blasphemy' his 'fathering on the scriptures the superiority of pastors above pastors', he retorted, 'Ye have mothered on the scriptures equality of pastors, which is anabaptistry.'[13] Besides, the lands north of the Tay, which showed a persistent record of conservative outlook, had little sympathy with anything as radical as Melville's proposals. There was thus, even within the Reformed Church itself, a certain amount of support for any government which would oppose Presbyterianism.

The entire ecclesiastical situation, and the Government's attitude to it, were affected by the existence of what can be called, though only with some qualifications, a Roman Catholic faction. This was in some respects the heir of the party which had supported Mary after her deposition in 1567 and had carried on a civil war against the party of the king and his regents until 1573. The Marian party had not itself been predominantly Roman Catholic in composition but was based partly on opposition to the propriety of deposing a sovereign and partly on opposition, for personal and dynastic reasons, to the group of Protestant lords who had crowned James. It may also be presumed to have had an appeal to those who were generally conservative in their outlook. Active or militant Roman Catholicism was in truth a barely significant element in the Scotland of James VI, for it lacked leadership of single-minded prelates or peers, and Roman Catholic practice was severely restricted owing to the dearth of priests. Yet there was much latent sympathy with Catholicism in certain parts of the north-east, the west Highlands and islands and the south-west, and no one could have predicted how much support a skilfully led Roman Catholic revival might have enjoyed. At any rate, while the number of Mary's supporters dwindled over the years, as long as she lived she was not without sympathisers and her existence was a threat to James almost as much as it was to Elizabeth. There was therefore what may be called broadly a conservative faction, not unwilling to see Mary's restoration, favourable to some extent to Roman Catholicism, to some extent to episcopacy, and anxious for the alignment of Scotland with France or Spain. This faction lost some of its political force after Mary's execution, but it continued to intrigue with Roman Catholic agents, who entertained hopes of converting James and were wildly over-optimistic over the amount of support a papal or Spanish force would receive should one land in Scotland.

On the other hand there was an ultra-Protestant faction, which was eager for a firm alignment of Scotland and England against the Romanist powers of the Continent. This party was hand-in-glove with the English Puritan politicians who were always trying to divert Elizabeth's foreign policy in the direction of an anti-Catholic crusade. In the purely ecclesiastical field there was much communication between Scottish Presbyterians and English Puritans and some between Scottish Episcopalians and English bishops; but, whereas English Puritan politicians encouraged Scottish Presbyterians, Queen Elizabeth does not seem to have thought of Anglicanism as a commodity for export and never used her influence in the cause of episcopacy in Scotland. It was not until as late as 1590 that she awoke to the danger of Presbyterianism, and wrote to James warning him of the existence in both kingdoms of 'a sect of perilous consequences such as would have no kings but a presbytery'.[14] By that time James had been contending with the peril for years, but his anti-Presbyterian efforts had brought him no favour from England, and it was the Presbyterian faction in Scotland which was always represented as the true friend of an English alliance. The ultra-Protestant and pro-English party naturally enjoyed the support of the Presbyterian ministers, whose pulpits were the most powerful propaganda machine in the land.

All the elements in a complex struggle for the power to direct Scottish policy were in existence before James came of age. The regent Morton, who held office from 1572 until 1580 with a brief intermission, and who obtained English help to destroy Edinburgh Castle, the last stronghold of the Marian party, in 1573, was a good friend to England, though he was not prepared to accept dictation from England. He was equally a good friend to episcopacy and a critic of Melville, but he took no action to prevent the growing domination of the Presbyterian party in the Church. In 1578 the General Assembly adopted a Second Book of Discipline, embodying what are assumed to be Melville's proposals, and it went on to condemn the office of bishop. This in itself was bound to lead to a clash with the State, for the place of bishops in ecclesiastical administration, as well as much more that Melville proposed to sweep away, was founded on statute law: the Assembly could adopt the Second Book of Discipline as a programme, but only Crown and Parliament could pass the legislation to put it into effect.

Conflict intensified after Morton's fall in 1580. The king, now fourteen, was under the domination of a cousin from France, Esmé Stewart, whom he created duke of Lennox. Lennox remains a somewhat enigmatic figure, and there is little reason to believe that he had any real interest in either the revival of Roman Catholicism or the restoration of Mary, but he was regarded with wild optimism by Roman Catholic agents and with the utmost suspicion by the ultra-Protestants, even although he agreed to the Negative Confession, drawn up in 1581, as a test of adherence to Protestantism. He also defied the General Assembly's ruling by making a fresh appointment to the archbishopric of Glasgow. A reaction against Lennox's regime came in 1582, when a party of ultra-Protestant lords seized the king's person in the Ruthven Raid and formed an administration which lasted for ten months. Besides trying to make a firm understanding with Elizabeth, they gave some countenance to the Presbyterians, whose organisation developed in certain areas, though still without statutory authority.

When the king escaped from the Ruthven Raiders in June 1583, his former favourite, Lennox, was dead, but an administration was formed under James Stewart, created earl of Arran, who brought back into office some of the former Marians and other conservatives who had been excluded from office under Morton. This administration drove Andrew Melville and about a score of his followers into exile in England, where they were warmly welcomed by both politicians and ministers of their own outlook, and in May 1584 it passed the 'Black Acts', which re-affirmed episcopal government and made it plain that supremacy over the Church was to rest with the Crown-in-Parliament. This very emphatic code of statutes was the effective retort to Melville and all he stood for. At the end of 1585 Arran was displaced by yet another *coup d'état*, but the Government which was then formed was a kind of coalition, in which some men who had been in office under Arran were retained. There was therefore no return to the ultra-Protestant policy of the Ruthven Raiders. The Black Acts remained the law, and no official countenance was given to the Presbyterians, but, after it became evident that a compromise settlement which would have combined Episcopalian and Presbyterian elements proved to be unacceptable to either side, the Presbyterians went ahead with the unofficial development of their system. By 1592 presbyteries were in operation quite widely and had taken over some of the functions, in the admission and oversight of ministers, which still in law pertained to bishops. In the course of this development the Government passed an act which, though purely secular in its scope, had an indirect effect on ecclesiastical developments. By an Act of Annexation (1587) all the ecclesiastical temporalities, of bishoprics and abbeys alike, were formally annexed to the Crown. This did not result in anything like a clean sweep of existing holders from their properties, for many exceptions were made and many properties soon regranted to their former possessors, but it did affect the bishops, who in the main lost the bulk of their properties and the prestige which went with them. Taken in conjunction with the concurrent drift towards Presbyterianism, the result was a temporary eclipse of episcopacy. It was thoughtlessly said by one of the older historians that the Act of Annexation once and for all made impossible the revival in Scotland of an episcopacy comparable to the Church of England's.[15] but of course the Act of Annexation was capable of repeal and was in fact repealed in 1606.

King James himself until his later years was probably not a strong party man by temperament, and he aimed at some kind of *via media* to which he could reconcile the great majority—he hoped all—of his people. At precisely what point his own views began to shape policy it is hard to say, but already when he was only seventeen he had announced his intention to be a 'catholic' or 'universal' king, that is, one above faction and able to choose his ministers at his pleasure.[16] His own interests besides led to an element of duality in his proceedings. His ultimate objective, never lost sight of, was his acceptance as Elizabeth's heir, and this inclined him to court the favour of the Protestants who prevailed in England and not to ignore the more moderate of the Puritans. On the other hand there was always a possibility that continental Roman Catholic powers, notably Spain, might intervene in England either before or at Elizabeth's death, and James had hopes—though they grew fainter with the years—that if he maintained amicable relations with Roman Catholics at home and abroad he might commend himself to English and foreign Romanists and might succeed to England under papal auspices. Besides he always had a prudential regard for his own safety, and to show himself an intransigent Protestant might cause the pope to authorise a fanatical Roman Catholic to assassinate him.

But to be a universal king, to be superior to faction, required either force or diplomacy. As James knew well that he had neither money nor men to make coercion possible, he had to resort to the tactical skill with which he was amply endowed. Therefore, although he would ideally have preferred all-round conciliation from the outset, the only course open to him was to be all things to all men or at least to endeavour to appease each party in turn.

From 1586 the king's chief minister was John Maitland of Thirlestane, of whom it was said that 'he kept the king on two grounds sure, neither to cast out with the kirk or with England.'[17] Maitland formally concluded a league with England which went a long way to guarantee Scotland's acquiescence in Mary's execution in 1587 and Scotland's neutrality in the Armada year, 1588. The league with England and the Act of Annexation of 1587 were both satisfactory to the ultra-Protestants in Scotland, though the Act of Annexation was not followed, as the Presbyterians hoped it would be, by a transference of ecclesiastical property to the Reformed Church. The Scottish Government was meantime much troubled by the activities of the so-called Roman Catholic faction, led mainly by the earls of Huntly and Errol, who were persistently intriguing with Spanish agents. The king was not disposed to take severe action against them, for that would have been contrary to his general aim of impartiality and conciliation, and his lenient attitude to them went a long way to nullify the policies which had appeased the Protestants.

It must have become increasingly evident that the policy of a *via media*, or of conciliation all round, was at this stage premature. While there is no direct evidence to indicate the trend of James's thought, the necessary inference would appear to be that he decided to lean on one faction until he had destroyed the political force of the other. His choice was to rely on the Presbyterians while he dealt with the 'Roman Catholic' menace. As already mentioned, the Presbyterians had been developing their organisation, illegally but without opposition, and in 1592 an act of Parliament officially authorised the Presbyterian system of courts and formally deprived the bishops of authority. It did not grant anything like all that Andrew Melville had contended for, because the king in effect retained the power to name the time and place of meetings of the General Assembly, patronage was preserved, the office of bishop was not explicitly abolished and nothing was done for the endowment of the Reformed Church. In other words James was being extremely amiable, but his concessions were qualified and they cost nothing in financial terms.

However he had done enough to gain a great measure of support from the ultra-Protestants, and with their help he put increasing pressure on the recalcitrant northern earls to abandon their intrigues. They made a formal submission to the Reformed Church in 1596. This menace being removed, it was possible to turn on the Presbyterians, and the king did this with a rapidity which makes the conclusion inescapable that his policy had been planned. He had ample opportunities for the course he pursued. For one thing the Presbyterians, in the years since 1592, had felt so confident that they tended to interfere more and more in secular affairs: not only did the ministers rebuke the king and queen for their personal behaviour, but they attempted to interfere in both domestic and foreign policy. It was at this stage—in 1596 to be precise—that Andrew Melville had the famous interview with the king in which he called him 'God's silly vassal'[18] and lectured him on his subordination to the Church. But it was soon evident that the Presbyterians had over-reached themselves. A rather mysterious and confused riot in Edinburgh in December 1596 may have arisen from an attempt to rouse public opinion against the Government on the strength of a kind of 'popish scare', but it was interpreted to mean that, unless firm action were taken, the civil Government was going to fall into disrepute, or be undermined. Public opinion was no longer supporting the ministers in their extreme courses, and the king was able to turn the riot to account by representing it as an object lesson in the dangers of clerical power. By threatening Edinburgh with displacement from its position as capital of the kingdom, he brought the town to grovelling submission and secured to himself rights in the appointment of ministers both in Edinburgh and certain other leading towns.

The king's next moves were practicable largely because of the im-perfections—from the Presbyterian point of view—of the legislation of 1592, and the failure of the Presbyterian system to establish itself uni-formly throughout the land. For one thing there was the question of clerical representation in Parliament. There were still some more or less titular bishops in existence, and they, along with laymen who held abbeys as commendators, sat in Parliament as the so-called 'clerical estate'. The General Assembly was not at this point opposed to clerical representation in Parliament, and indeed demanded it, but went to ex-cess in claiming a number of members which might have swamped the house, and ultimately agreed to a compromise which provided for the appointment to vacant sees of 'parliamentary bishops' in the shape of ministers who would hold the titles of sees and sit in Parliament but have no ecclesiastical jurisdiction or status. Another channel which opened the way to a revival of something like episcopacy was the con-tinued weakness of presbyteries as effective organs of church govern-ment. Again and again the General Assembly had to appoint 'com-missioners' or 'visitors' to exercise oversight in various areas, so the practice of committing jurisdiction to individuals was not entirely ef-faced. Clearly, if a minister who had been appointed to a see as a 'parliamentary bishop' were also appointed as 'commissioner' of his diocese, something like an episcopal system would begin to re-emerge.

The first 'parliamentary bishops' were in fact appointed in 1600, and in subsequent years some of them were commissioned to act as visitors. But it was evident that James was not going to be able to proceed much further until he had tamed the General Assembly. The assemblies which had been supporting the Presbyterian policy had had a heavy preponderance of members from southern Scotland: for example that of 1590 had 160 members, of whom only six came from the whole country north and west of Angus and Perthshire. James had already realised that, as the act of 1592 had given to him or his representatives the power to name the place of meeting for an Assembly, he could call assemblies in places like Montrose and Aberdeen, which would be easier of access for the northern conservatives, instead of invariably holding them in Fife or Edinburgh, where they were apt to be swamped by the Melvillian radicals. He could also pay travelling expenses to encourage the attendance of northern ministers. He next proceeded to exploit the power which the act of 1592 had given him to name the date of meeting of the Assembly. If he chose, as he first did in 1597, to change the prearranged date by advancing it, it was difficult for anyone to object, and once his power to advance the date had been admitted, he could go on, as he did in 1602, to postpone the date by four months. But when an Assembly called to meet in 1604 was first postponed to 1605 and then postponed indefinitely, there was alarm lest the regular course of meetings of assemblies might cease altogether. Consequently a number of ministers assembled at Aberdeen in 1605 and formally constituted an Assembly in defiance of the king's prorogation. They were prosecuted, but were ably defended and their condemnation was secured only with some difficulty. However James had gained his point, and from this stage there was no question of any assembly meeting except when he summoned it. Besides curbing the Assembly, the king had to take special measures with Andrew Melville and a few of the other most zealous Presbyterians. They were summoned to London in 1606, ostensibly for a conference, but were in effect kidnapped. Melville did not improve his standing by writing a squib attacking the furnishings of the chapel royal and by shaking the archbishop of Canterbury's sleeves and calling them 'Romish rags'.[19] He was committed to the Tower and then exiled. His fellows were subjected to various kinds of restraint and were never again able to lead a party in Scotland. The consequence of the prosecution of the ministers who had constituted the assembly at Aberdeen and of the penalties imposed on the ministers kidnapped in London was that, for the remainder of the reign, while assemblies might be restive, they would not be defiant.

All the machinery was now at the king's disposal for further measures to strengthen his nascent episcopate. In 1607 he obtained the consent of a General Assembly to the appointment of 'constant moderators', that is, permanent chairmen, of presbyteries, and then, evidently by the simple process of falsifying the minutes, he proclaimed that consent had been given also to constant moderators of synods, who of course looked much more like diocesan bishops. Some bishops did then begin to act as constant moderators of both presbyteries and synods. Before he had taken these measures, James had already made another move which he could make without consulting the General Assembly at all, and this was to restore by act of Parliament, in 1606, the properties which had been taken from the bishoprics by the Act of Annexation in 1587. This act, called an Act for the Restitution of the Estate of Bishops, was purely civil and financial in its purpose, but it was clearly going to improve the prestige of churchmen who were already parliamentary bishops, visitors of their dioceses and permanent moderators. In 1609 came another act of Parliament, restoring to the bishops their consistorial jurisdiction, which by Mary's act of 1564 had been transferred to new secular courts: the bishops thus had power to appoint the 'commissaries' who acted in executry and matrimonial causes. Finally in 1610 a General Assembly at Glasgow, in which ministers from the north almost equalled in number those from the south, gave its approval to the transference of certain powers, especially in the admission of ministers, from presbyteries to bishops, and its acts were confirmed (with the judicious elimination of certain qualifying clauses) by act of Parliament in 1612. In 1610 the normal episcopal succession had been restored to Scotland by the consecration at Westminster of three Scottish bishops at the hands of English bishops.

This was the antithesis of what Andrew Melville had striven for, but it met with a considerable measure of acquiescence, and not only because of the king's display of severity towards the leaders of the opposition. For one thing the king could count on the support of most of the nobles, who had no taste for Melville's financial schemes and were all the time benefiting increasingly by the judicious distribution among them of the monastic property. Besides not only did the revival of ancient institutions appeal to those of conservative outlook, but all the changes did not make much difference to the everyday working of the Church and certainly did hardly anything which the ordinary church member was likely to disapprove of, if he noticed the change at all. The kirk sessions continued to function at congregational level, with their elders (still subject to periodical election, as the reformers had proposed, for Melville's proposal for life-elders had never been put into effect), and exercised their firm moral discipline on the best reformed model. The bishops, so far from discouraging the sessions, took some pains to increase their numbers and effectiveness. Presbyteries still met, and carried out many of their functions without any need to refer to the bishop. The synods, which in any event met only twice yearly and were of less importance, also still met, though they were now bishops' synods, just as they had originally been superintendents' synods. Even the General Assembly continued to meet intermittently, down to 1618. There was no reordination of ministers who had been presbyterially ordained.[20]

The vexed question of the location of supreme authority over the Church was, if not quite left in abeyance, at any rate not pressed to a definition which might have met wide repugnance. King James admittedly had no doubts in his own mind. He had fostered a belief in the divine right of his kingship, in his responsibility to God alone. This was in a sense as much the answer to the Presbyterians now as it had been to the pope earlier. To put the antithesis between James and Melville in direct terms, James believed not in Two Kingdoms, but in One Kingdom, comprising both Church and State, over which he ruled as God's viceregent, without the need of clerical mentors. An act of 1606 did refer in sweeping terms to the king's powers in church affairs in right of his prerogative, but James, who remarked with characteristic shrewdness that 'prerogative is a secret that ryves (tears) in the stretching',[21] preferred to carry through his changes in church government, and even up to a point, the later changes he made in worship, through the agency of manipulated general assemblies rather than even by Parliament. It is significant of his dexterity that, whereas episcopacy had been reaffirmed by Parliament in 1584 and presbytery authorised by Parliament in 1592, in 1610, it was a General Assembly which passed acts to restore episcopacy and it was left to Parliament to confirm its legislation.

After 1603 James had been removed from everyday contact with Scottish subjects who could presume on their familiarity to criticise him; he was surrounded instead by obsequious and flattering courtiers and prelates. Even when the English House of Commons criticised him, it did so in language little removed from adulation. This all went to his head, especially as the years went by and he was less willing to attend to business with his old shrewdness. It has been remarked that he was more admirable in the days of his adversity, when he had challenge after challenge to meet, than in the better fortune of his later days, when there was less to stir him to use his abilities.[22] James came to believe that he could not make a false move, and whereas there had been a period when he hardly ever put a foot wrong, in his later years he lost his sureness of touch.

Not content with carrying through his changes in church government, and gaining a considerable measure of acquiescence in them, James, from 1612 onwards, began to move towards changes in worship. Any changes of this kind were highly dangerous, because, unlike his bishops, they affected what the ordinary worshipper saw in his church Sunday by Sunday. There were many besides the king who thought that the Book of Common Order, which had been the basis of Scottish worship since the 1560s, required revision, and as early as 1601 the General Assembly had considered the subject. It was only after 1612, when he had completed his changes in polity, that the king began to press his own views and indicate a preference for the English Prayer Book. A General Assembly at Aberdeen in 1616 initiated a process of liturgical revision which went on, more or less continuously, for two or three years, and produced three drafts of a revised service-book.[23] The first and second represented native desires for improvement rather than alien influence, but the third was much more like a simplified version of the Prayer Book.

Meantime, while liturgical revision was proceeding, the king brought forward additional proposals which finally took shape in the Five Articles of Perth: the observance of the main holy days in the Christian year; kneeling at Communion; private Communion; private baptism; and confirmation by bishops. When these were put before a General Assembly in 1617 it was evident that they would encounter severe opposition, and the king had already given some offence, when he visited Scotland in that year, by using the English service in the chapel royal and proposing to decorate the building with figures of the apostles. He also demanded an act which would have recognised his right to impose the changes he wanted without consulting a General Assembly, and although he withdrew this, he did it with a bad grace: he said that he could act by his prerogative in any event and uttered the threat; 'Your Scottish Church hath so far contemned my clemency. Now they shall find what it is to draw the anger of a king upon them.'[24] Even now however he still sought the approval of a General Assembly for his Five Articles, and obtained it at Perth in 1618.

The resort to a General Assembly, even at this late stage, showed that James had not lost all his common sense. Besides the opposition had increased to a point when there was, for the first time, something like separatism in the Scottish Reformed Church and some activity of extreme sects, including Anabaptists. The situation was a warning to the king that he must go no further. Although a licence for the printing of the third draft liturgy was issued, the book was not printed. Then in 1621, when parliamentary approval of the Five Articles was sought and reluctantly given—again through the support of representatives from the north—it seems that James gave some kind of undertaking that if this measure were approved he would propose no more innovations. Not only did he keep his word, but his bishops had the good sense not to press the Five Articles on the clergy and people. As a result, by the time of his death, overt opposition within the Church had again dwindled.

In assessing James's success in his dealings with the Church, one must remember the background of the order and prosperity which the country had of late enjoyed under his rule. There might be occasional grumblings, over his later ecclesiastical innovations as over his taxations, but it was no mere flattery when one of his subjects referred to 'this dilectable time of peace under your majesty's rule and most excellent government',[25] and the days were to come when men would look back with regret to the 'great wisdom' of 'Blessed King James'.[26]

3. The Economy of Scotland under James VI and I

S. G. E. LYTHE

THE Scotland to which James succeeded had changed appreciably from that of his early Stewart ancestors. Especially under James IV and V—broadly in the fifty years after 1498—the impact of the Renaissance had been evident in a great flowering of Scottish literature and music; printing had been introduced in 1508; the professionalised supreme court set up in 1541 provided the mechanism if not always the reality of justice; architecture became more decorative and less formidable; for brief periods at least the King's writ had some sort of significance beyond the Lowlands. And in 1560 the Scottish Parliament renounced the supreme symbol of medievalism, obedience to Rome.

It seems paradoxical that, whilst the cultural life of the nation was breaking ancient fetters, the economic remained essentially medieval, indeed it is arguable that economic life reached its medieval apogee in the reign of Queen Mary.[1] In western Europe at large the urban craft gild can be taken as a typical medieval economic institution. In Scotland urban craftsmen seem to have lost ground from the mid-fourteenth century, craft incorporations do not appear until towards 1500 and their role in town government remained fragile for yet another hundred years. The consequence was that they stayed on the defensive and by their anxiety for self-preservation they remained a barrier to structural and technical change in industry.

The economic institutional framework was further stiffened in the middle decades of the sixteenth century by the great vigour of one old body, the Convention of Royal Burghs,[2] and the emergence of another, the Staple at Veere,[3] both nationwide in their impact. The former had its roots in the 'Court of the Four Burghs' (originally Berwick, Edinburgh, Roxburgh and Stirling) of the thirteenth century, and with the passing of time and the greater reliance of kings on burghal fiscal support, it expanded to include all the Royal Burghs. By the middle decades of the sixteenth century it was meeting with increasing regularity, involving itself (generally with royal approval) in matters of common

For Notes to Chapter 3, see pages 230–32; for Bibliography, see pages 218–19.

burghal interest, allocating the burgh's share in national taxation, in a sense a kind of economic parliament but one which spoke for a sectional interest only. One of its responsibilities (shared with the Crown on unspecified terms) was the management of the Staple at Veere. From the early years of the previous century the Scots had tried to maintain some sort of trading base in the Low Countries, and, after a series of changes of location, it was fixed in 1541 at Campvere ('Veere' to contemporaries) where, apart from breaks in the 1570s, it was to remain until the late eighteenth century. As the Royal Burghs had a monopoly of foreign trade it clearly suited their administrative convenience that all Scottish trade with one of its principal markets should pass through a single clearing house, and this canalisation similarly simplified customs procedures. Unlike the English equivalent, the Scottish staple never involved any 'stint' or quantitive restriction on the individual trader, and unquestionably the facilities at Veere—both social and commercial—were an asset to the Scottish merchant. Furthermore the locals were good Protestants. But one cannot fail to be struck by the fact that, at a time when in the more advanced economies medieval institutions were under challenge, in Scotland they were still in a phase of active growth.

Similarly both in distribution and in social structure the population of the Scotland of 1567 retained medieval characteristics. Virtually nothing can be written with certainty of its overall size. If, as has been postulated, it stood to that of England in the ratio of one to five,[4] and—to continue the process of hypothesis—we use currently accepted English estimates,[5] then Scotland in 1545 would have had about 700,000 people, rising to perhaps 800,000 in 1603. Against contemporary verbal evidence of the fecundity of Scottish women (the result, some said, of a plain homely diet) must be set the clear evidence of such classic Malthusian-type checks as war, famine and plague, and, though death from violence almost certainly diminished as the reign of James VI went on, it is likely that the ravages of plague periodically produced a slowing down in the rate of population growth.

If the population was anything like the estimates just given it is hard to see how much more than one-tenth of it lived in conditions which—by any reasonable definition—could be called urban. The south and east were freely peppered by legally constituted burghs, the chief of them enjoying 'Royal Burgh' status; the west, north of the Clyde, was almost destitute of burghs of any kind. The only available index of relative town size derives from their shares in national taxation of which Edinburgh always contributed most, normally paying about three times as much as Dundee or Aberdeen. Despite ingenious calculations by modern demographers, absolute population figures are scarce in the extreme. It is clear however from such relatively firm evidence as the musters of 'fencible' men (roughly the able-bodied between the ages of sixteen and sixty) and lists of burgess holdings that, at the time of James's accession, there were many influential middle-range burghs in Scotland with a population of not more than about a thousand. In 1560 for example Haddington had 264 burgess holdings; in 1570 Peebles could muster about 170 able-bodied adult males; in 1571 the forty-five absentees at Lanark from an election meeting represented 'the third part' of the burgess population. And though Aberdeen and Dundee may have been six times as large, and Edinburgh perhaps ten or twelve times as large, not even they had achieved a way of life which could be called exclusively urban. Of his examination of personal inventories Professor Donaldson has written that 'it is indeed a somewhat tedious task to find testaments which relate only to what we should consider to be urban interests.'[6] The very physical compactness of the burgh meant that open country was rarely more than a few minutes walk away: farming interests so merged with commercial that for example in 1559 the Dundee Council ordained that the 'Nethergait Port' be kept open during harvest time,[7] while the frequent occurrence of the name 'Cowgait' tells its own story.

The Scotland of 1567 was not only essentially a rural nation but a nation whose rural economy was for the most part primitive. It is true that since the fifteenth century the practice of feuing land (in rough terms a form of perpetual tenancy) induced by financial pressures on Crown, Church and baronial landowners, had introduced some element of stability of tenure, but it was still far from general. Over vast areas insecurity of tenure rendered cultivators the victims of the fluctuating fortunes of their social and legal superiors. Equally it is true that occasional leases embodied clauses which seem to presage agricultural 'improvement', and by the end of the reign there were at least some lowland areas where farmers were beginning to use lime to combat the natural acidity of the soil. By primitive wooden implements, reinforced by an abundance of labour, the arable soil in an average year yielded enough oats to fill most stomachs and enough flax to occupy many fingers. Some regions, mainly on the east and around the firths, enjoyed a high reputation for productivity, stemming from a natural fertility of their soils. The Carse of Gowrie, according to George Buchanan was 'a noble corn country'; Moray was *'la petite France'*, and the Lothians, at least to Boece, were 'the most plentious ground of Scotland'. In accounts of the Western Isles, spanning the second half of the sixteenth century, expressions such as 'fertile and fruitful' and 'inhabit and manurit' (tilled) are applied to islands which today have scarcely any of these characteristics.

But however skilfully the merits are marshalled, the agricultural economy of Scotland was on the whole static in technology and inefficient in organisation. The typical tenant had neither the status nor the resources to break with the traditional infield-outfield system of cultivation and all the inhibiting features of joint tenancy which went with it. Quite unlike the text-book English nucleated village, the typical Scottish rural settlement was a small group of cottages housing the families which made up the farming unit—the 'farmtown', or 'kirktown' if it ran to a church. The immediately adjacent arable land—the infield —was kept under perpetual cultivation and fed by manure from the folded stock: beyond that a further area of outfield was cultivated until the natural fertility of the soil was exhausted and then abandoned in favour of a freshly ploughed piece of pasture. The one saving grace of the outfield lay in its flexibility: more or less could be ploughed and cropped according to short-term needs. For various reasons, but mainly because of the size of the team needed for ploughing, arable farming was generally—though by no means universally—based on the collective efforts of the group of families whose relationship to the landowner was increasingly controlled by an intermediary, the tacksman. His interest, and that of his superior, lay in rents which, paid either in kind or money, often absorbed up to a third of the value of the product of the land. By any modern standards the land, certainly in the Lowlands, was underutilised even by the then-known agricultural techniques. In the Highlands the situation was different. The sheer facts of physical geography restricted the potentially usable acreage, and the clan system was conceived in terms of military and social relationships rather than of economic production.

So the real strength of the rural economy rested on the prodigality of nature. Foreign observers, except those doing a public relations job, almost unanimously damned Scottish arable farming, but equally unanimously marvelled at the abundance of fish and animals.[8] Their evidence is substantiated by commercial statistics. Between 1611 and 1614 for example fish represented nearly one-fifth (by value) of Scotland's exports, and there were years when a quarter of a million skins and hides were sent to the Baltic alone. But the notion of the Highlands as a great sheep territory belongs to a later age: the Highland sheep of this period were frail little beasts cosseted by their owners and kept for milking as much as for mutton and wool. The hardier goats were everywhere, but the real pastoral wealth of Scotland lay in cattle. By utilising upland pastures in summer and by vigilance against predators the herdsmen maintained, despite the chronic shortage of winter fodder, a massive output of cattle products. And to this must be added a contribution of an even more elementary economic type: the skins and flesh of deer and the eggs and feathers of wild birds.

But whilst James VI inherited an essentially medieval economy, his reign coincided with a period of considerable economic dynamism even on the periphery of western Europe. Thus Sweden, a country physically even more cut off from the mainstream of change than Scotland, emerged under the Vasas as a major element in the European metal markets and, on the strength of that, as a major military power. The task confronting the various regents and then James himself was, in its simplest form, how to create the appropriate infrastructure for economic growth within a society which presented a bewildering complex of instability and rigidity. The instability arose basically from the weakness and inefficiency of government. In the conditions of the mid-sixteenth century there could be no assured strong government in Scotland until relations with England were stabilised. The agreements reached in 1560, though strained, survived to be reinforced by the Union of the Crowns in 1603. In short the major obstacle to stable government was removed. Parallel to this was the church settlement. Protestantism, legally established in 1560, was the complement to diplomatic agreement with England. Under Melville it produced a fresh threat, for even if the theory of the Two Kingdoms acknowledged the temporal throne as such, it certainly challenged the single authority of the occupant in the establishment of strong central government. James's success in resisting theocracy was just as vital as his pacific foreign policy. But the process was slow. Until after 1603 local insubordination in the Borders restricted the best use of their grazings, and it was only from the safety of London that James took the final vigorous measure to subdue the overmighty chiefs of the Western Isles and Earl Patrick of Orkney. Over much of the country James had enforced the king's peace. Locally —as indeed they did in Elizabethan England—men might resort to violence to settle disputes, but by and large Scotland settled down to that condition of internal security which was the essential prerequisite for economic growth.

But security by itself was not a promoter of economic growth: it was simply a condition. Growth depended upon a confluence of positive factors among which release of resources, effective demand and government stimulus may be isolated for examination. Though it is true that the industries of the period were in broad terms labour-intensive, it is nevertheless evident that some, for example mining, salt, soap and glassmaking and shipbuilding, could not develop without the infusion of capital. Perhaps because of the traditional social division between merchants and craftsmen, the direct involvement of merchant capital in manufacturing was relatively rare, and in so far as evidences of capital flows are identifiable they were mainly to or from landowning. Relatively little is yet known about the changing anatomy of Scottish landowning but certainly, because of its limited nature, the redistribution of old church lands in Scotland was less socially influential than in England. Nevertheless the classic example of a capital-intensive industrial enterprise involved the reopening and development of the old monastic coal mine at Culross.[9] The lease of 1575, by which Sir George Bruce acquired the colliery from the commendator of Culross Abbey, spoke of him as one with 'great knowledge and skill in machinery' and as 'the likeliest person to re-establish again the Colliery at Culross'.[10] Though, as his name implies, of ancient descent, Bruce rose in prestige by his own abilities and by the patronage of the Crown, and by about 1590 he was converting the old mine into one of the showpieces of contemporary industrial technology. The installation of a horse-drawn chain-and-bucket pump enabled him to pursue the coal seam down to forty fathoms and the sinking of a second shaft at the lowest point of the foreshore allowed him to load coal directly on to waiting ships. Entrepreneurial capital, technological skill and the ability to meet a known demand ensured for Bruce's mine a unique place in the industrial history of James's reign.

A passing reference in the Dunfermline burgh records to 'Laurence Musgrave, Englishman, servant to Sir George Bruce's works' and to other 'Englishmen . . . at the said work'[11] prompts inquiry into the extent and role of alien skill in the Scottish industry of the period. Away to the north-west, at Letterewe on the shore of Loch Maree, Sir George Hay established a colony of Englishmen as part of his project to make iron from locally available bog-ore and timber. At Wemyss (Fife) the same Hay's glassworks made its first significant impact on the market in glass products (even outside Scotland) after the arrival in Scotland of the Venetian expert John Maria dell' Acqua. The history of precious metal mining and extraction is a catalogue of foreign names. In 1568 for example Cornelius de Vos obtained a licence to work the mines on Crawford Muir in Lanarkshire and set up a company with himself, Abraham Peterson (an alien famous among other things for the length of his beard) and three Scots as partners.[12] Within months de Vos was writing to Daniel Hochstetter (of an Augsburg family) asking for skilled workmen. Cornelius de Vos fades from the record in the late 1570s, only to be succeeded by a Fleming, Eustachius Roche, whose rights were annulled in 1592, and five years later in effect transferred to the Englishman Bevis Bulmer, 'the accepted Croesus amongst industrial speculators'.[13] Bulmer operated not only in the classic gold and silver territory of Crawford Muir and Wanlockhead but was involved also in opening a new silver mine near Linlithgow which in 1613 passed into fresh ownership, with a Portuguese, Paulo Pinto, as one of the partners.

The textiles presented a special technical problem. They were old-established with entrenched craft organisations but, except perhaps in knitted hose and linen yarn, Scottish products were notoriously inferior in a period when demand in western Europe was becoming increasingly sophisticated and when the advanced textile technology of the Low Countries was setting new standards. The weakness was recognised in acts of the Scottish Parliament from 1582 onwards, and in 1604 the Convention of Royal Burghs sent an expert to England and Flanders 'for homebringing of Flemings and others for making of broad cloth ... and other stuffs'.[14] This, and other similar missions, induced a few specialists to come, only in general to batter against a wall of stubborn conservatism.

There was obviously an alternative method of obtaining technical knowledge. For centuries Scotsmen had gone to the Continent to train in medicine. So Peter Lowe, after long experience as a member of the Faculty of Surgery in Paris, returned home in 1598 and, to remedy the 'great abuses [in surgery] committed by ignorant . . . and unlearned persons', was authorised to set up an examining body from which sprang the present Royal College of Physicians and Surgeons of Glasgow. Traces of the same pattern can be found in industrial technology. Seeking a patent of monopoly for making 'engines' for the transport of coal, Thomas Tulloch in 1606 claimed to be offering knowledge gained from years of being among 'uncouth nations'.[15] But sophisticated skill is a tender plant. In 1537 Aberdeen Town Council had sent Andrew Cullam to Flanders 'with regard to receiving useful instructions how to keep in order the Kirk clock . . . and the College orloges', yet eighty years later the same body was bemoaning the 'want of skilful men' to look after the public clocks.[16]

It is tolerably clear that even in the more favourable environment which developed as the reign of James VI proceeded, and even with the more active spirit of entrepreneurial enterprise, industrialisation in Scotland made relatively little permanent headway in areas involving advanced techniques. Glassmaking, which at first sight seems an exception, got off to a good start at Wemyss on a site well located for raw materials and for marketing via Leith. Quite rapidly their 'braid' (window) glass was as good as that imported from Danzig, and, with the aid of foreign craftsmen, they were soon competing in the English drinking-glass market against the products of a powerful English monopolist, Robert Mansell. Then, by a process more familiar to the twentieth than to the seventeenth century, Mansell acquired control of the Wemyss works, and by 1631 production had ceased. The ironworks at Letterewe, after a phase of success, was reduced to importing ore from Ulverston (Lancs) and seems to have closed when Hay's patent expired in 1626. Patents for the making of gunpowder have led to the belief that mills for its manufacture existed in the 1620s,[17] but when Edinburgh needed powder in 1625 it authorised Sir William Dick to buy supplies in England or the Low Countries. The soapmakers, among whom the versatile Edinburgh citizen Nathaniel Udward was prominent, encountered such opposition from importing merchants that they got only a qualified form of protection from overseas competition.

Whilst it is true that industry remained a minor element in the economy of James VI, and whilst no distinct self-generating industrial sector emerged, it is nevertheless clear that considerable expansion in industrial output took place. The clearest evidences lie in primary production, notably coal and salt, especially in those coastal areas of Fife and the Firth of Forth traditionally linked with west European seaborne commerce. Controlled by a politically influential group of landowners, these industries secured exemption from the restrictions on exporting and, perhaps even more significantly, secured under an act of 1606 a system of labour recruitment and control which amounted to little short of serfdom. Coastal location, low labour costs and the unwillingness of the English to sell their coal to foreigners combined to win for Scottish coal a strong export position. Precise quantification is impossible, but whilst the estimates made by J. U. Nef of Scottish coal exports—averaging 1000 modern tons annually in 1551–60 to 60,000 modern tons in the 1630s[18]—may exaggerate the rise, they are certainly a fair reflection of the general trend. By the early 1600s for example very substantial shipments of coal in Scottish ships were going both to London and to the Baltic. Scottish complaints around 1620 about the shortage of coal on the domestic market are matched by Dutch evidence of the amount of Scottish coal arriving there: in a single year fifty cargoes were entered at Veere alone.[19] The link between coal and salt was close. Often the proprietors were identical, and salt production involved the evaporation of sea water and pans heated by coal fires. The west European salt market was a highly complex affair, for whilst the French salines dominated in terms of productive capacity, consideration of distance and sometimes uncertainty of supply provided opportunities for more local producers. Compared with the quantity of salt carried into the Baltic from Biscay by Dutchmen, Scottish shipments were at best microscopic, but the trend over James's reign was decisively upwards. Even in an exceptionally high year in the 1570s the Scottish contribution was only 308 lasts, whereas in the 1620s only 1621 and 1622 were below that figure, and in the final year of the reign it rose to 1338.[20] A sampling of English Port Books from the 1580s reveals a surprisingly frequent traffic in Scottish salt to most eastern English ports. In 1621, to take one example, of the 134 Scottish arrivals recorded at London, one vessel in four carried some salt and one in five carried some coal.[21]

What however is more surprising is that of the same 134 vessels no fewer than 90 carried parcels of textiles. The dominance of 'Scotch yarn' in this trade, coupled with the regularity of raw flax imports from Danzig and elsewhere, suggests that Scotland had acquired the capacity to compete internationally at that point in the chain of textile production where cheap labour was more important than technical sophistication. At the more advanced levels the country clearly remained backward—materials were for example still being sent to France or the Low Countries to be dyed and the better cloths were being imported—but equally clearly spinning was contributing substantially to the credit side of the trade balance. Elsewhere within the industrial field the evidences are at best hypothetical. Before 1590 it was only in an exceptional year such as 1576 that imports of iron from the Baltic rose to above 100 lasts whereas the average for the 1620s was over 300. Bearing in mind that by the early 1600s Scotland's domestic output had also been stepped up we might fairly assume that the production of ironware—which could range from the homely girdles of Culross to elaborate door fittings for Huntly or Linlithgow—increased substantially. If, and this qualification must be stressed, Baltic raw material imports as a whole were any valid index of Scotland's industrial health, then we should hazard an inference of irregular but marked growth in the 1590s and early 1600s, then a well-defined recession from about 1611 to 1618 and finally a quite spectacular recovery and boom in the 1620s. In so far as such measures of material achievement are valid, the reign of James VI seems to have ended on a strong note.

He had reigned in a period when, throughout western Europe, governments were devising positive economic policies, designed broadly to limit imports, create domestic employment and build up national strength. It becomes increasingly clear that, even in the more advanced and settled states, this 'mercantilism' contained all manner of inconsistencies, and it would be optimistic indeed to expect anything better in Scotland. It is hard at times even to say what was the supreme economic policy-making body, for alongside Parliament the Privy Council and the Convention of Royal Burghs both exercised quasi-legislative powers and could—as over the ban on the export of wool in 1597–8—be in open conflict. Restrictions on the use of wood fuel for industrial purposes or on the export of wool and coal, whilst supported by high moral phrases about 'the general benefit of the commonwealth', were incompatible with the widening opportunities of the time and repeatedly broke down either because of the resulting loss of customs revenue or because of the exemptions which the Crown was willing to issue. For all his own lofty sentiments, James was more likely to be influenced by the political weight of the coal-masters and by the 'great deal of treasure . . . yearly brought within the country'[22] by their exports than by the vestiges of medieval theorising about domestic plenty. Superficially at least economic policy underwent a major change in 1597 with the introduction of a general *ad valorem* import tariff. It went only a little way to meeting the demands of the burghs, voiced from the 1570s onwards, for restrictions in cloth imports, but it brought a valuable contribution to royal revenue and there is a strong suspicion that the motive had been fiscal, with protection of industry as only an incidental consideration.

As in England the granting of monopolies similarly reflects a complex of financial and more general economic considerations. An industrial history of the Scotland of James VI based only on patents of monopoly would present a nation bursting with entrepreneurial skill, new technology and insatiable customers.[23] Some, notably that to Lord

Erskine for leather and that to Udward for soap, were conditional upon technical improvement of the product; some, like that to Peter Groot Heres for papermaking, produced no results of which record survives; others, such as George Hay's glassmaking licence, were followed by major developments. They had two features in common: they were all potential sources of revenue to the Crown and they all in some fashion cut into the liberty of other Scotsmen. In this area too the reign ended on a note of optimism. Prompted, it would seem, by the agitation in England which led to the Statute of Monopolies of 1624, James instructed the Council in Scotland to establish a Commission for Grievances, which, having examined complaints about the issuing of several monopolies, reached decisions which seem full of good economic and technical sense.

For most of the reign the economic body suffered nagging complaints, some of which certainly reflect the ineptitude of its political guardians. In its handling of the currency Scottish Government, at least down to about 1600, appears at its worst. Certainly there were complications and tensions beyond its control: the changing price ratio between gold and silver and the Europe-wide 'price revolution'. The causes and consequences, the relationship to population growth and commodity supplies, both present difficulties of interpretation even in the context of nations where data are relatively abundant.[24] In terms of its own money Scotland saw some startling shifts in commodity prices. In the year of James's accession wheat at Stirling was assessed at £1. 17s. od. the boll and ale at about 3s. a gallon. For 1600 (not, so far as can be judged, a year of exceptional shortage) the corresponding figures were £8 and 8s. Deep non-monetary factors were at work, but their effects were unquestionably aggravated by the inability (or indeed unwillingness) of Scottish Governments even to attempt a sound monetary policy. 'The Scottish coinage of this reign', wrote Burns, 'is remarkable for the extraordinary variety of types, and for the frequent changes in the qualities and weights of the coins', and, he went on, 'what lay at the root of these constant tamperings with the coinage under James VI was the wretched state of the King's private exchequer.'[25] Coinage, lying within the royal prerogative, was a profitable exercise and in the short run there were additional attractions in debasement. Contemporaries at least were in no doubts about the link between debasement and prices. Thus the debased money of the 1570s occasioned 'a great alteration of prices', and 'what farther harm appears to follow by the unskilful handling of the money . . . it is horrible to be spoken and almost incredible.'[26] The problem for the unsophisticated buyer in the market-place was always complicated by the general circulation of a wide assortment of foreign coins, often of uncertain value, adding a further dimension to the chaotic state of the domestic currency. Improvement in standards certainly came after 1603 when the major Scottish coins were issued in conformity with English counterparts, and the indications are that the behaviour of domestic prices in the last twenty years of the reign was more restrained and tolerable than in the previous forty.

Whether the domestic currency problem was aggravated by adverse trade balances cannot, in the present state of knowledge, be determined. But there is good reason to argue that the currency was subject to periodic strains arising from shortfalls in the domestic harvest and the consequent need for heavy grain purchases overseas. The evidence of heavy rye shipments from the East Baltic in Scottish vessels, supported by domestic literary references, indicates that the reign of James VI witnessed some phases of acute food scarcity in Scotland: 1574–8; 1586–7; 1595–8; 1606 (relatively minor); and 1622–3. There is some indication of a response in terms of increased Scottish exports. Thus salt and skins to the Baltic in 1578 were both well above the average of the previous five years; skins were very high in 1588; cloth rose suddenly in 1596 and skins in 1597, and in 1622 salt rose well above any level hitherto recorded in the seventeenth century. Against this must be set the fact that the dispatch of ships to the Baltic in ballast was almost entirely confined to these phases of heavy grain purchase; the activities of a Scottish merchant who in each of the years 1595–7 took or sent coin to the Baltic to buy rye or peas;[27] and the view of the Privy Council in 1624 that the recent importations of grain had been so great that 'the most part of the moneys of this Kingdom has been bestowed to that use'.[28]

This recourse to the granaries of Danzig and Königsberg illustrates one facet of Scotland's participation in the economic life of north-western Europe. An analysis of the 483 ships arriving at Dundee from 1580 (with breaks) to 1618 shows that 259 were from Baltic or Scandinavian ports. The reign of James VI saw one important change in the geographical pattern. As has long been suspected, and is now proven, direct Scottish commercial contact with eastern Sweden was exceptional before about 1580 [29] but grew rapidly in volume and regularity in the next twenty or thirty years, providing, as we have seen, a supply of high-grade iron for Scottish smiths. This change was in part responsible for some erosion of the dominance of Danzig in Baltic–Scottish commerce: there were periods in the early part of James's reign when three-quarters of the Scottish ships leaving the Baltic had been freighted there, but by the end of the reign the fraction had fallen to one-half and that of Königsberg had risen to a quarter. At the Scottish end about half the total was shared by Leith and Dundee. Set against its ancient links with the Eastern trade, Aberdeen's contribution was relatively small, often indeed less (in terms at least of number of ships) than that of Montrose and of several of the small Fife ports. For obvious geographical reasons the Clyde ports were poorly placed and it looks as if the south-west generally got its Baltic goods overland, possibly from Bo'ness on the Firth of Forth.

Some timber came from the Baltic, but the overwhelming quantity was Norwegian. The evidence of the Dundee Shipping Lists is that every third ship arriving there from foreign ports was from Norway, laden almost invariably wholly with timber. The favours bestowed on the trade, for example the exceptions from export bans granted to timber merchants in a statute of 1573, emphasize its crucial role in the economy, and serve as circumstantial evidence of the relative treelessness of eastern Scotland. How far the allegedly extensive primeval forests of Scotland had been devastated and how far natural regeneration had been thwarted by goats and other vegetarians remain largely conjectural. There are evidences of some internal timber trading around Loch Ness and elsewhere, but on the whole the economics of the timber market operated against the remote inland producers. Whilst they were employing primitive methods and were faced with long hauls, the Norwegians—impelled by the need to supplement their traditional earnings from fish—adopted the new water-powered saw to process logs in areas within easy reach of seaborne transport.

Without this northern trade the craftsmen of Scotland must have been deprived of many of their key raw materials and, as we have seen, at times hunger must have bitten more deeply. But for infusion of colour and variety, for sophistication and contact with the mainstream of European culture, Scotland depended upon more southerly commercial links, notably with the Low Countries, with France and with England. If, as Lithgow said, the south-east Baltic was the 'Girnell [granary] of Western Europe',[30] the Low Countries could equally claim to be its emporium. In Scottish eyes the Low Countries were a key area of commerce. The trade was organised as no other through the Staple at Veere, the sea-crossing was relatively short and relatively storm-free, and personal relationships were increasingly smoothed by common adherence to Calvinism. And not only could the Dutchmen supply anything from pins to apples or from paper to onions, but their own vast commercial mechanism enabled them to buy in bulk and, certainly by the early 1600s, to pay in sound currency. So, to give but one example, whilst Scottish coal was certainly sent direct to the Baltic, it seems tolerably clear that Dutch demand for both coal and salt provided a major stimulus to the expansion of these industries in and around the Forth Valley.

Consideration of the commercial relationship with France raises the question of whether it was in any real sense an economic facet of the Auld Alliance. Geographically the pattern was simple: one limb terminated in the Norman ports and handled a trade quite similar in composition to that with the Low Countries; the other moved south to the Bay of Biscay concentrating almost exclusively on the salt and wine ports, broadly La Rochelle and Bordeaux. Scotsmen represented only a trifling component of the great salt armadas which, dominated by the Dutch, moved northward each autumn from the salines, but in an age when salt was the universal chemical and when survival could depend on salted meat and fish, the regular supply of 'Bay' salt was critical to Scotland. For despite the great expansion of Scottish domestic production, and despite the cooling of political relations with France, French salt continued to arrive in great quantity throughout James's reign at all major Scottish ports including, at least from the 1590s, those of the Clyde area.[31] According to the Privy Council in 1610 'the most part of the wines brought yearly within the kingdom' were sold in Leith and Edinburgh.[32] A rough calculation, based on a local wine impost there, suggests that this 'part' was of the order of a quarter of a million modern gallons.[33] In some years up to 100,000 modern gallons arrived also in Dundee, and again there are evidences going back to the 1560s of some wine traffic on the shorter 'West Sea' route to Ayr and the Clyde. Sometimes the wine ships brought a few barrels of vinegar, dried fruits, olive oil or of dyestuffs. The trading privileges enjoyed by Scotsmen in France were by no means lost even after 1603, and the wine trade, like the salt, clearly symbolised a form of commercial relationship which could and did continue strongly irrespective of any change in the general diplomatic relationship between the two nations.

A related problem is posed by the political *rapprochement* with England. The mind of James is nowhere more clearly reflected than in the motto *'Quae Deus Coniunxit Nemo Separet'* on the post-1603 Scottish crown piece: his concept of the two nations joined in marital union, reposing, as he told the English Commons, 'under One Roof, or rather in One Bed, together',[34] with all that such a union might imply in terms of intimacy and productive outcome. To him the regnal Union of 1603 was but the preface to a complete economic integration, and for a brief spell he was able to employ his prerogative powers to erode the trade barriers between the two countries.[35] But within eight years, save in the possible case of infants born after 1603, the legal framework of economic relationship between the two had reverted to the pre-1603 condition. Clearly there were changes of indirect economic impact: both executives were responsive to the same royal voice; though there had been no flood of migrants there were many more Scotsmen in England; the Borders had become safe enough for a regular royal postal service and for a sharp rise in estate values on both sides; whereas Elizabeth had fortified Berwick, James built a bridge over the Tweed; the ratio between the two currencies was at long last reasonably stabilised. In the absence of adequate historical research (which must be based mainly on English records because few Scottish survive) it cannot yet be categorically stated whether the Union materially influenced either the volume or the pattern of Anglo-Scottish economic relationships. One point however has already emerged; these relationships, at least in terms of commerce, were more substantial before 1603 than used to be supposed. A sampling of English Port Books for the 1580s and 1590s from Newcastle down to London reveals evidence of regular arrivals from Scotland (especially from the Fife ports and Leith) with salt, fish, yarn and cloth and miscellaneous small items. In one year, 1583–4, twenty-six were entered at Hull, nine of them from Kirkcaldy,[36] and in the last three months of 1585 twelve were entered at King's Lynn, again with Kirkcaldy prominent.[37] After 1603 the broad characteristics seem to be much the same with (by Scottish standards) an extensive trade with London and with coal occupying a very clear role among Scottish shipments. The return cargoes, certainly those from London, bear a remarkable resemblance to those from Holland: knives, scissors, gloves, belts and buttons, harness fittings, lanterns and spectacles, fine fabrics, taffeta night caps, bowstrings and writing materials. Perhaps, as Scotsmen became more familiar with London, they tended to look to it rather than to the Continent for their miscellaneous small wares. There are signs too of changes in the trans-Border trade. The 'Account of English goods consumed at Dumfries' for the early 1620s includes scythes, cloth and 'hwkis' (reaping hooks?) against, for 1621, 'the account of 4640 sheep and 2531 cattle' transported in to England by way of the west

Marches.[38] In other words the livestock droving was beginning. Similarly just over the Border at Naworth, where Dacres and Howards had withstood centuries of Scottish assault, by the early 1600s the lady of the castle was buying cheap cloth and wine from 'a Scottish merchant'.[39] The Scottish pedlar was also on his way south.

Important as overseas commerce may have been to Scotland, it needs to be viewed in the wider perspective of the North Sea economy as a whole. Thus the 1554 lasts of rye shipped from the Baltic to Scotland in 1587 (a 'famine' year in Scotland) must be set against the 28,866 lasts simultaneously shipped by the Dutch and the 6383 shipped by the English. Similarly, except perhaps in skins and coal, there is no indication that Scotland could exercise any lasting influence on North Sea prices, and consequently her economic well-being could be determined by events at points as widespread as Danzig and La Rochelle over which she had little or no control. Viewed thus, the economy of the Scotland of James VI was at best peripheral. It is true that a peripheral producer, especially one with low labour costs, can display enough opportunism to take advantage of the periodic misfortunes of the major members of the group. But the inherent rigidity of most sectors of her economy, the reliance on established and often personal overseas links, and the lack of 'risk' capital, combined to prevent Scotland from making much impact as an economic freelance. Indeed, so far as one can judge, the only international field in which Scotsmen attempted this role was in the seaborne carrying trade. No doubt, in the debates after 1603 on James's project for economic integration, the English overstated their case, but their repeated emphasis on the competitive capacity of Scottish carriers cannot be wholly ignored.[40] Just, they said, as the Scottish merchants (openly called 'Pedlars' in the House of Commons) traded in small lots where they could with next to no overheads, so the Scottish skipper, his crew baking their oatcakes on the open deck, could undercut the well provisioned bulky merchantmen of the major trading nations. Though neither the scale of the carrying trade nor its value to Scotland in invisible earnings can be accurately determined, there are various pointers. Some are misleading. In 1576 for example, of the sixty-seven Scottish ships entering the Baltic, seventeen had sailed from French ports, but this was a year of food shortage in Scotland and it looks as if, by some method of communication of which we are ignorant, Scottish vessels lying in French ports had been routed to the Baltic to load grain for Scotland. Furthermore against this must be set the significant number of Hanse and other foreign ships—often as much as a third of the total—

engaged in the normal Baltic-Scottish trade. Equally suspect is the statement to the Privy Council in 1619 that 'the best ships of Scotland are continually employed in the service of Frenchmen',[41] though there are evidences that, because of the somewhat indeterminate diplomatic status of Scotland, her ships had for some time been used by both France and England to enter waters where their own nationals would have been at peril.[42] But the evidence of the English Port Books, both before and after 1603, seems indisputable. It shows that Scottish vessels were frequently engaged in the traffic between the Continent and the ports of eastern England and that some, such as the *Bruce* of Kirkcaldy in the early 1600s, appear to have been regularly so employed.[43]

By the standards of the nationals for whom they worked, the native land of these seamen was poor and its economy backward. But their own activities, like the enterprise at home of the new industrial entrepreneurs, provide evidence of at least traces of dynamic quality. Unfortunately the available materials, such as they are, relate heavily to the coastlands of Scotland, and so far we know little in any direct way of how the economic life of the interior was faring. What we can surmise, for example from inventories of private estates, supports the proposition that under the more stable conditions gradually imposed by James VI there was some dissemination of prosperity, especially in the concluding years of his reign. In the economy at large there remained grave deficiencies. Fishing methods and equipment for example were still so undeveloped that Dutchmen could come to reap the great herring harvest within sight of Scottish headlands; improvements in husbandry and estate management were still exceptional and tentative; the quality of most manufactures was still low and the move into the more sophisticated branches was in its infancy. Yet for all these deficiencies the concluding impression must be that the economic heart of Scotland was beating more soundly in 1625 than it had done in 1567: indeed perhaps more soundly than it had ever beaten before.

4. James VI and I and Witchcraft

CHRISTINA LARNER

IN primitive societies two types of witchcraft are identified: white witchcraft or the craft of healing, and black witchcraft or *maleficium.* The distinction was known to Roman law, and dominated all dealings with witchcraft accusations in Europe until the late fifteenth century. It is also common ground in most studies of contemporary primitive societies. Historians of the sixteenth and seventeenth centuries however have to add a third witchcraft which existed only from the fifteenth to the early eighteenth century and which has no contemporary equivalent. It differed from the simple concepts of black and white witchcraft in its origins. Far from being an experience of village life, it was evolved by churchmen and lawyers from Christian theology, canon law and certain philosophical ideas. It differed also in content. Christian witch theorists gave a central position to the idea of the demonic pact. The witch became a witch by virtue of a personal arrangement with the devil who appeared to his potential recruit in some physical form. At this meeting, in return for renunciation of baptism, services on earth and the soul of the witch at death, the devil promised material advantages and magical powers. In addition an integral part of the Christian witch theory was that the witch did not operate alone. Witchcraft involved midnight meetings to worship the devil, to receive his orders and to have sexual intercourse with him or his subordinate spirits.

The development of this theory in Europe, and its application in witchcraft trials, had a drastic effect on the rate of prosecutions. The change from the isolated local harrying of individuals to a widespread crusade against witchcraft, to a recognisable mania and persecution, began fairly abruptly in northern Italy and southern Germany in the late fifteenth century, and spread widely through the Continent during the following century. There are three main reasons why the introduction of the Christian witch theory had such a catastrophic effect. The first is that it was developed by the ruling classes. If we except the traditional vulnerability of rulers to soothsayers and astrologers, there had previously been a fairly sharp contrast between village credulity

For Notes to Chapter 4, see pages 232–3; for Bibliography, see pages 219–20.

and intellectual scepticism. Now the power of the local witch was heavily reinforced by the conviction of the authorities that her power was real and to be feared. At the same time the capacity to punish her was intensified by the codification of laws against witchcraft, both in canon law and later in the statute law of Protestant countries. The other reasons are connected with the theory itself. The logical conclusion of the idea of the demonic pact was the abolition of the traditional distinction between black and white magic. The power of the witch sprang from the demonic pact and was therefore evil, whether it was used for healing or harming. This meant that the village healer was as likely to be prosecuted as the local scold. Above all the idea that witchcraft was organised and that witches worked in groups, was responsible for the way in which witch prosecutions, once initiated, spread rapidly. An accused witch would be invited under torture to name colleagues, and would do so. Figures for executions for witchcraft in Europe in the sixteenth and seventeenth centuries are not very precise, but estimates are always in thousands.

The mania reached different places at different times. An important factor appears to have been geographical proximity to the area in which it originated. The most severe persecution was in Germany and France. Scotland, Ireland, Scandinavia and America, acquired the persecution late; Spain, apart from the Basque country, and southern Italy avoided it almost altogether. England was a special case. Witchcraft entered statute law in 1542 and witches were prosecuted in large numbers, but, by virtue of a different legal system, without the full logic and relentlessness of continental law. English witches were rarely tortured; English lawyers maintained throughout the distinction between black and white magic in the severity of the punishments they meted out, and the demonic pact was scarcely heard of.

Scotland, although it might well like England have remained a special case, did receive the full continental demonology and become a persecuting state, but not until the winter of 1590–91 by which time the theory had already been current and the persecution endemic in parts of Europe for over a century. The two reigns of James VI and I in Scotland and England, so far as witchcraft is concerned, cover three phases. The first is the period of his minority and early manhood in Scotland. During this period witchcraft was a criminal offence, but it was not pursued with much ferocity or with any reference to the demonic pact. The second was the last thirteen years of his resident reign in Scotland during which continental demonology was applied in Scotland and witches vigorously hunted out and persecuted. In the third period, his reign in England, James encountered an atmosphere in which continental demonology had impinged only marginally on theology, philosophy and law, and in which scepticism was becoming increasingly acceptable. It is the theme of the present essay that James was relatively uninterested in demonology until 1590, intensely interested from the sorcery trials of 1590 until the publication of his *Daemonologie* in 1597, and slightly embarrassed and anxious to make the least of this former enthusiasm thereafter. In this he was simply exhibiting the somewhat chameleon-like nature of his intellectual interests. He tended to pick up and play around with fashionable ideas; and in these three periods he was reflecting the intellectual and religious climate first of the Scotland of the mid-sixteenth century; second of the Danish Court of the late sixteenth century in which continental demonology was current; and third the more relaxed and sophisticated atmosphere of the English Court.

So far as the first period is concerned, it has been assumed and frequently repeated that the persecution of witchcraft in Scotland began with the introduction of a Calvinist form of reformed religion, and in particular with the Witchcraft Act of 1563.[1] There are really two problems about this. The first concerns the responsibility for the passing of the Witchcraft Act; the second the nature and intensity of the prosecutions which followed it.

On the first it was thought that the Witchcraft Act was passed in response to direct pressure from John Knox and his clergy. The actual evidence is scanty and the emphasis given to the part played by the clergy and the laity respectively is a matter of interpretation. Knox certainly applauded the passing of a whole series of statutes on an assortment of moral issues amongst which he mentioned, but did not single out, witchcraft.[2] But in the initial request of the General Assembly to the Privy Council that one or other of them should step in and fill the legal void left by the ecclesiastical courts on a number of quasi-criminal, quasi-moral issues, to which these acts were a response, the Assembly had not included witchcraft in the proposed list at all.[3] One can assume from this that the new crime was simply added by the legal drafters in a general process of tidying up the law.

It is also clear, from our knowledge of the existence of a sermon preached by Knox at a condemned witch,[4] and from complaints of moral slackness, which included laxity about witchcraft, by the General Assembly,[5] that the clergy at this time were more interested than the laity in the prosecution of witches. But again this sermon would have to be set in the context of other unknown and perhaps less newsworthy sermons, and the Assembly's complaints set in the context of their other complaints, to get a fair picture of the extent to which that body was really interested in hunting witches. In the articles of the General Assembly of 1583 to be presented to the king there was the complaint, 'That there is no punishment for incest, adultery, witchcraft, murders, abominable and horrid oaths, in such sort that daily sin increaseth and provoketh the wrath of God against the whole country.'[6] From this, and from the accounts of the proceedings of the General Assembly throughout this period it appears that among its various obsessions—power, money, mass-mongering and sex—witchcraft was a subordinate problem. Its role in the development of the persecution remains elusive and ambiguous.

On the second question, that of the nature and intensity of the witch-craft persecution between 1563 and 1590, the evidence is a little clearer. Such statistical information as we have shows that there were very few cases in this period compared with the seventy years that followed, and many of these cases did not result in executions.[7] Beliefs about witch-craft too, even among the clergy, were simple, and uncomplicated by the demonic pact, incubi and succubi, and night-flying. The actual wording of the Witchcraft Act, severe though it is in providing the death penalty even for those who only consult witches, is as sceptical in tone as the eighteenth century Act[8] that repealed it. It speaks of 'The heavy and abominable superstition used by divers of the lieges of this Realm by using of Witchcraft, Sorcery, and Necromancy, and credence given thereto in times bygone . . . and for avoiding and away putting of all such vain superstition in times to come,' and states that 'no persons . . . shall take upon hand in any times hereafter to use any manner of Witch-craft Sorcery or Necromancy nor give themselves forth to have any such craft or knowledge thereof, therethrough abusing the people.'[9]

The lack of any knowledge in Scotland of continental demonology prior to the treason trials which began at the end of the year 1590 was pointed out by F. Legge in 1891,[10] though his findings are still not widely known. An example of the negative evidence on demonology before this date is found in the sermon preached by Robert Bruce at the earl of Bothwell in November 1589. The earl, who was to be a central figure in the trials of the following year, was up on the stool of repent-ance in the High Kirk of St Giles. The significant aspect of the sermon he had to listen to is the attitude taken by the preacher to the idea of the devil: an attitude typical of pre-1590 thought in Scotland. By the gift of repentance, said Bruce, 'he shall be delivered from the snare of the Devil, in which he was held captive to do him service.'[11] So short a time as a year later it would have been quite impossible to use such a phrase without meaning that the person referred to had made a physical pact with the devil, for by that time everyone knew that this was the manner by which a man was 'held captive to do him service'. In the context of the sermon however it is quite clear that throughout Bruce is talking about the devil in a spiritual sense and is assuming that the evil that Bothwell had done was the murdering and rebellion which the devil, or spirit of evil, had driven him to, rather than the physical worship of Satan himself. For example he exhorted the congregation as follows: 'Therefore, every one of you in the fear of God, examine your affections, examine your minds, and see whereto you are addicted; suspect ever your affections, whatever enticement they have to cloak the self with; suspect ever the motion of them, for the Devil is in them.'[12]

Here, and throughout this sermon, Bruce is talking of the devil in the manner of the early and medieval Church. The devil is a corrupter of the spirit and the cause of rifts between man and his God; he is not a worker of impious physical miracles. The greatest sin you can commit, said Bruce, is, 'When a man in his heart will match the gravity of his iniquity with the infinite weight of the mercy of God; when the Devil by his suggestion, maketh thee to believe, that thy sins are greater than the mercy of God.'[13] This was the manner in which Bruce could preach about the devil as late as 1589. Yet on 6 June 1591 he was admonishing the king from the pulpit to execute justice upon the witches 'although it should be with the hazard of his life'.[14]

Indeed the fact that the events of the winter of 1590–91 were related to a sudden change in the beliefs and attitudes of the educated classes is not really now in dispute. Prior to 1590 there were no serious or consistent attempts to persecute witchcraft in Scotland and no sign of any interest among lawyers or theologians in the theory of the demonic pact. It is not therefore surpising that James had no interest in the subject of witchcraft. Yet all James's biographers in the last fifty years have suggested that he had,[15] so it is worth briefly indicating some of the negative evidence.[16]

There are no works on witchcraft in any catalogues of books known to have been available to James in his youth, and no direct statements by James before 1590 on the subject at all. If one looks for signs of a general interest in demonological matters in his early published works, references to Satan and to the devil are plentiful: in this his biographers are right, though it is doubtful whether he really used the terminology more frequently than his contemporaries. What is telling is the way in which he used it. In his commentary on a passage from the Book of Revelation which was written in 1588 [17] he refers to the millennium when Satan will rampage about the earth freely, deceiving the people. The time has now come, wrote James, when 'Satan's instruments' are loosed to trouble the Kirk. But 'Satan's instruments' and 'Satan and his Congregation' are not the devil with his congregation of witches and wizards of whom he was to write in his own *Daemonologie*; they are the Roman Church. James writes as though he knows of no other meaning for the phrase 'Satan's instruments' except that of 'anti-Christ and his clergy'. Other agents of the devil are the Princes of the Earth, the Turk, and also the Spaniard. It seems unlikely that had he known of any other he would have missed an opportunity to inform and impress.

The dramatic change in the climate of opinion in Scotland, and in James himself became apparent during the massive trials for treason by scorcery of 1590–91. Which came first is not quite clear. The evidence about these trials is incomplete and the full truth about them will probably never be known.[18] What actually happened—whether there was a genuine conspiracy to kill the king, a scare that snowballed or a government plot to incriminate the earl of Bothwell—it is now impossible to say. During the course of these trials it was alleged that over 300 witches had gathered at various times to perform treason against the king. They were supposed to have raised storms while the king and his bride were at sea, to have attempted to effect his death by melting his effigy in wax, to have indulged in hitherto unheard of obscene rituals in the kirk of North Berwick in the physical presence of their master, the devil. The trials lasted from November 1590 to May 1591; more than 100 suspects were examined and a large, but unknown, number were executed.[19]

Some of the elements in the accusations were old and familiar, some new. Most of the witches were accused of physical harming and healing. This was an ingredient as old as any form of witchcraft and one which featured in initial accusations at village level so long as the prosecutions continued. The political aspect of the trial, which so far as the king was concerned was undoubtedly the most important one, was also familiar. The trials were treason trials, and the fact that the witches were supposed to have attempted the life of the king was the main reason for the ferocity and tenacity of the interrogations. The fear that Bothwell was involved, or (a possible alternative) the attempt to incriminate him, exacerbated the proceedings. In their political aspect the trials were akin to the old type of witch trial, in which the accusation of witchcraft was used, sometimes cynically, as a means to convict, or make popular the conviction, of a particular person. One is reminded of the situation a hundred years earlier when the earl of Mar, a source of faction, was accused of attempting to bewitch his brother, King James III. The earl of Mar was assassinated, and several witches and warlocks who were supposed to have conspired with him were executed to discredit his name.

The trials of 1590–91 were the last of this type of treason-cum-sorcery trial in Scotland. Here Scotland was following a pattern already seen in England and on the Continent where early prosecutions had been initiated for political reasons. Once the persecution of witchcraft became an end in itself, prosecutions were mainly of obscure people.

The features which were new to Scotland in the trials were the demonic pact, and the witches' meetings to worship the devil; and these became central points in many later Scottish prosecutions. And the mere fact of a mass trial for treason by sorcery does not explain the presence of these elements. Indeed, despite the fact that Scotland was more dependent on Roman law than England, there seems no reason why Scotland could not have continued on the same course that had prevailed between 1563 and 1590 and like England avoided the full horrors of European demonic beliefs.

In considering this problem it is difficult to escape the conclusion that James himself was the principal, if not the sole, purveyor to his people of the concept of the demonic pact. In the autumn of 1589 the king had gone on a gallant voyage to Denmark to collect his bride. She had already set out for Scotland once and had had to turn back because of bad weather. James had never enjoyed himself so much as he did at the Danish Court, and he stayed through the winter, dancing, feasting, hunting, engaging in learned disputations; flattered, wooed and listened to. When at last the Scottish party set sail in the spring of 1590 they had a very rough passage and one of the attendant ships was lost. Despite the fact that the phenomenon of equinoctial gales was a familiar one, the ferocity of these gales was blamed on witchcraft. Witches were apprehended in Copenhagen on charges of storm-raising against the King of Scotland. The Scots were not long in looking for culprits on their side of the North Sea. Rumours are said to have been current that the storms were caused by witches working in both Denmark and Scotland.[20]

The whole problem of tracing the beginning of the panic is the problem of detecting the origins of rumour. It is possible that it was the Danish connection which helped to stimulate witch persecution in Scotland. Certainly witch-hunting was endemic in Denmark at the time and James may well have been influenced by this during his six-month stay there. So far as demonology is concerned, he is known to have enjoyed his discussions with Lutheran theologians, and with the astronomer Tycho Brahe. And he also visited Hemmingius, whom he later cited with approval in *Daemonologie*.[21] It was James's first encounter with continental thinkers and he must have been introduced to many new ideas then. He is likely to have been impressed by the fact that the learned and important in that country took the terrors and menace of witchcraft seriously. Such ideas may have been further spread among the Scottish ruling classes during the return visit paid by the Danish Court in the month of May 1590. This is all speculative, but it is at least suggestive, for, by whatever means the ideas travelled, it is clear that they were unknown in 1589; they were in the air by the end of 1590, and during the winter trials the king was their principal exponent.

G. L. Kittredge, who successfully established that James rapidly became a sceptic on demonology after his arrival in England, attempted, on much less secure grounds, to exonerate him from blame in the Scottish persecution. His argument was that the worst period of persecution in Scotland did not come till long after James's reign, that James did not initiate the prosecutions in 1590, and that, 'he did not teach the Scottish nation the witch creed: that creed was the heritage of the human race and was nowhere less questioned by all classes and all professions than in Scotland.'[22] The first point is true, but irrelevant. The second is dubious. The third is again dubious, and to back it up by suggestion that the outbreak of prosecutions was the result of a great popular panic which James could not possibly have resisted is to overstrain the evidence that has come down to us. The facts are that James from time to time exhorted jurors to convict, sometimes unsuccessfully, that he took an intense interest in all the trials, and that by the spring of 1591 he was one of the principal agents in keeping them alive. He showed particular zeal for example in the case of Barbara Napier who was arrested for consulting with witches for treasonable purposes, and who was known to be a friend of Bothwell. She claimed to be with child, and James wrote to Maitland in April 1591: 'Try by the mediciners' oaths if Barbara Napier be with bairn or not. Take no delaying answer. If you find she be not, to the fire with her presently, and cause bowel her publicly.' [23] One of the reasons, apart from her pregnancy, why the jury were reluctant to convict was that the clause in the 1563 act which imposed death merely for consulting witches had never before been enforced, and that therefore it was felt hard to execute her. It was presumably her connection with Bothwell which made James quite so vindictive towards her. Certainly the case of Bothwell was *sub judice* at the time. One correspondent was writing from Durham to a friend in Ireland:

> The Lord Bothwell of Scotland is committed to Edinburgh Castle for conspiring the King's death by sorcery as they say. He stands upon his truth and craves that by combat against his accuser, though however so mean a person, he may defend himself. We say that he shall die. The Scots would be the contrary; but if he die they spare not to speak that to him as to others we make their King a butcher to serve our turns.[24]

And Bowes, the English ambassador, writing to Burghley: 'The King's forwardness in these matters persuades many that they shall not fall so suddenly to such end' (i.e. that Bothwell might yet escape the country).[25]

The implication of these comments is that the country was not behind the king or the Government in their attempt to implicate Bothwell and his friends in the witches' conspiracy. It was James who was determined to see the matter through. The reasons why he moved so rapidly from a position of indifference to witches before 1590 to that of being the most ardent prosecutor in these trials cannot be stated categorically. The most convincing explanation does seem to be a two-fold one: that he was introduced to demonology and titillated by it in Denmark, and returned to Scotland suggestible and ready to see witchcraft where he had seen none before. When the rumours of treasonable sorcery started he was receptive rather than sceptical. He was doubly receptive because the attack was directly on himself. It was that assault on his kingly person that consolidated his convictions about the reality of the sorcery threat.

Certainly the trials were to James treason trials before they were sorcery trials. The most appalling aspect of the affair to him was the attempt upon his sacred life. The method was secondary, but once the method had been accepted it fell easily into place. It was entirely natural that the force behind the attempt to kill him should be the devil himself. The king was the Lord's Anointed; therefore he was the greatest enemy in Scotland that the devil could have. James early fell into a state of mind in which any attempt on the part of the judiciary to acquit an accused witch was seen as a failure to take seriously the treasonable threat to the king's majesty. The importance of taking no risks with persons who would be a further potential threat to his life took precedence over the question of the actual guilt or otherwise of the accused. It was not the witch theory which James had been incubating during his fearful and clergy-ridden youth; it was the doctrine of the divine right of kings.

This attitude is well illustrated in the speech[26] which James made to the recalcitrant jurors on their acquittal of Barbara Napier. This has often been cited by historians in support of the view that James already regarded himself as an expert on the subject of witchcraft, one ready to instruct the unenlightened, but in fact there are only three brief references to the crime of witchcraft as such in the long speech. In the tenor of the speech taken as a whole, it is quite plain that his primary anxiety is not that a witch might go free, but that a king, endeavouring at twenty-four to exercise the benevolent paternalism which was his responsibility, might be thwarted. He was deeply mortified by the presumption of this jury in acquitting a woman he believed to be guilty of treason. The greater part of the speech is an expression of this paternal grievance. He began by explaining that the reason why no monarch had ever before interfered in criminal matters was because of the 'nonage of my forbears', and continued:

> Yet this I say, that—howsoever matters have gone against my will I am innocent of all injustice in these behalfs, and for my part my conscience doth set me clear, as did the conscience of Samuel, and I call you to be my judges herein. And suppose I be your king, yet I submit myself to the accusations of you my subjects in this behalf, and let any one say what I have done. And as I have this begun, so purpose I to go forward; not because I am James Stuart, and can command so many thousands of men, but because God hath made me a king and judge to judge righteous judgement.

He emphasised how narrowly he had escaped death through the activities of the witches, and protested that he personally did not fear death, but was only concerned for 'the common good of this country, which enjoyeth peace by my life. . . as you may collect by mine absence, for if such troubles were in breeding whilst I retained life, what would have been done if my life had been taken from me'.

Treason dominated sorcery at the time, but in the aftermath when the immediate fear of treason had died down and Bothwell had finally fled the country, the fear of witchcraft, which had been implanted during that winter of trials, began to increase. The authorities, including the king, had taken witchcraft seriously. The principal wise women, and the most cantakerous cursers in every village within earshot of Edinburgh, assumed a new importance and a new menace. Commissions were set up to hunt out witches, and naturally they found them.

The effect on James himself was equally marked. The picture of himself as the principal target for witches became an integral part of the myth of kingship which James was using to glamorise his personality. But there was a delicate balance to be maintained here. There was a possibility that his new-found interest in witchcraft, unless carefully stated and defined, could equally well damage his image, especially in England. It was probably this anxiety which led to his further researches, justifications and at length the publication of *Daemonologie* in 1597.

In the immediate aftermath, the saga of the North Berwick witches was used to enhance James's credit in England in the tract *News from Scotland*, published in London in 1591 'according to the Scottish copie'. Whether this is supposed to refer to a published work, to a manuscript, or to nothing at all, is not clear, but on internal evidence there is a high degree of probability that the tract was written directly for an English reading public. The work belongs to the English type of witch tract: it purports to inform and educate; in practice it titillates and tells a gruesomely enjoyable story. The orthography is English rather than Scottish and the English term 'deputy bailiffe' is used instead of the local 'baillie depute'. Two clear points are made to the English public about the part played by James: the first was that he was said to be initially sceptical about the possibility of magic being used against him. According to the pamphlet when James first heard the accounts of the witches' performances at North Berwick he was not impressed and accused them all of lying. Agnes Sampson, a principal suspect in the early stages, took him aside and told him

the very words which passed between the King's Majesty and his Queen at Upslo in Norway the first night of marriage, with the answers each to other, whereat the King's Majesty wondered greatly, and swore by the living God, that he believed all the devils in hell could not have discovered the same, acknowledging her words to be most true, and therefore gave the more credit to the rest that is before declared'.[27]

It was a familiar feature of witch tracts to have in them some sceptical figure who was later convinced by some infallible proof such as that just given. The second point put across was that James, according to the witches who might be supposed to have known, was regarded as the greatest enemy that the devil had on the earth. The whole saga was a piece of high flattery to James. Messages and accounts from ambassadors served the same purpose.

The principal threat to the success of this novel attempt to enhance James's stock in England was the work of Reginald Scot, whose book *The Discoverie of Witchcraft* had been published in 1584. It was a widely known, well documented and courageous attack on the belief in witchcraft. It was courageous in that sceptics about witchcraft always laid themselves open to accusations of atheism. But it was respectably learned, influential and to James potentially dangerous. The story that on his arrival in England he caused all known copies of the book to be publicly burned may be apocryphal, but certainly the prime declared purpose of writing *Daemonologie* was to refute 'the damnable opinion of two principally in our age, whereof the one called SCOT, an Englishman, is not ashamed in public print to deny that there can be such a thing as witchcraft: and so maintains the old error of the Sadducees, in denying of spirits'.[28]

James's intention was to produce a significant contribution to the general international debate, and in the process instruct those of his subjects, and his potential subjects, who were still doubtful or ignorant on the subject of witchcraft. In fact his book is not in the same league as Scot's. It is a great deal shorter: some eighty pages as opposed to Scot's 600 odd; it is derivative, and, in marked contrast to Scot, who gives in his first edition an alphabetical bibliography of 216 foreign and twenty-four English authors, he gives very few references, all of which are to be found in Scot.

Daemonologie is written as a dialogue between one Philomathes, who asks sceptical and sometimes highly pertinent questions, and Epistemon, who gives learned but often unsatisfactory answers which Philomathes invariably accepts gratefully. There are three books, dealing with magic in general, with sorcery and witchcraft, and with spirits and ghosts. James makes the demonic pact the centre of the second book, and repeats the standard theories about the renunciation of baptism and the bestowal of the devil's mark. He credits witches with power to harm or kill by incantations over wax images which they melt over a fire, and adds that they

> can raise storms and tempests in the air, either upon the sea or land, though not universally, but in such a particular place and prescribed bounds, as God will permit them so to trouble: which likewise is very easy to be discerned from any other natural tempests that are not nature's, in respect of the sudden and violent raising thereof, together with the short enduring of the same. And this is likewise very possible to their master to do.[29]

All this suggests that the justification of his part in the treason scare was still uppermost in James's mind, and an important part of the motivation for writing the book.

The point which gives him the most obvious difficulty, and is apparent in the passage cited above, is that of the relative power of God and the devil. Throughout his treatise James vacillates between a Calvinist and a dualist position, with the emphasis, though rather confused, on the ultimate omnipotence of God. 'It is true', he allows Epistemon to admit, 'that the devil cannot foretell all things in the future', but he does have considerable knowledge and 'he knows it only as his being worldly wise and taught by a continual experience, ever since the creation.'[30] The idea that the power of the devil comes from an excess of worldly wisdom gained by having been around the place for a very long time is novel by any standards, but one which James does not develop.

Perhaps his most interesting point is a psycho-sociological observation of the reasons why people take up witchcraft. They are led, he wrote, 'even by these three passions that are within ourselves: curiosity in great ingines [ingenia = minds]; thirst of revenge for some torts deeply apprehended; or greedy appetite of gear, caused through great poverty. As to the first of these, curiosity, it is only the enticement of magicians, or necromancers—and the other two are the allures of sorcerers or witches.'[31]

In the same year in which *Daemonologie* was published James showed signs of anxiety about the rate of prosecutions for witchcraft. It is possible that having justified the panic in which he was personally involved he felt free to stem the panic persecution of others. At any rate in 1597 he revoked the standing commissions against witchcraft. But although this temporarily halted the number of prosecutions, the witch doctrine had by this time taken an almost complete hold of the clergy, gentry and legal profession of Scotland. This in its turn encouraged already existing village belief, and allowed villagers and townsmen complete licence in their accusations. Only occasionally did they meet an independent-minded and brave judiciary.

James's departure for England in 1603 in fact ensured that the persecution of witchcraft in Scotland would continue, for he made no attempt, after that, to interfere in the Scottish prosecutions. The Scottish Privy Council granted commissions for trying witches on its own initiative through the rest of his reign. During this period there seems to have been an average of about twenty cases of witchcraft a year, about half of which resulted in executions. While James's part in contributing to this situation cannot be denied, he was far from being the sole force behind it. The clergy and the legal profession took up the hunt with zeal; for the populace it was a major diversion in their harsh and bleak lives.

By the time that James rode to England he had lost his intense interest in witchcraft. The English Crown had pushed everything else into the background. Furthermore England was a different world. James, despite loyalty to his Scottish courtiers and old favourites, reacted immediately and with characteristic flexibility, to the immense gulf in sophistication between the styles of the Scottish and English Courts.

Two features are worth re-emphasising here about the state of the witch belief in England. The first is that continental demonic witchcraft never loomed large in the English prosecutions. Simple *maleficium* remained the staple diet. The second is that by this time the number of prosecutions was declining. Seventeenth-century England has a more lurid reputation for witchcraft than the England of the sixteenth century. But this can be accounted for by the few large-scale panics such as those of Lancashire in 1612 and Essex in 1645, which were much written about; and by the general increase in pamphlet literature in this century. Statistical work on the Home Circuit records has suggested that the high period for prosecutions was the reign of Elizabeth.[32] Thereafter prosecutions and convictions waned. For the elite it was fast becoming a subject for lewd, if slightly dangerous, humour.

Yet James could not but arrive with a reputation for a high level of interest in witchcraft. His own propaganda in England had ensured that. An indication of this reputation is that Macbeth is thought to have been specially written as a court play for performance to James in 1604. Its unusually short length (James was known to fidget through full-length theatre), the flattering references to Banquo's line and the centrality of the theme of prophecy by witchcraft, all suggest this.[33] The reputation of James as a perpetual and consistent demonologist has in the past, and even quite lately, been accepted as justified by historians. This older view was that James came to England as a triumphant witch-hunter ready to do for England what he had done for Scotland, and root out the pestilence of sorcery there as well; also that his arrival did give a new impetus to the persecution in England and marked the beginning of a reign of terror. This picture was built up before the statistical work of C. L'Estrange Ewen was published in 1929 but it has clung.[34] It was based partly on the fact that the new English Witchcraft Act of 1604 was more severe than the Elizabethan act of 1563 and the assumption that this was necessarily followed by more severe proceedings. It was also thought that James took a vigorous and interested part (similar to that played by him during the North Berwick investigations) in the trials of the Lancashire witches of 1612, although the sole source for this last story appears to be the imagination of Harrison Ainsworth in his novel *The Lancashire Witches*.

The picture altered on close inspection. G. L. Kittredge was on firmer ground in his attempt to clear James of having intensified an English persecution than he was in clearing him of helping to initiate the Scottish one. He compared the Elizabethan Witchcraft Act clause by clause with that of 1604, and showed that the later act was more severe in one clause only: that ordaining death for a first conviction of raising up evil spirits. This clause, he showed, was not in fact enforced in James's reign at all, and was only used during the Essex outbreak of 1645. Though he did not know of Ewen's work, he estimated that there were certainly no more executions in James's reign in England than under Elizabeth, and very possibly fewer. He also made it clear that not only did James not attend the trials of the Lancashire witches; he knew nothing about them until after they were hanged. He showed that James's main interest in witches during his reign in England was not to hound them down but to detect impostors.

It is possible that his interest in this aspect of witch detection may have stemmed from a continued anxiety to correct a possible unfavourable reputation for panicking easily on witchcraft, and to emphasise that his interest in demonology was not overcredulous or unsophisticated. Some indication of the way in which his reputation for expert knowledge was received is shown in the well-known letter of Sir John Harrington to Sir Amyas Paulet in which he records a conversation with the king:

His Majesty did much press for my opinion touching the power of Satan in matters of witchcraft; and asked me, with much gravity, if I did truly understand why the devil did work more with ancient women than others? I did not refrain from a scurvy jest, and even said (notwithstanding to whom it was said) that we were taught hereof in scripture, where it is told that the devil walketh in dry places. . . . More serious discourse did next ensue. . . .[35]

Such theology as James wrote during his years in England also shows a greatly reduced interest in the demonic. In his *Meditation on the Lord's Prayer* published in 1619, he makes no attempt to use the 'deliver us from evil' phrase as a starting point for a discourse on Satan. This phrase, he wrote, follows on from 'lead us not into temptation', and refers to the evil of temptation and punishment: an explanation which would have come as easily from a contemporary liberal theologian. 'The Greek hath it,' he goes on to admit, 'from the evil one; and these words put us in mind what need we have of continual prayer to God, to be preserved from that old traiterous and restless enemy—*qui circundet terram.*' 'The Latin, *a malo,*' he continued, can mean 'any evil thing or the evil one—whether by means of Satan or otherwise'.[36] King James at fifty-three appeared to have lost sight of demonology.

In conclusion it is worth pointing out that while witchcraft loomed larger in Scotland after 1590 than it did in England, it is in the field of English witchcraft that important new research has recently been done. Alan Macfarlane's book on Essex witchcraft[37] and Keith Thomas's more general work[38] covering all aspects of religion and magic in England in the sixteenth and seventeenth centuries, were inspired by the methods and ideas of social anthropologists. These writers have laid stress on the collection of statistical information about witchcraft accusations and prosecutions from hitherto unexplored manuscript sources, and in this way have enormously enriched the picture that previous historians had gained from chap-books, pamphlets and published trials.

English witchcraft beliefs, unlike those of the rest of Europe at the time, were simple, related to local experience and not very closely integrated with official Christianity. It is this resemblance of English witchcraft to the beliefs and practices of modern single-culture societies which has made it appear sensible to apply concepts developed by social anthropologists from twentieth-century field-work to an historical situation. Their anthropological framework has caused these historians to look principally at the experience of the accused and accusing villager rather than the administrative system under which they were judged, and to explain the rise and fall of witchcraft accusations in terms of the replacement of a neighbourly by a commercial ethic, and consequent social tension.

The subject matter of the present chapter gives a special opportunity for setting the Scottish witchcraft experience alongside the English. No comparable work has been done on accusations at village level in Scotland, but if the picture given in this essay of the way in which the persecution developed in Scotland is anywhere near accurate, it shows the witch panic developing from the beliefs and attitudes of the elite, rather than as a spontaneous expression from below. One cannot discount the possibility that social forces in late sixteenth-century Scotland were an important factor; all one can say is that explanations in these terms would be a great deal more vague than those given here for the Scottish outbreak. To stress the importance of political activity and elitist ideas may not explain the persecution in any psychological depth, but it does at least account for its appearance at a specific point in time.

There is a question left open. Given that English society at this time had more than one cultural level, it resembled that of Scotland more closely than any primitive monocultural society. What part, therefore in the English persecution can be ascribed to clergy, magistrates and gentry? Despite the great differences in intensity and quality, it would seem that the English villager with an accusation to make was as dependent for getting his case heard on the attitude of the local authorities as his Scottish counterpart. It is clear that it was the prosecuting class that helped to reduce the incidence of cases in both countries in the late seventeenth century. It seems reasonable that their more sympathetic attitude in earlier times must have encouraged those who thought themselves bewitched to bring forward their accusations. There are three parties to a witch trial: the accuser, the accused and the judge; and it is the role of the last that tends to be left out of the explanation by social tension. Future researchers may yet have to return to the study of the world-view of the social and political elite.[39] In the meantime what better mirror to elitist opinion than the utterances of a fashion-conscious king?

5. The English Catholic Community 1603-1625

JOHN BOSSY

THE Catholic community has a shadowy existence in histories of the reign of James I. From Gardiner's narrative we get a good deal of information on the oscillations of official policy towards recusants and priests, on the Gunpowder Plot and its sequel, and on problems faced by the king in formulating a guarantee of good intentions towards his Catholic subjects which would satisfy a king of Spain or France contemplating a marriage between his daughter and James's son; we discover that Catholic beliefs were making progress at Court. But about the Catholic community itself, and about its contribution to the emergence of religious plurality among Englishmen, we learn practically nothing: Gardiner's thoughts on the subject were contained in a single paragraph. Here he remarked that the Catholics were 'no petty sect to which a contemptuous toleration might be accorded', but 'a very considerable proportion of the community'; that they were increasing to an extent which represented a threat to English liberties; and that, though their present condition might in general be acceptable to the Catholic laity, it was not acceptable to the clergy, who 'could not be content . . . with the edification of their existing congregations' and were driven by a continuing urge to 'fulfil the mission on which they had come'.[1] This was vague indeed, though not entirely misleading. Gardiner was admittedly a nineteenth-century political historian, and his treatment of other religious bodies may not have been much more adequate than this; but, while more recent historians have amply made up what Gardiner lacked in his treatment of English Protestantism, they do not seem to have made much progress with the Catholics: the latest notes laconically that they 'survived'.[2] The position is not in fact as bad as this would indicate, but there is still a strong tendency for research and interest in English Catholicism to fade after 1603, and it is not easy to get a clear impression of what was happening to it in the Jacobean period. In the circumstances it seems wise to eschew anything too ambitious, and to pursue a few themes chosen because they have a certain coherence among themselves, and because they indicate areas where

For Notes to Chapter 5, see pages 233–6; for Bibliography, see page 220.

the experience of English Catholics may have something to contribute to the comprehension of English society as a whole.

What was most obviously new about the English Catholic body after 1603 was its retreat from the political engagements which had marked the Elizabethan period. This was true in two senses. After 1603 there was a sharp decline in the interest which the major Catholic governments of Europe showed in its potentialities as a political force. Few now believed that it was a serious deterrent which might be used to influence or undermine the actions of an English Government, far less to replace it by a different one. For the Spaniards this conviction was expressed in the peace of 1604. Philip III had tried to insist on concessions to English Catholics as a condition for making peace, but his counsellors were sceptical and the idea was quietly abandoned; it was not worth their while antagonising James by trying to maintain some sort of protectorate over his Catholic subjects. The French soon came to the same conclusion. By 1605 they had given up trying to make anything of the anti-Jesuit movement among English Catholics, and Henry IV returned a fairly tepid response when the Jesuits, disgruntled at being let down by the Spaniards, offered to transfer their affections to him. During the last decade or so of the reign, in the course of James's marriage negotiations first with the Spaniards and then with the French, the notion of doing something for Catholics in England cropped up a good deal, and both governments made some gesture in this direction a condition of any treaty; but this was chiefly in order to get a marriage dispensation from the pope, and does not imply that they thought the goodwill of English Catholics was worth much. At the very close of the reign there was a revival of foreign intervention in their affairs, due largely to the progress of the Counter-Reformation in France, but in essentials they were on their own politically after 1604.[3]

Left to their own devices, they found it on the whole congenial to forget about political issues altogether. It may seem surprising to say this of a period when several of them were deeply engaged in arguments about political allegiance set off by the statute of 1606, which made Catholics not members of the nobility liable to be required to swear, among other things, that they abhorred and detested as impious and heretical the damnable doctrine 'that Princes which be excommunicated or deprived by the Pope may be deposed or murdered by their subjects'. The dispute about whether or not they were entitled to take this oath has been described as a 'cross-issue', not falling into the existing grooves of internal controversy within the community; it might also be described as a non-issue, since by the time the argument was over the question was no longer of any significance.[4]

What was happening may be gathered from the tactics of the chief English supporter of the oath, the Benedictine Thomas Preston. Preston wrote under the name of a well-known Catholic layman, the Northumbrian Roger Widdrington, and his arguments were well adjusted to the feelings of the Catholic gentry. He claimed that the pope's deposing power was not a matter of faith but a 'probable' opinion on which the clergy could not legitimately give binding advice. There was no obligation on the laity, in defence of this opinion, 'to be deprived of all their goods, to be accounted traitors to their prince and country, and moreover to suffer their children, nephews, kinsmen and their whole posterity, which this our age doth so much labour to advance, to be brought to perpetual beggary'.[5] Widdrington was a symptom of a shift in the balance of power in the community from the clergy, who had dominated the Elizabethan decades, towards the nobility and gentry; the surviving leaders of Elizabethan Catholicism were obliged to adapt themselves to it. Robert Parsons, who remained a formidable figure until his death in 1610, had not gone out of his way to conciliate landowning Catholics before 1603, and was among other things identified with a populist political theory. Against the statutory oath, which was intended to eradicate this theory, Parsons did indeed defend the deposing power; but in some respects his position was now not very far from Widdrington's, in that privately at least he conceded that Catholics were not under an obligation to do anything about carrying it into effect. It was only an extended version of Parsons's argument which led the archpriest George Blackwell to conclude that the oath was admissible. This moderation is one of several indications that after 1603 Parsons had decided to do what he could to appease the gentry; it was part of a more general shift towards envisaging as permanent for English Catholics the sectarian condition which, as Professor Jordan has rightly pointed out, most of the gentry were already anxious to settle for.[6]

The attitude of the secular clergy leaders calls for a little more comment. The Appellant priests, who had composed and signed the familiar 'Protestation' of allegiance to Queen Elizabeth in January 1603, were precisely those, one might have thought, who would have proved most willing to accept the statutory oath; it was in fact they more than anyone who ensured that James's effort should prove abortive. This may puzzle those who have accepted the view that the Appellants were motivated above all by feelings of political loyalty or nationalism.[7] To understand it, one must look for a moment at the background to the Protestation itself. What seems to have happened in 1602-3 was that Elizabeth's Privy Council was favourable to the idea of a corporal oath of allegiance, to be taken in person by individual priests, as a means of distinguishing the seditious from the rest. The idea was accepted by the more extreme members of the party, notably by William Watson, but rejected by a majority which included most of the responsible members and in particular the experienced northern missioner John Mush. Their instinct was that taking an oath of this kind in this manner derogated from their clerical status, and would lead to a disintegration of the body of Catholic secular clergy in England, whose unity they were struggling to preserve. This was much strengthened when it emerged in discussion that the Council—or at least a majority of the councillors, since there may have been some division on this point —would only guarantee immunity from penal legislation to priests who, having taken an oath, ceased thereafter to perform their priestly ministry in England. On these grounds the Appellants refused to offer any formula for an oath, and produced instead their Protestation: a written declaration, signed by those who agreed with it—which excluded Watson and others—and presented by deputies acting on behalf of the signatories. By implication this was a collective act of the whole body of the Catholic secular clergy of England, and they added to the text a stiff declaration making it clear that they intended to go on behaving as priests, and affirming their submission to the spiritual authority of the see of Rome. In this form and with this content the Protestation was dismissed as unacceptable: the Council and the majority of the Appellants were at cross-purposes, and had not come to any sort of agreement at all.[8]

In this light the apparently contradictory attitude of the same priests three years later is easily understood. What they were now presented with was much what they had rejected in 1603, and once again it seems to have been Mush who took the lead in turning it down; two signatories of the Protestation were executed after having refused to take the statutory oath. This decision isolated the clerical oath-takers like Preston and Blackwell and ensured that the Catholic clergy as a body would survive the controversy with little damage. One should add that after the papacy had condemned the oath the secular clergy leaders were extremely sensitive to the damage which suspicions of their unreliability on this score might do to their reputation in Rome.[9] But from this also one may deduce that they were first and foremost Roman Catholic priests, and their concerns ecclesiastical rather than political; in offering formulae of allegiance they had been trespassing on ground which was best left to the gentry, and after one unsuccessful experience they were anxious enough to abandon it. In their own way they too were abstracting themselves from the political concerns which had been interwoven with the experience of the Elizabethan mission.

The immediate cause of the oath controversy, and the most memorable political action undertaken by English Catholics during the reign, was of course the Gunpowder Plot. I do not pretend to expertise on this subject, but will venture three remarks. First I do not think it was all got up by the Government, or that the conspirators were *agents provocateurs* let loose by Robert Cecil on the Catholic community and the English Jesuits to provide an excuse for delivering them a knock-out blow; no such blow followed.[10] Second I am sure that one must in some sense regard the conspiracy as the last fling of the Elizabethan tradition of a politically engaged Catholicism. One must surely recognise in the mind of Robert Catesby, its moving spirit, a garbled version of political themes which had been enunciated by pro-Spanish Catholics during the reign of Elizabeth: his case of conscience about the legitimacy of killing innocent parties in a good cause presented a problem which must have occurred to many of their readers; his hostility to the aristocracy recalls Parsons's own. It would be most unfair to treat the conspiracy as a natural consequence of Elizabethan Catholic political theory, which it caricatured, or of Jesuit preaching. Henry Garnet, the Jesuit superior in England, was a loyalist; he seems always to have thought that missionary work could go on perfectly well without political afterthoughts, and did as much as could reasonably have been expected, though not perhaps as much as he might have been advised to do, to get the *coup* called off. All the same James was probably right in believing that the attempt would not have been made if there had not been abroad among some of the Catholic gentry notions about overthrowing supposedly tyrannical governments derived, probably at second or third hand, from the political literature of Elizabethan Catholicism.[11] Finally the immediate occasion of the plot has normally been seen in James's failure to fulfil undertakings about toleration of Catholics understood to have been given before his accession. This is no doubt true in a general way, but what turned a sense of disgruntlement into the plot as it actually emerged was the retraction of international political interest in the English Catholics: it is probably best placed among the after-effects of the Anglo-Spanish peace of 1604. The

Government was not merely being tender to foreign powers when it went out of its way to announce, in publishing the news of the plot, that there was no evidence that any of them had had anything to do with it. The conspirators were set on the path of melodramatic violence because they had discovered that the Spaniards were neither interested in more orthodox forms of assault nor prepared to subsidise those who suggested them.[12] At the same time Garnet had fallen out with the Spaniards over the peace treaty, and so had no chance to bring effective external pressure to bear on Catesby and his friends.[13] So the plot went forward. In the history of English Catholicism it seems to me of rather more significance than recent historians have usually granted it. In its own grotesque way it figured the end of an epoch; it helped to precipitate a withdrawal of Catholics from the general concerns of the commonwealth which was probably in their circumstances the lesser of two evils.[14] It clarified the terms on which a Catholic community could come into existence in a Protestant England.

Unwarranted political ambitions were not the only obstacle to this readjustment: in the long run, it was the ecclesiastical obstacles which proved more difficult to surmount. In the ecclesiastical politics of English Catholicism, King James's reign occupied a pause between two confrontations, the Archpriest controversy of 1598–1602, and the so-called Chalcedon controversy of 1625–31. Both of these arose from attempts to create a Catholic ecclesiastical structure in a Protestant country, and involved a conflict of missionary and hierarchical conceptions of what that structure ought to be.

During the reign hierarchical aspirations in the form of a claim for 'ordinary' episcopal government, made rapid progress among the secular clergy. The movement, which was throughout the chief concern of the Appellant priests, had got under way in the 1590s, and may be considered part of the wider conservative revival characteristic of the English ecclesiastical scene during that decade. By 1603, although they had failed to persuade the papacy to abandon its invention of government by archpriest, they had achieved a compromise by which this regime was continued, but those who objected to it were in effect invited to take it over. In 1602 Pope Clement VIII had instructed Blackwell to see that some of the twelve 'assistants' who were to act as his advisers and local representatives should be drawn from priests who had led the agitation against him; five years later, when Blackwell had been removed from office for taking the oath of allegiance, they constituted a majority firm enough to carry his successor with them. Parsons was able to block further progress during his lifetime, but the movement advanced steadily after his death. In 1613 the college at Douai was transferred from hostile into friendly hands; from 1621 the archpriest regime was in abeyance; in 1623 a bishop was finally secured, in the person of William Bishop, one of the original Appellants. In the short time at his disposal, since he died after a few months in office, Bishop was able to replace the *ad hoc* organisation of the archpriests by an orthodox structure of vicars-general, archdeacons and rural deans; he also erected a dean and chapter. This was an important step for various reasons. It was the expression of a claim that his office was that of a bishop-in-ordinary, not a mere delegate of papal authority; it provided for the continuity of the hierarchical structure in case the papacy should fail to maintain the future succession of bishops, as in fact it did; perhaps most important of all, it gave an institutional embodiment to what had been one of the principal claims of the Appellant clergy from the first—the claim that the existing body of Catholic secular clergy in England was legally and historically speaking identical with the *Ecclesia Anglicana* as it had stood before the Reformation. This claim to continuity the chapter was designed to preserve: as Bishop expressed it, there could be no properly constituted church without bishop, cathedral and chapter; though its material structures and revenues might be in other hands, spiritually the *Ecclesia Anglicana* was intact. It maintained its claims and the historic jurisdiction which belonged to it by the ordinary course of canon law.[15]

If we look at it from a political point of view, and confine ourselves to its earlier phases, we may well see the Appellant or secular clergy movement as forward-looking, an attempt to face the facts and come to terms with the realities of post-Reformation England.[16] If we look at it from an ecclesiastical point of view, we get precisely the opposite impression. The two judgements may be equally correct; but there seems a case, in interpreting the secular clergy leaders' conduct, for thinking less of Acton and Cavour, and more of Bancroft and Laud. This was certainly the comparison which came to suggest itself to the Catholic gentry, whose hostility explains the collapse of hierarchical ambitions during the reign of Charles I.

For their own sake, the seculars might have devoted some of the time which they spent on questions of ecclesiastical structure attending more closely to the practical problems of the missions. While they were achieving a series of successes in high ecclesiastical politics, their antagonists were quietly cutting the ground from under their feet; for the

English Jesuits the reign, which had not begun under very promising auspices, turned out surprisingly well. Parsons's concern, at the close of his career, to disarm some of the antagonisms which had accumulated against him, helped to clear the way for a redirection of Jesuit efforts in England. They set to work to restore good relations with the gentry and aristocracy, and to build up the independent missionary organisation which was now required, since as part of his settlement of the Archpriest controversy in 1602 Clement VIII had ordered the separation of secular and Jesuit missions.[17] Garnet, Richard Blount, superior in England after 1615, and Thomas Fitzherbert, who succeeded Parsons as rector of the English College in Rome, were between them well qualified to accomplish both these tasks. Garnet was the most impressive figure of the three, and had taken several of the steps required before his execution in 1606; the long regime of Blount and Fitzherbert, which lasted practically until the Civil War, built very successfully on his foundations, though it may be that they did not quite achieve Garnet's balance between the two objectives of pacifying the gentry and building up the mission, and were inclined, when in doubt, to settle for the first.[18]

The first sign of their success was a rapid expansion of the number of Jesuit missioners working in England. In 1600 there were hardly more than a dozen; by 1620 there were more than a hundred, and the number continued to rise until the Civil War, reaching a peak between 150 and 200 at which it remained for more than a century.[19] Since the days of the Elizabethan mission, the English Jesuits had transformed themselves from a tiny self-conscious elite into a mass missionary body. Several factors lay behind this transformation. Although after 1602 formal connections between the Jesuits and the secular clergy had been severed, a high proportion of the secular missioners had got used to working with Jesuit support and under Jesuit supervision; influences of loyalty, spiritual formation and practical assistance worked strongly to maintain the attachment. The simplest way of securing this was to apply for admission to the Society; Garnet was able to persuade his general, Acquaviva, to give him authority to admit those he judged suitable, and after his death Blount established in and around London a series of houses in which a period of novitiate might be passed. The last of these was the so-called 'Jesuit college' in Clerkenwell exposed in 1628.[20] Besides, the experience of their pioneers had given the English Jesuits an accumulation of missionary competence which had as yet no equivalent elsewhere. They had thought

seriously about problems of organisation, distribution and finance, about
the practicalities of a missionary life, and about methods of approaching
the laity and responding to their needs. The Jesuit annual letters, which
begin soon after 1600, contain a great deal of propaganda and some
dubious statistics, but they do testify to a genuine concern for missionary problems, and the expansion of the order in England was a justified response to this concern.[21] It also reflected their determination to
cultivate the gentry, as one may see from the volume of financial support which now began to accrue to the Jesuits from the resources of
English landownership.

Here there were two problems: the support of individual missioners,
and the resources of the mission as a whole. Since the days of Parsons
and Campion, the Jesuits in England had shown themselves anxious to
avoid dependence on income provided directly by an individual patron,
but after 1600 they were obliged to settle a growing number of priests
as permanent residents in gentry houses, 'sitting'—as a description of
their condition put it—'like sparrows upon the housetop'.[22] Garnet had
been able to build a central fund of fairly considerable size to serve the
general needs of the mission, and in particular to support priests in areas
and among classes of the population which were hardly able to support
them themselves. Large benefactions from the gentry and aristocracy
had been put into this fund, and by the close of James's reign these
were coming in at a steady rate. There was one from the Somersets, not
apparently from the head of the family, the fourth earl of Worcester,
but from his daughter Lady Francis Somerset, made on her deathbed
in 1620; another seems to have come about the same time from the two
daughters of the Elizabethan Lord Vaux, Anne Vaux and Eleanor
Brooksby; a large endowment from the second Lord Petre followed a
few years later. But in this case too earlier plans had to be modified, in
that these benefactions were tied to areas of particular interest to the
testators, and in most cases the family held on to the capital. This
meant that they could not be incorporated into a single fund for the
use of the mission as a whole, and that local arrangements had to be
made for exploiting them.[23] Largely for this reason the organisational
structure of the Jesuit mission as it emerged during the reign put more
stress on the local bodies known as 'districts' or 'residences' than on the
centre; and this distribution was not really altered when, between 1619
and 1623, the process was completed by the erection of the mission,
along with its supporting establishments abroad, into a full province of
the Society, with Richard Blount as its first provincial. Here too the

influence of the gentry and a financial motive were visible, since it was held that benefactions would flow more freely to a body which possessed full autonomy and a superior resident in England.[24]

Altogether, during the twenty years which followed their separation from the secular clergy, the English Jesuits had acquired a position of formidable strength. This had been achieved at some cost. Not only had they renounced the grand reforming designs and concern for common-wealth matters which had characterised the middle career of Parsons; they had also made renunciations in the strictly missionary field. Culti-vating the gentry meant tolerating maldistributions which, roughly speaking, left them with most resources in parts of the country where there were fewest Catholics, actual or potential; together with the drift from the circulating mission to the stable residence, it meant that the poorer and remoter regions, where missionary activity should have been most rewarding, were comparatively neglected, and a vacuum created which various kinds of Protestant nonconformity were sooner or later to fill. Yet one may hesitate before making too stringent criti-cisms of Jesuit missionary policy at this time. At least until the Civil War there were numerous Jesuits working in extremely rough condi-tions, at or below the poverty line, in the remoter uplands and especially in the north-east.[25] It is also true that these problems and deficiencies affected not only the Jesuits but the Catholic clergy as a whole. They reflected the constitution of the Catholic community itself, and the conditions in which it was to survive, if at all; and it may well be that one sees them more clearly among the Jesuits because they were the first really to face them. Besides they were not problems which confronted only the Catholic clergy: the Puritan mission, if one may so describe it, was faced with them too. Puritans also had their difficulties in 'set[ting] up some lights in all the dark corners of the kingdom', and devising 'a competent maintenance . . . for the poor ministry, that they may live by the gospel that preach the gospel'; though they were perhaps more successful in persuading their lay supporters to do something about it.[26]

During James's reign there also emerged an English Benedictine mission which, despite the differing tradition it represented, tended to reproduce the experience of the Jesuits on a smaller scale, and to find that its interests were identified with theirs;[27] its presence helped to give a more general form to a fundamental issue which now began to emerge. By 1623 the secular clergy had come to stand for a traditional hierarchy, claiming continuity with the past and affirming that the rela-tion of clergy to laity was still one of jurisdiction and authority. On their side the bodies of regular clergy, which by now constituted getting on for half of the total, had come to rest in the missionary condition; they took it that the proper model for the operations of a Catholic priesthood in seventeenth-century England was not how it had operated in fifteenth-century England, but how it was operating in, say, Holland or Japan. To this degree they were rejecting institutional continuity with the pre-Reformation Church, and claiming that in the Catholic community as it stood traditional or continental forms of episcopal government were inappropriate. They were also asserting that in these circumstances parochial organisation did not apply, and that the relation of priest to layman was not one of exterior authority or government.[28] In practice the most important question was whether the laity had freedom in the choice of its pastors. In standing for this freedom Jesuits and Benedictines were occupying a position well designed to appeal to the English gentry, and it stood them in good stead when the two divergent clerical traditions came into conflict at the beginning of the following reign.[29]

Meanwhile beneath layers of parliamentary enactment, political controversy and ecclesiastical in-fighting, a distinctive religious community was beginning to emerge. To speak of 'emergence' in this context may seem to be flying in the face of a common-sense view that post-Reformation English Catholicism was the remnant of an old dispensation, and that the unexpected vitality it had shown during the Elizabethan period was no more than a temporary rally on the part of a patient who could not be expected to last much longer.[30] Although this last point of view has found expression in a recent treatment of the Elizabethan period, it must seem demonstrably incorrect to historians of seventeenth-century England. The relations of the post-Reformation Catholic community with pre-Reformation Christianity in England are far from simple, and from most points of view it seems more realistic to treat the community as a novel creation of the seminary priests. Seen in this light the early seventeenth century will appear a period of modest progress rather than of decline. If we abandon vague and unverifiable impressions like Gardiner's, and stick to what may reasonably be deduced from the recusancy statistics, we may judge that the real membership of the Catholic community, considered as the more or less regular clientele of the missionary priests, was something like 35,000 in 1603 and something like 60,000 in 1640;[31] the number of its priests increased a good deal faster, from about 250 to about 750. In the light of these figures Aveling's contention that during the seventeenth century the Catholic revival in England reached its peak looks nearer the truth than the suggestions of Jordan and Trimble that after 1603 English Catholicism was teetering on the verge of extinction, or David Mathew's less drastic notion of 'a gradually receding community', 'constantly dissolving at its edges'.[32] In this sense those who thought that popery was increasing were right, though their notions about the absolute number of its adherents were wildly exaggerated and their ideas about why it was increasing were usually wrong.

For in so far as they were fearful of the effect of the progress of Catholicism at Court in changing the religious composition of the country their fears were, at least in the short run, groundless. Connections between court and country Catholicism, while possible to trace, were on the whole tangential.[33] There is more to be said in favour of Lawrence Stone's view that what mattered in the community was a small group of aristocratic families; but while Somersets, Talbots (earls of Shrewsbury), Paulets (Marquises of Winchester), Brownes (Viscounts Montague), Petres, Arundells and others were a solid buffer against its enemies, and do a good deal to account for its relative strength in particular regions, like the southern Welsh border, or Hampshire and west Sussex, they strike one as playing a comparatively passive role in its history. Most of the Howard family, whose general prominence in Jacobean politics and society is well known, maintained a prudent distance from Catholicism during this period; in Lancashire, where it was strongest, it got on without help from the earls of Derby; and it might be argued that the Catholicism of the earls of Worcester was as much an effect as a cause of its popularity among the gentry and people of Monmouthshire.[34] Even the inflation of honours, which brought numerous Catholics into the peerage, still left the backbone of the community, and the most active or typical figures among its laity, in the ranks of the armigerous gentry. Among the variously active, one might think of the principal Gunpowder plotters; of the original Roger Widdrington, leader of the Northumbrian Catholic gentry and a prominent figure on the Border; or of Midlanders like Sir Thomas Brudenell and Sir Basil Brooke, a pair of entrepreneurial brothers-in-law who provided the lay leadership for the anti-episcopal movement of the following reign.[35] Among the typical one may think of quiet northerners like the Yorkshireman Thomas Meynell of Kilvington or the Lancastrian William Blundell of Crosby, concerned with their modest acres, family relations, country pursuits and the state of their souls.[36] Despite some appearances, the Catholic community was country rather than court.

It was the gentry whose interests were primarily served by the reconstruction of the clerical mission: frustrated in their wider ambitions, the clergy tended to concentrate on the task of household reformation which remained open to them, and the most detailed accounts of the religious life of the community which we possess are all examples of this. The three most accessible of these refer to the households of Lady Montague at Battle Abbey in Sussex, of the Babthorpe family at Osgodby in Yorkshire and of Dorothy Lawson at St Anthony's near Newcastle.[37] What they reveal is an intensely cultivated cycle of domestic religious observance, quasi-monastic in character, which might embody a more or less purely traditional feeling for Catholicism according to how little or how much instruction and self-examination was infused into it. At one end of the scale we have Lady Montague's multiple masses and obsession with fasting and abstinence, at the other Dorothy Lawson's determination to take personally in hand the catechising of her household and neighbours.[38] It seems clear that, within this restricted framework, a good deal of progress towards modernity was being made: it took some time for practice to filter down from the model households to more workaday establishments like that at Little Crosby, but by the outbreak of the Civil War the gentry and their families seem to have been well instructed in their religion, conscious of their moral and social duties, and firmly embedded in a pattern of daily life whose traditional elements were carried with a good deal of sophistication, and did not form a barrier to contact with the world outside.

Comparisons have been suggested between the practice of household reformation among Catholics and Puritans, and these seem in general apposite.[39] The concern was in both cases a response to the failure of Elizabethan aspirations for universal public reformation, though Puritans might more easily feel that such ambitions had been postponed rather than abandoned. But there were also contrasts, and without probing very deeply one may mention two of them. As a general rule it might be suggested that in Catholic households the initiative in domestic reformation was more likely to come from a wife or widow than from the paterfamilias. This may have reflected a greater underlying susceptibility to Catholicism in women than in men; but the most obvious occasion for it was the continued prevalence among the gentry of arrangements whereby the husband attended Anglican services and the wife did not. After about 1620, when this practice was dying out, there are indications of a patriarchal reaction; during the last years of the reign much alarm was caused by the efforts of the Yorkshirewoman

Mary Ward to make formal provision within the missionary organisation for women to participate in the work of household reform, and
these were defeated by a powerful masculine reaction shortly after its
close.[40] After this I doubt if there was much difference between the
balance of power obtaining in Catholic and in Protestant households.
The other contrast was more tenacious: in its Catholic form household
reformation, at this time and for some time to come, does not seem to
have extended beyond the milieu of the gentry. A gap seems to have
been widening, inside the community, between a gentry which was
being formed by the modernised Catholicism of the Counter-Reformation, and the poorer Catholics who largely remained in unreformed
ignorance and superstition. The evidence accumulated by Keith Thomas
in his *Religion and the Decline of Magic* for a persisting popular
notion of the Catholic priest as a wonder-worker and a shield against
witchcraft and the devil points in this direction; it is noticeable
that these feelings seem to have been most strongly entrenched in
Lancashire, where Catholicism was most markedly a religion of
the people.[41] The level of literacy among poorer Catholics seems
to have been low: a story from the Jesuit letters of a poor woman who
became a Catholic after listening to a Protestant preacher whom she
understood to have said that the illiterate could not be saved, may I
think be taken as having some representative value.[42] It would be wrong
to neglect evidence that missionary priests were prepared to ignore the
gentry and able to instil a high level of Catholic belief and practice into
popular congregations;[43] the religious sophistication of a gentry household might be expected to communicate itself to its poorer neighbours.
But in general one can detect a fairly sharp distinction; and clerical
accommodation with the gentry maintained and perhaps intensified it,
since the gentry were becoming sensitive about forms of popular prose-
lytism which might upset a tolerable relation with the authorities,
secular and ecclesiastical.[44]

The strange consequence of this was that during the early seventeenth century the popular mission of the Catholic clergy was perhaps
more effectively to English Protestants than to English Catholics. The
widespread influence of Catholic spiritual writing in England has been
observed in various contexts, notably in literature.[45] But Catholic
spirituality did more for Englishmen of this age than exercise the minds
of metaphysical poets: it offered guidance and inspiration in a region
of Christian sensibility which Protestants had been slow to cultivate,
the field of devotion, of the 'practic' as distinguished from the 'theoric';

it could bring some positive refreshment to the sense—ultimately no doubt the Renaissance sense—that there was a limit to the good which could be done in Christianity by refining the formulation of its truths. During the seventeenth century English Protestants were to make up for lost time in this respect, but meanwhile there had been a gap which Catholic authors were well equipped to fill. This was only partly a foreign invasion; it was partly too a paradoxical fulfilment of the ambitions of those who had launched the Elizabethan mission. English Catholicism, in its post-Reformation shape, had begun life as a particular type of activism; this had in some senses been discredited, and within the community the movement was now towards the monastic, the contemplative and the quietistic. But an impulse which could not well expand in the circumstances of a body entrenching itself for a long siege might, detached from its specific origins, prove communicable to people who did not have such difficulties to contend with. A generation of godly Englishmen, who were not Catholics, grew up in the early seventeenth century on a little book whose most lapidary phrase seems to have entered deeply into the consciousness of their descendants: 'The things that a man hath to believe are much fewer, than the things he hath to do.'[46] Its author was Robert Parsons, perhaps more influential after his death than during his life, and better appreciated outside than within the community which he had helped, if mainly as a sleep-walker, to create.

6. England's Overseas Trade in the Reign of James I

BRIAN DIETZ

DESPITE the extension and diversification of routes and markets from
the 1550s England's position in the general framework of European
trade in 1603 was relatively simple and circumscribed. Geographical
expansion had not been accompanied, as far as can be judged, by any
sustained or marked growth in the volume and value of trade; and if
anything it had confirmed the dominance of London, where about
eight-tenths of the country's trade were, as the outports would have it,
'engrossed'. Perhaps the east coast ports had increased their share
through the Eastland trade, but elsewhere the balance between London and the provinces had almost certainly shifted in the capital's
favour. Even privateering, a vital substitute for normal trade in
the south and west during the long Spanish war, had passed increasingly
under the control of a dozen or so metropolitan merchant-princes. Nor
had the rerouting of trade reduced its dependence on a single commodity for export. The 'balance of trade', a concept that was soon to
become familiar, hinged on the sale of woollen cloths. New types had
been introduced with the 'new draperies', a wide range of 'stuffs' or
mixed fabrics distinguished by their lightness, variety of pattern and
cheapness. But at the end of the Tudor period the cloth trade was still
dominated by the traditional woollens of the old drapery, some dyed
but most undressed. Such specialisation is both the basis and an inevitable consequence of commercial exchange. No special gift of hindsight was needed however to grasp the disadvantages and dangers of
such a high degree of specialisation in a manufacture—or more properly
semi-manufacture—for which demand could not be expected to remain
predictable and steady. Growth even in normal conditions in established
markets tended to be slow. With increasing competition from foreign
manufactures and after long experience of the random forces which
could affect demand overseas there was an obvious need to improve
sales by widening markets. For a half-century awareness of this need
had been an impetus for expansion. Nevertheless trade remained pri-

For Notes to Chapter 6, see pages 236–8; for Bibliography, see page 221.

marily intra-European, with a further concentration on a few ports in the west and north. About eight-tenths of London's exports went to France (mainly Rouen), the Low Countries, Germany and the Baltic; and using traffic movements as an indicator roughly the same proportion of imports came from this region.[1] For most merchants, the glorious exploits of Elizabeth's sea-dogs notwithstanding, their best and certainly their safest opportunities seemed to lie across the North Sea and the Channel. A few did however have wider horizons and it was through their search for more distant markets that the latent possibilities of real growth were revealed. This would not apply perhaps to the Russian and African trades in which the rate of growth over fifty years had not been impressive; nor to the spectacular but abortive efforts at settlement in North America; but in the Mediterranean the Levant Company had laid firm foundations for such expansion, and in 1600 members provided much of the inspiration and capital for the East India Company. Organised, like the Muscovy Company, on a joint-stock basis, the last of the great Elizabethan trading organisations was a speculative but necessary venture to follow the Dutch around the Cape to seek oriental goods at their source.[2]

I

If commercial prospects in the Mediterranean and more dimly in the Orient were hopeful, elsewhere in 1603 they were not obviously encouraging. The last years of Elizabeth's reign had been difficult in most of the main markets. In Germany the Merchant Adventurers were discomfited by the imperial ban on their cloth shipments in 1597, while in the Baltic the Eastland Company's sales had fallen sharply from the high level of the late 1590s. And soon after James's accession the London plague made trade 'marvellous bad' for several months. There were however some grounds for optimism. The treaty of 1598 between France and Spain, rejoining each country to its most important market, had begun a trend towards peace which, in the integrated commercial economy of the time, prepared the way for a general recovery in which England shared. In 1604 James made his own peace with Spain and two years later he signed a commercial treaty with France. The following year the imperial ban was lifted, while in 1609 Spain accepted the truce with the rebel Dutch. Thus the political environment, so long inimical to trade, had become exceptionally favourable for investment and growth. And concurrently a series of good home harvests provided a further stimulus to trade.[3] Confidence was restored, capital was released and the country entered a period of undoubted prosperity.

All the chief ports seem to have shared in the post-war recovery. Its rate and duration varied however from region to region and port to port according to differences in the markets served and in the types of cloth exported. In the north-west, where trade was concentrated on the relatively stable markets of Ireland and France, progress was steady but unspectacular. But for the ports in the south and west, from Southampton to Bristol, the resumption of trade with Spain and Portugal was most significant: hence their determined opposition in the Commons' 'free trade' debates at the beginning of the reign to the restrictions imposed on trade by the Spanish Company charter when it was renewed in 1604.[4] France was also an important market, but more northerly contacts were so slight that few of the ports west of Southampton were affected directly by the later recession in that area. The main centres of cloth distribution in the south and west were Lyme Regis and Exeter. All the cloths were produced locally with the warmer southern climate in mind. Exeter shipped large quantities of Devon dozens—a traditional but relatively light-weight cloth that was technically close to a worsted or new drapery—and a smaller but increasing amount of actual 'stuffs' or serge. At Plymouth and Dartmouth cloth was not an important export. Both specialised in fishing and were the chief beneficiaries of the rapid growth of a multilateral trade based on the Newfoundland Banks. Large resources of capital, ships and men were employed in the fishing itself, in importing salt to process the fish, and in carrying the catch home or to markets overseas. With the reopening of Iberian ports and more secure access to the Mediterranean, 1604 marked the beginning of a period of unprecedented and largely unimpeded activity in this trade. Newfoundland was 'the India to the west of England'.[5]

The trading pattern and potentialities of the east coast ports differed considerably from those of the south and west. With the exception of Great Yarmouth, where herring was in steady demand for shipment through the Straits, direct regular contacts with markets south of Bordeaux and La Rochelle were slight. Trade was concentrated in western and northern Europe, with the Eastland the main point of growth during the Elizabethan period of expansion. Hull in particular, but also Ipswich and Newcastle, had developed a considerable trade through the Sound; in the case of Hull cloth shipments to the Baltic rivalled those of London. With this northerly concentration the east coast ports, which had been relatively unharmed by the war, benefited only indirectly from the peace. Nevertheless exports were buoyant after 1604 and it

seems that the outports rode the difficulties in the Baltic more successfully than London. The metropolitan merchants indeed blamed the
cheapness of Hull's Yorkshire kerseys for the sluggish sales of their own
more costly broadcloths. But they blamed the Dutch more, and for all
their disagreements the London and provincial members of the Eastland Company were at one in seeing in the Dutch a persistent and
growing threat to their trade. Exports were undermined by competition
in cloth, woven in England but dyed and dressed in the Netherlands;
and, more seriously it seems, the Dutch, with marked advantages in
freight costs and profit margins, encroached on England's west-bound
traffic in grain, pitch and tar, timber and other Eastland goods. After the
Truce of 1609 with Spain the number of Dutch carriers entering Hull
rose steadily, while parallel with this direct intrusion of foreign competition was the growth of a transit-trade in Baltic wares from Amsterdam and other Dutch ports. Rather later—the trend is most marked
after 1625—exports moved in the same direction when the cloth markets
of Hull and Ipswich shifted from the Baltic to the Netherlands and
Germany. By 1640 it was clear that their overseas trade had failed to
sustain the vigorous growth of the Elizabethan period. Its value and
volume had risen little, if at all, and the tendency was for the area to
contract under pressure from the Dutch.[6] Part of the problem of the
east coast ports was their limited opportunity for diversification. Geography had confined overseas trade to a region where conditions were
difficult and beyond which there was little scope for expansion. With
few fixed assets mercantile capital could seek alternative outlets: in
whaling at Spitzbergen (a Hull enterprise much resented by the London-
based Russia Company), in Newcastle's expanding coal trade and in
providing transport for other ports. But none of these opportunities lay
clearly within the sphere of international trade and for the merchant
who had acquired even a few of Thomas Mun's twelve 'excellent qualities which are required in a perfect merchant'[7] such alternative investments were a prodigal waste of hard-earned skills and experience. It
may be that with limited opportunities elsewhere the Hull merchant
had a special inducement to persist in the difficult northern trades; and
if this was so he had a further edge over the London merchant, whose
scope and opportunities for diversifying or simply transferring his business and capital to other markets were unique.

'Merchants of London', a provincial spokesman complained in the
Commons, 'have all trades . . . [and] go round about the world.'[8] The
capital had indeed a truly international port which served a huge and

growing market through direct contact with every major trading area in and beyond Europe. The congested wharfs and quays on the north bank of the Thames above Tower Dock handled far more ships of much greater tonnage than any of the outports;[9] and they travelled as far north as St Nicholas in Muscovy, south through the Mediterranean into the Black Sea, west to Africa and across the Atlantic, and after 1600 they regularly rounded the Cape in the East India Company's service. Whether it was liked or not, and many deplored her massive commercial superiority, London's prosperity was vital to the nation's health. In the immediate post-war years this prosperity was undoubted.[10] Imports rose from £840,466 in 1603 to £1,057,001 in 1607. Lord Salisbury's controversial Impositions and high food prices in 1608 apparently checked this growth until the moderation of both in 1610 aided a recovery, though not to the previous high level. In 1614 imports were valued at £969,374. Evidence on commodities is scanty but there was a predictable rise in the import of those originating in Spain, the Mediterranean and the Orient—spices, indigo and cochineal, Spanish and sweet wines and currants. Not all came direct from their source. The transit-trade from the Netherlands and to a lesser extent from Germany was substantial, with aliens taking a large share of it. At the turn of the century they accounted for about a quarter of all imports. After the Truce of 1609 their share was over a third. When the post-war recovery was halted these facts figured prominently in the debates and policies which attended the recession. Because of heavy discriminatory duties however the aliens' share of the export trade was small. As exports rose—from £1,011,061 in 1605 (a much higher level obviously than the plague year of 1603) to £1,286,500 in 1614—the chief beneficiaries were native merchants, and in particular the Merchant Adventurers who shipped about three-quarters of the cloth. The withdrawal of the imperial ban allowed the company to make a welcome return to normalcy, and in the years up to 1614 their trade resumed its traditional characteristics of concentration and specialisation. Cloth was distributed through only two outlets: Middelburg, where the affluent Dutch bought the better quality woollens, and the staple in Germany, which was moved in 1611 from Stade to Hamburg, where the coarser kerseys also sold well, if more erratically. The trade was also handled by relatively few members. Just over 200 were effectively in control, and of these twenty-six exported half the cloths in 1606, a proportion which apparently remains constant throughout the period.[11] This oligopolistic tendency was also marked in other trades, for example in the Levant,

and at other ports.[12] A further characteristic the Adventurers shared
with other companies was to specialise in the one market. 'I will not by
any means encourage you to have too many irons in the fire' was the
advice given to one of their most distinguished members,[13] and on the
whole they preferred not to widen their business activities.

The merits of such specialisation were and are open to debate. In
normal conditions the specialist's knowledge of commodities and market
conditions must have worked to his and the country's advantage. So at
least it was argued by the company merchants against the 'straggling
trade' of inexperienced 'interlopers' who flooded the market and sold
cheap. But in difficult times specialisation may have been an obstacle
to diversifying or transferring business elsewhere. For the Merchant
Adventurers the testing time came in 1614 when the post-war recovery
ended abruptly and a period of short-run crises and long-term decline
clearly began. The first assault on their position came from an unexpected quarter—the king, whose interest in trade was untypical, and
Alderman Cockayne, whose notorious Project received royal approval
in 1614. With cloth exports at a high peak further shipments by the
company were banned in July. Shortly afterwards it was disbanded in
favour of a new organisation which included Cockayne and other
Eastland merchants. Their ostensible purpose and pledge was to substitute for cloths 'in the white' a fully manufactured article which would,
it was argued, provide employment, increase turnover and profit and
create revenue for the Crown. In all probability their real aim was
simply to break into the Adventurers' market. But they needed at least
some of the old company's capital and experience to back the new, and
not surprisingly little was offered. Predictably also the Dutch retaliated
against the attack on their finishing industry with a ban on the import
of dressed and dyed cloths. Shipments, whether dyed or white, fell
catastrophically until belatedly the king's unusual persistence in
Cockayne's support yielded to the almost universal condemnation of his
Project. Late in 1617 the new company was dissolved and the old re-
instated. The old order was thus restored; but not the former prosperity.
After a brief recovery in 1618, when cloth sold well in the slack German
and Dutch markets, the London cloth merchants faced an even greater
crisis. By 1620 their trade was unmistakably in recession. Two years
later the bottom of a disastrous slump was reached when shipments fell
by a quarter from the level of 1618 and even to a point below that
of 1616. With markets shrinking, credit tight and money scarce, with
falling wool prices and rising stocks of unsold cloths, with widespread

bankruptcies and unemployment, trade was in the grip of the gravest crisis in living memory. 'When', it was asked, 'was it seen a land so distressed without war?'

II

As with the recovery at the beginning of the reign the recession at the end varied in time and pace from port to port and market to market. London it seems was worse affected than the outports, and within the city traders to northern Europe had the greatest difficulties. Exports to Germany and Poland fell first. While the Dutch mart was firm in 1620, shipments to Hamburg and the Baltic were respectively a third and almost two-thirds down on 1618. In 1622 the trend was reversed: the Polish and German markets had recovered slightly, but exports to the Netherlands had fallen heavily. Why there should have been these variations is not immediately apparent. For the general crisis however the explanation is not hard to find.[14] It was not a consequence of Cockayne's Project, although that ill-conceived experiment did weaken the Adventurers' trade at a critical time. Nor was the contraction of overseas markets a direct consequence of the Thirty Years War. Contemporaries were aware that war could increase the demand for cloth, although it is likely that local manufacturers of cheaper articles would benefit most. The point where the war clearly connects with the recession is in the 'unparalleled outburst of monetary confusion and currency manipulation' inflicted on Germany and eastern Europe by local magnates and mint-controllers in search of short-term gains and partly to meet the cost of war. The effect of these widespread debasements was to undermine confidence generally, and for the merchant shipping to the area of the debased currencies they worked like a modern devaluation. Imports were discouraged while local produce for export became significantly cheaper. Thus English cloth was almost priced out of the market, and the merchants' hope of profit lay in the cheaper imports. For those trading with Hamburg or the Netherlands there were no serious obstacles to such profits, and the high level of imports in the early 1620s suggests that advantage was duly taken by the Merchant Adventurers. For the Eastland Company however the sudden shift in the terms of trade was an unqualified disaster. Largely this was because, as one observer put it, 'exportation and importation stand in such relation that the one prospers not without the other.' Imports had in effect to be paid for by exports in a trade in which cash transactions and bills of exchange played little part. And in so far as bullion exports could be used to subsidise imports in this exceptional situation, the Dutch were generally believed to be much better placed than the English. A further difficulty facing the company was the extreme elasticity of demand in England for Baltic wares. As the Sound Toll Registers show, the west-bound trade was closely geared to the demand for grain, which fluctuated violently. It was therefore a particular misfortune that the currency manipulations coincided with good harvests at home in 1618, 1619 and 1620. To emphasise the interdependence of imports and exports harvest failures in 1622 and 1623 occasioned heavy grain shipments and in 1622 —there are no figures for 1623—cloth exports rose sharply.

By 1624 the worst of the crisis was over for the Eastland Company, as it was for the Merchant Adventurers. It had however made a deep impression on both their trades. Confidence was shaken not only by the direct impact of the crisis, but also by the disturbing way it emphasised how fundamentally adverse the longer-term trends were in this region. The early 1620s did indeed bring into sharp focus changes in the terms of trade that had been apparent for some time and could not easily be reversed: the shift in demand from high-quality English woollens to cheaper local cloths; the related trends for trade to become import-ed and money to flow out of the country; and the growing competition from the Dutch. Although it did so in a most emphatic way, the crisis had merely underlined the evident dangers and disadvantages of depend-ence on markets where the staple export was becoming less competitive, and foreigners had such a powerful position in the import trade. Hence, or so it would seem, the very high turnover rate among merchants trading in these markets even before the decline became obvious. Between 1606 and 1614, a relatively prosperous period, 66 per cent of Eastland merchants had apparently withdrawn from the Baltic. The figure for the Merchant Adventurers was 50 per cent. Some seem to have retired altogether from overseas trade, but a signficant number, especially of the former Baltic traders, appear in 1614 to be buying and selling exclusively in south-European markets[15] This is firm if fragment-ary evidence of what is perhaps the most significant commercial develop-ment in the early Stuart period: the shift of investment and activity from north and eastern Europe to the seemingly more promising mar-kets in the south, and beyond Europe itself to the Orient and America. It was far from complete by 1625 or by 1640, and it was not made without difficulty. The depression of the early 1620s in particular cast a shadow far beyond the traditional European markets. But by the end of James's reign the Elizabethan invasion of the Mediterranean and the extra-European investments had been firmly advanced and exploited.

In this redirection of metropolitan trade the reopening of Spanish ports was less important perhaps than might be expected. A recent study of this hitherto neglected area of English trade has revealed unexpected difficulties in the London branch. As in the Eastland trade the outports may have prospered more than London, where the high hopes of easy profits after 1604 soon evaporated. 'It was generally thought', as one disillusioned and probably inexperienced merchant put it, 'that our peace with Spain would bring in mountains of gold, but it now proveth molehills of earth.' Those who could remember the pre-war demand for the old draperies in Spain found it weakened by changes in taste and competition from cheaper local and Italian cloths. Merchants also complained that in the same interval money in Spain had become so scarce, disordered and debased that they had to look for their returns in commodities like wine, tobacco and oil, for which prices and demand fluctuated sharply. And at both terminals of the trade the 'mere merchants' of London blamed the unskilled and unapprenticed in-and-out traders for many of their difficulties. Such complaints were often made in fact in the context of the debate for and against a regulated company trade with Spain which began in 1604, and to that extent they must be viewed with some suspicion. It does seem however that despite a sharp rise in some imports from Spain, the peace did prove disappointing for London if not for the outports. The unexpected conclusion might be that while the northern trades recovered strongly in the first decade of the reign, the Spanish market, which was depressed by conditions similar to those encountered later in the north, stubbornly refused to come to vigorous life. In due course stronger sales of the new draperies improved the terms of trade and attracted the greater merchant, but initially at least the difficulties and disappointments seem to have discouraged all but 'the relatively unimportant small traders . . . often operating on small margins of capital and credit'.[16]

This characterisation of the Spanish trade in the immediate post-war years contrasts strongly with what is known about the Levant Company. From its earliest days the Turkey trade had involved the exchange of expensive commodities in large quantities with heavy transport costs, and when dyed and dressed Suffolk and Essex broadcloths replaced the cheaper kerseys from about 1600 the need for extensive capital and credit was increased. Hence the company's high admission fees, its general reputation for exclusiveness and wealth, and the strong tendency towards oligopoly. In addition the Turkey merchant tended to be a specialist, though he was likely to invest in the cognate East India trade. In these respects he was not so dissimilar to his colleagues in the northern trades; but in the early seventeenth century he enjoyed advantages which they were obviously denied. Indeed the terms of trade in the Mediterranean were in all the main essentials in England's favour. The success of her merchants and ships coincided with and contributed to the decline of Venice which began about 1600. As the main supports of the Venetian economy were undermined—her dominance of the commercial exchange between the Orient and Europe, her shipping, shipbuilding and woollen-cloth industries[17]—the English advanced strongly in the Mediterranean. Competition was faced from other quarters but on generally favourable terms. England's main rivals in the early seventeenth century were the other northern invaders: the French, who made the first inroads on Venice's commercial hegemony, and the Dutch, who arrived in force as grain shippers in the 1590s. After 1600 the French were themselves in retreat, while the Dutch were much less formidable competitors in the southern trades than they were in the north. In particular they lacked their usual advantages in transportation. The highly economical *fluit* which commanded the northern trade routes was too ponderous and vulnerable in waters where politics and piracy put a premium on speed and security as well as size and economy. Even in competition with the Dutch therefore the English merchantmen with their 'warlike reputation' were much in demand in the local trades. The Mediterranean was indeed the first and for many years the only region in Europe where English ships combined a firm hold over the bilateral exchange with a significant share of the local carrying trade—what William Petyt later called 'huxtering from port to port'. Often they were away for a year or more as they plied intricate and profitable routes inside the Straits; and since the owners were frequently merchants as well there was a direct and fruitful alliance between the transport and trading accounts. In the latter two commodities dominated the export side. Cloth was much the most valuable export to the eastern Mediterranean, where it found ready sales at the expense of the more costly high-quality Italian textiles. Even in Italy itself the new draperies sold well through the free port of Leghorn which gave access to the populous Lombardy Plain. The most valuable export to Italy however was probably the herring. The fact that the 'Leghorn cask' was a standard container at Yarmouth is an indication of the importance of this trade. That the English should profit from the 'puissant red herring' even in competition with the Dutch was a satisfying reversal of their usual roles.[18]

While progress through the Straits was impressive it was not unimpeded. Almost simultaneously with the northern companies the Levant Company in particular encountered difficulties in a trade that was very susceptible to local political disturbances and the attention of pirates. From about 1618 these problems were intensified. A further embarrassment was provided by the organisation which the Turkey merchants had 'fathered' in 1600. By 1618 the East India Company, which they had promoted mainly out of fear of Dutch competition in eastern commodities by the direct Cape route, had itself become a competitor. This position had not been achieved easily. The company's first voyage with four ships in 1601—the Dutch sent out sixty-five in that year—had been attended by difficulties on all sides. Capital was short, suitable ships were hard to find and expensive. Demand in the East for European goods was slight, while the European market for pepper was dangerously unstable. And there was the powerful presence of the Dutch. None the less the youthful and harassed company showed a remarkable capacity for survival and growth, and after a decade of experiment the trade prospered. High returns on the early voyages eased the problem of attracting capital and the shortage of suitable ships forced the company to build for itself. The problem of developing a balanced and stable commodity exchange was more intractable. On the export side the company was forced to rely largely on bullion, a necessary but in some quarters unpopular policy. On the import side however the dangers of relying on pepper were partly offset by adding indigo and calicoes; and while Dutch opposition continued, a brief *modus vivendi* was achieved from 1613 which allowed the English to stabilise and develop their organisation overseas. The port-to-port trade in Asia flourished and the years from 1613 to 1620 saw a rapid expansion in the other two interlocking sections of the company's trade—the bilateral trade and the intra-European re-exports, which were essential for the purchase of specie on the Continent. About 1620 however the company ran into difficulties. It may have expanded too far too quickly. Certainly in the last years of James's reign it was forced on to the defensive by Dutch hostility, culminating in the massacre at Amboina, heavy losses of shipping, and by the waning confidence of investors who expected quick returns in all circumstances. The policy of expansion gave way to one of retrenchment, the trading area contracted and business was at best stabilised. Even the East India Company, seemingly so remote from the main stream of English trade, struggled against the strong tide of dislocation and depression.[19]

III

A crisis as comprehensive and severe as that of the early 1620s naturally aroused deep and widespread concern. The mood was caught when Parliament began a thorough inquiry in 1621. 'All grievances in the Kingdom are trifles', Sir Edwin Sandys told the Commons, 'compared with the decay in trade.' A year later a special trade commission was appointed to continue the investigation. Commercial and financial experts were invited to add their advice to that of individual merchants, trading companies, clothiers and other vested interests. Not surprisingly what emerged from the debates was confused and contradictory, but the discussions did prove to be a landmark in English economic thought and commercial policy.

On the essential features of the crisis commentators were in broad agreement. Where they differed was in distinguishing between cause and effect and in their order of priorities. Many assumed without question that the acute 'want of money' was the prime cause of the depression, thereby mistaking—though in the short-run situation the emphasis was 'only partly false'[20]—symptom for cause. One who made this confusion, Edward Misselden, proceeded to explain the shortage as a consequence of the undervaluation of English silver and coin in relation to continental currencies. The disparity, which had been of some concern to the Government for about a decade and acutely so from 1618, drew an 'abundance of money' out of the country. To stop the flow Misselden proposed a revaluation of English silver coin. While agreeing that monetary scarcity was the crucial factor, Gerard Malynes offered the alternative explanation that money was drawn out of the country by the speculative dealings of foreign bankers who kept the rate of exchange well below specie export point. His solution was some means of governmental control to ensure transactions at par value. Thus Malynes was one of many who confused the means whereby the export of specie was made profitable with the cause of that export. The confusion was quickly noted by Thomas Mun who, in a remarkably succinct and influential thesis, compelled attention away from these 'secondary means'. The 'principal effecient' of the outflow of money was, he insisted, the adverse balance of trade. 'I never knew yet a decay in our trade and treasure . . . but . . . by excessive consumption of foreign wares at home, or by declination in the vent of our commodities abroad.' With a confidence that was partly misplaced he dismissed as irrelevant currency manipulations, exchange rates and all other factors in the crisis. The possibility that they could affect as well as reflect the 'balance of payments' crisis, as in the short run they clearly did, was rejected in favour of a sophisticated but misleadingly monocausal explanation.

Although Mun's concern with the balance of trade was too narrow in the context of the immediate crisis, it did draw attention to the longer-term problems facing English merchants. His observations in particular gave strong theoretical support to the simpler but similar diagnosis of the Government's own expert, Lionel Cranfield. As early as 1614 Cranfield had predicted monetary shortages and a change against England in the terms of trade. The following year an inquiry into the commercial records appeared to confirm these fears. In 1621 he was further convinced that, as he told the Commons, 'trade is as great as ever but not so good. It increases inwards and decreases outwards, and we cannot in a short time alter them'; furthermore, 'the want of money is because trade is sick, and as long as trade is sick, we shall be in want of money.' Secondary complications in the disordered state of trade were the volume of manufactures and transit-goods entering the country; the import of 'vain, unnecessary things' like wine and tobacco; the large aliens' share in the import trade, and the loss of transport earnings through the employment of foreign carriers. For London this diagnosis appears to be correct in most essentials. From evidence collected by Cranfield himself and other data [21] it is clear that metropolitan trade had become import-led. In the year from Christmas 1621 imports stood at £1,291,720, a significantly higher level than at any time in the years of prosperity before 1614, while in the same year cloth exports had fallen well below the average level of that earlier period. Of imports from the Netherlands in 1621 almost half were transit-goods, while 62 per cent of the same trade two years before was in manufactures. French imports were also mainly manufactures—linens, canvas and mixed fabrics—supported by wine. Aliens were responsible for about a third of the French trade, which was the most valuable from any one country. Imports from Germany were mainly in the Merchant Adventurers' account—over nine-tenths in 1622—but manufactures and transit-goods, including Italian silks and Baltic wares, were prominent. Shipments direct from the Baltic, being essential raw materials, 'had utility and begot visible gain'. The disturbing features of the Eastland trade were an adverse balance that had previously been favourable—as it was thought—and the prominence of alien merchants and carriers.

Attention throughout the crisis was focused on London and her most depressed markets in northern Europe. If provincial trade had been as closely scrutinised the situation might have seemed less alarming, and if attention had shifted away from northern Europe the balance and terms of metropolitan trade must have seemed more favourable. It may be that historians will have to qualify the widely held belief that there was a strong and steady flow of bullion from Spain;[22] but the exchange was advantageous to the extent that manufactures, that is, woollen cloths, bought primary produce and the trade was conducted by native merchants in English ships. From the 'mercantilist' viewpoint the flaw in the Spanish trade was the import of 'unnecessary' wines and tobacco. A like criticism was levelled against the Levant trade in currants which were the most valuable of the company's imports in the early 1620s. But almost as valuable as this 'liquorish stuff' were cotton wool and raw silk which supplied home industries. Moreover the trade was controlled by Englishmen, as was that with Italy. If one includes the large invisible earnings from freight and port-to-port trading in the Mediterranean there seems no reason to question the common assumption of the time that the balance of trade within the Straits was firmly in England's favour. Less certain is the contribution of extra-European investment. At the time the position of the East India Company was ambiguous and controversial. According to its critics in the 1620s the company's huge exports of specie were a prime cause of the shortage of money and therefore of the depression. But in its defence Thomas Mun argued, *inter alia*, that re-exports to the Continent compensated for the loss, and it is indeed difficult to see how the silver could have been bought without them. Lastly the contribution of investment in North America to the 'balance of payments' is difficult to assess. But clearly a distinction must be made between the substantial earnings from the Newfoundland fisheries and the negligible returns in interest and profit from the plantations. On the estimated outlay on the latter of £300,000 up to 1624[23] quick returns could not be expected. The Virginia Company was aware of this when it based its early appeals to investors on the non-commercial and long-range goals of national honour, prestige and religious sentiment. Later the emphasis shifted to the more conventional profit motive, but this carried little conviction when the company's record was scrutinised. Although tobacco exports had risen rapidly after the second charter was granted in 1609, the profit margin was slight. By 1624 the company was near bankruptcy and the New England settlements to the north had only just been founded.[24]

Although the crisis debates from 1621 to 1624 encouraged analysts like Mun to develop their theories and so make a major contribution to economic thought, this was not their purpose. The Government wanted practical solutions to pressing problems, not general theories of durable value; and this was precisely what the theoreticians could not offer. Misselden's advice was unacceptable because revaluation was bound to be inflationary, and for obvious social and political reasons price rises in the midst of a depression were hardly to be welcomed. Moreover Mun did make the point that the current deflation helped to lower export prices. Nor was Malynes's prescription attractive to the Government. Apart from the logical objection that manipulation of the exchange rates would be effective only in the short run, the mechanism of control was clearly beyond its resources. This left Mun's diagnosis which, although more logical and perceptive, was not reassuring either since all the economic ills were seen to be rooted in an adverse balance of trade which could not be corrected easily. Mun's own advice on this fundamental point was to reduce cloth prices, a panacea which Malynes dismissed, with some justification, as 'hunting after shadows'. Over a long period cloth production costs had been virtually fixed, and the Government's own contribution to the export price through heavy duties was unlikely to be reduced. Prices could still be cut by reducing the quality of the cloth, but this was a dangerous expedient which no one, given the universal hostility to 'false manufactures', was anxious to propose. One chance thus remained: that of 'selling cheap' abroad by making trade more free and competitive. A familiar theme—the monopolistic trading companies were conventional villains in any economic drama—it was taken up by Parliament in 1621 and under strong pressure the Merchant Adventurers, who came under the most severe criticism, were forced to open up their membership and allow outsiders free trade in certain cloths. The Eastland Company on the other hand was offered protection because its position was seen in a different light. In the Baltic the struggle was not between English merchants—'free' or 'unfree', metropolitan or provincial—but between the company and aliens; and not for the first time Dutch competition reinforced the arguments for a regulated trade. In 1622 a proclamation confined the import of Eastland wares to company members and English ships, or to ships of the country of origin. The Government further attacked the aliens' import trade by reinforcing the old Statute of Employments which required foreigners to take away some of their profits in commodities. The 'over balance' also prompted measures to encourage domestic manufacture, especially of linen; to prohibit wool exports in order to weaken foreign competition in the cloth trade; and to restrain bullion exports. None of these measures was new, and if set against the weighty and trenchant advice that it was offered the Government's strategy might seem unduly conventional and unimaginative. But it is difficult to see what else could be done, and in so far as it was conceived in a strong spirit of economic nationalism and in the name of the balance of trade, an idea which was central to economic thinking for almost two centuries, it was a pointer to and a basis for more elaborate policies.

IV

Early in 1625 James told his trade commissioners that trade was recovering, an impression figures for the previous year confirmed. But the reign did not end on a note of prosperity. It closed, rather, as it began with a severe outbreak of plague. Such were the 'random perturbations' which, while lying outside the commercial structure, could shake it so severely. And if the disruptive influences from within are taken into account the force of the argument that 'equilibrium . . . was always unstable'[25] can be appreciated. As this implies, the extreme fluctuations in trade at this time did not necessarily effect radical changes in its structure: rather they were above and below a line of development which over the long run had considerable continuity. This becomes apparent if the pattern of English trade in 1625 is compared with that of 1603. Although the Government had been sympathetic to pressure from the outports, London's predominance is undisturbed; and despite the relaxation of monopolistic company controls the 'unproportionable paucity of sellers' that was complained of at the beginning of the reign seems to have been a characteristic of trade at the end. The continued application of the joint-stock principle to maritime enterprise had certainly widened investment opportunities for gentlemen as well as merchants. Even so it is clear that the circle of share-holders and of traders generally remained a tight one. Commerce was for the specialist and continued to favour the greater merchant. And on the export side it was still dominated by the dealer in woollen cloths, for despite the growing awareness of the need to diversify these still accounted for eight- to nine-tenths of London's exports. The massive growth by 1700 of re-exports in oriental and American goods, reflecting the extent to which trade had become dependent upon the extra-European world, is barely foreshadowed in the figures for the early Stuart period.[26] Trade was thus firmly anchored still in Europe. There had however been developments of enduring importance in these two decades. Although difficult to measure, the most marked had been the shift in investment within Europe from north to south. This is indicated in the changing pattern of shipping movements,[27] and in the contrasting fortunes of the old and the new draperies. As the old declined through the contraction of markets in the north, the new expanded through the developing markets to the south. A positive gain from this redirection of trade along more distant routes was the rapid growth of shipping and shipbuilding. In the development of England's ocean-going merchant marine the twenty years of peace under James were at least as important as the equivalent period of war under Elizabeth. The East India Company had also made a major contribution to this growth, as it had to the widening frontiers of England's trade. What had seemed a very speculative venture in 1603 had become a mature and powerful institution within two decades. More fragile and less immediate in their contribution were the American plantations. Yet the Jacobean settlers had shown what their predecessors lacked, persistence and a grasp of the need for continuous, large-scale planning—enough at least to ensure the future. Thus the gains in southern Europe and beyond helped to offset the losses in the traditional markets across the Channel and the North Sea. By 1625 it seemed far less certain than it did in 1603 that the shortest routes were the safest and most profitable.

7. Colonial Developments in the Reign of James I

LOUIS B. WRIGHT

ENGLAND was late in starting colonial ventures in the New World. Friendly relations with Spain during the reigns of the early Tudors, followed by a period of dangerous hostility in the later years of Queen Elizabeth, prevented the occupation of territory claimed by Spain. A group of expansionists led by Sir Francis Walsingham, the earl of Leicester, Sir Humphrey Gilbert and Sir Walter Raleigh, it is true, urged the necessity of seizing a portion of the new land before Spain occupied it all, but their tentative efforts ended in failure. Richard Hakluyt, the preacher-compiler of voyages, was their chief propagandist for colonial activity.

Gilbert and his half-brother, Raleigh, the most persistent of the Elizabethan expansionists, paved the way for later colonial settlements. Gilbert, by claiming Newfoundland for England in 1583, helped to fix interest upon that region. Raleigh, by his experiences and his establishment of the short-lived colonies on the coast of North Carolina in 1585–7, kept alive interest in 'Virginia', the region he had named after the Virgin Queen. The English were also fascinated by possibilities of colonisation in the tropics. Raleigh personally led an expedition up the Orinoco River as far as the falls of the Rio Caroni in 1595 in search of gold, diamonds and Indian allies against the Spaniards; he came home convinced that great riches could be found in Guiana, a belief that led to the fatal expedition of 1617 which ended in his own execution to appease the Spaniards. Raleigh's descriptive narrative, *The Discovery of the Large, Rich, and Beautiful Empire of Guiana* (1596) expressed his own enthusiasm for the country and influenced Englishmen in the reign of James I to attempt to colonise in tropical America. The Elizabethan efforts at making settlements in America ended in failure but they paved the way for successful ventures in the next reign. On James's accession in 1603, he at once began negotiations that led to peace with Spain the next year. Although Spain did not relinquish any of her claims to American territory, the way was now open for English pene-

For Notes to Chapter 7, see page 238; for Bibliography, see pages 221–2.

tration of regions not actually occupied. Spain was weaker than she had been under Philip II, and she was not disposed to make a great row over a few Englishmen huddling in discomfort in the far reaches of North America or in undesirable and unsettled spots in the tropics.

The reign of James I saw a growing interest in commercial enterprise and expansion overseas. The establishment of peace gave businessmen greater confidence and assurance, and the accumulation of capital, which had been increasing during the past generation, gave the merchants of London more scope and power. The success of the first two expeditions of the East India Company, which received its charter on 31 December, 1600, stimuated further oceanic enterprise. The first expedition, which sailed in April 1601 with four ships commanded by Sir James Lancaster, drifted back, ship by ship, between June and September 1603, with a million pounds of pepper and other spices. The net return to the investors was 95 per cent. A second expedition led by Sir Henry Middleton returned in 1606 and proved almost as profitable. No longer would Englishmen be content with trade across the Channel; the lure of profits would lead them to the ends of the earth, and they would establish trading stations and colonies in the four corners of the world.

It would be a mistake to believe however that the increase in oceanic trade and the new impetus to expansion overseas was a sudden and unexpected phenomenon. It had been building up gradually since the creation of the Muscovy Company in 1555 and the commercial explorations of Anthony Jenkinson across Russia to Persia in 1557–9. Many of the Jacobean investors and promoters had been important merchants in the previous reign. For example Sir Thomas Smith, named governor of the East India Company under Elizabeth, continued in that post until 1621. He also served as governor of the Muscovy Company and the Somers' Island Company, and as treasurer of the Virginia Company. Elizabethan merchants had been piling up capital which, now that Spain was no longer a threat, found an outlet in overseas expansion. Oceanic trade would inevitably lead to the establishment of trading posts and colonies overseas.

The expansion of oceanic commerce in the reign of James however created new economic problems and maladjustments that caused controversies in the business community. For example the East India Company brought rich cargoes from the East and stimulated a taste for luxuries that enriched merchants involved in the trade. But since the East as yet showed no great interest in English products much of the

East India Company's merchandise had to be paid for in bullion. The drain of precious metal from England caused economists of the day to cry ruin and to blame the company for exciting the country to extravagance. Satirists railed against the taste for 'baubles' and useless products; preachers condemned the public for its appetite for luxuries and the East India Company for supplying goods that weakened English character and impoverished hitherto honest citizens.

As a result of the drain of bullion a clamour arose for the discovery and establishment within the dominion of England of sources for the commodities that Englishmen now had to buy from foreigners. The argument ran that Englishmen could establish colonies that would produce exotic products without draining funds from the kingdom. Raleigh himself had held out this hope in *The Discovery of the Large, Rich and Beautiful Empire of Guiana,* a hope that helps to account for the concentration, over a considerable period, of colonial efforts in the tropics.

Not only would Guiana supply England with gold and silver, precious metals badly needed, but, Raleigh added:

> Where there is store of gold, it is in effect needless to remember other commodities for trade. But it [Guiana] hath towards the south part of the river great quantities of Brazil wood and of divers berries that dye a most perfect crimson and carnation. . . . All places yield abundance of cotton, of silk, of balsam, and of those kinds most excellent and never known in Europe; of all sorts of gums, of Indian pepper, and what else the countries may afford we know not. . . . The soil besides is so excellent and so full of rivers as it will carry sugar, ginger, and all those commodities which the West Indies hath.[1]

Raleigh's emphasis on silk, cotton, dye-stuff, pepper, sugar, ginger and other commodities would find constant iteration in later advocates of colonisation. These and other exotic products England had to buy from economic competitors—sometimes her enemies—at a great loss to the nation. Colonies might prove to be the remedy. The hope of discovering vast hoards of gold and silver, as the Spaniards had done, was never completely abandoned by Elizabethan and Jacobean adventurers overseas, but gradually they came to realise that profits from trade were more certain, and the production of exotic products within a colonial framework might confer great national benefits.

Guiana in Raleigh's optimistic description sounded like a land that would provide precious metals and even diamonds, as well as most of the tropical products so ardently desired. He had heard of a mountain of pure gold in the interior, a mountain that shone with such brilliance that it hurt the eyes of its viewers; another mountain of crystal was reported to be littered with diamonds and other precious stones. Raleigh thought he had a glimpse of this mountain through the distant haze, for he 'saw it afar off and it appeared like a white church tower of an exceeding height'. Somewhere in the interior lay the town of Manoa, the capital of a king who in his revels anointed himself with balsam and rolled in gold dust. This king, 'El Dorado, the gilded one', soon gave his name to the land, and El Dorado became the objective of many an adventurer in the early seventeenth century.

Small wonder is it that Charles Leigh in 1604 begged a charter from King James to make a settlement on the Wiapoco River in territory that now lies between Brazil and French Guiana. His efforts, after a two-year struggle, failed, but that failure did not prevent Robert Harcourt from trying in 1609, with a little group of thirty men, to establish a colony in the same area. They too had to give up. Undiscouraged, Harcourt applied to King James in 1613 for a charter to establish a proprietary colony in Guiana, but he was unable to find sufficient manpower to settle his grant.

Harcourt published an account of his experiences in 1613 as *A Relation of a Voyage to Guiana*, with a second edition in 1626. This narrative, like Raleigh's previous work, did much to excite Englishmen about the prospects for wealth from tropical colonies. Harcourt enumerated a long list of useful products including a leaf that cured the headache and sundry other drugs, gums and spices. Significantly he commented that 'there is yet another profitable commodity to be reaped in Guiana and that is by tobacco, which albeit some [including King James] dislike, yet the generality of men in this kingdom doth with great affection entertain it. . . . The price it holdeth is great; the benefit our merchants gain thereby is infinite.'[2] He emphasised the ease with which it could be grown in Guiana and the immense profits that would accrue from its cultivation. Harcourt also stressed the value of sugar-cane, 'whereof in those parts there is great plenty', cotton, hemp and flax, all of which Guiana produced in abundance. Surely no reader of the tract could help believing that here was an opportunity for settlement that should not be neglected.

So great was the hold of this region on English imaginations that Prince Henry in 1610 urged Sir Thomas Roe, later to distinguish himself as an ambassador of trade and commerce at the Court of the Great Mogul, to go to South America in search of gold and places for colonisation. During 1610–11 Roe travelled 300 miles up the Amazon River and decided that the territory offered alluring prospects for colonisation. To hold the country for England he left a forlorn group of twenty men at the mouth of the Amazon. A few of these apparently hung on for three or four years. Roe himself made two further voyages of discovery on the South American coast and explored the coastline from the Amazon to the Orinoco. He was searching for evidence of gold mines but, like Raleigh and others, he came back with only rumours of treasure for his pains.

In 1617 Raleigh, who had been languishing in the Tower of London since late in 1603 under sentence of death on a trumped-up charge of treason, obtained a warrant of release from the king to enable him once more to go to Guiana in search of the wealth that he believed to be there. He still dreamed of Englishmen established in an area from which they could eventually make a successful attack on Spain. Although King James's greed induced him to let Raleigh organise the Guiana venture, he expressly forbade him to attack any Spanish settlement.

With such money as Raleigh could raise from his friends and his wife's fortune, he equipped the expedition and sailed for the Orinoco in March 1617. The expedition was ill-fated from the start. Raleigh himself was ill with fever by the time he reached the American coast and consequently decided to stay in Trinidad while the remainder of the party under Captain Lawrence Keymis pushed up the Orinoco. In a fight with Spaniards encountered on the way, Raleigh's son Walter was killed. After returning with this ill news—and no clue to a mountain of gold—Keymis committed suicide.

Bitter and empty-handed, Raleigh returned to an enraged sovereign. Not only had he failed to find gold so desired by the avaricious king, but he had become embroiled with the Spaniards. The Spanish ambassador, Gondomar, demanded Raleigh's head, and James had him executed on Tower Hill on 29 October, 1618. (Legally speaking, he was executed in fulfilment of the suspended sentence for treason of 1603.) Thus ended the career of the most persistent of the early English colonialists.

Despite Spanish protests about Raleigh's expedition to Guiana, King James in 1619 issued a charter to one of Raleigh's captains, Roger North, to organise the Amazon Company and to establish a small colony on the great river. Once more Gondomar complained, but North managed to sail in 1620 and land his men on the Amazon delta. To his surprise he found a few Englishmen and Irishmen in the vicinity, remnants of other ventures to South America. For his efforts North, like

Raleigh, was sent to the Tower but escaped with his life. His little colony on the Amazon struggled along until the Portuguese wiped it out in 1623. North managed to get another charter in the next reign to establish the Guiana Company (1627), which attempted to plant colonies on both the Amazon and the Orinoco, but these projects also met with disaster. Englishmen never gained a permanent foothold in this tropical region. They would have to try elsewhere to find sources for the exotic commodities they required.

While some promoters were still trying to establish colonies in South America, others were turning again to Virginia. Raleigh himself had never given up hope of a colony on the North American coast and in 1589 had turned over certain of his chartered rights to a syndicate of London merchants headed by Sir Thomas Smith. Still others thought they might find sites for colonies further north. The earl of Southampton and Sir Thomas Arundel conceived a plan to found a colony with English Catholics unhappy over their treatment at home; to that end in 1605 they sent Captain George Weymouth to explore in the north. Weymouth landed on the coast of Maine, thought well of the country and returned to praise its prospects. He also brought back five Indian captives who were taught enough English to boast about the fruitfulness of their country.

To promote colonisation in North America, the King in 1606 created the Royal Council for Virginia. A few Englishmen were excited by reports of renewed French interest in the north, for in 1606 Samuel Champlain sailed on an expedition organised by the Canada Company. If England intended to occupy any of North America it would have to bestir itself.

King James himself apparently decided that England should establish colonies between the 34th and 45th degrees of north latitude. Two chartered companies were created to manage the business, the Virginia Company of London, which would have the right to colonise between the 34th and 41st parallels, and the Plymouth Company, which could occupy territory extending south from the 45th parallel to the 38th. To prevent friction in the overlapping territory, the rules provided that neither colony could make a settlement within 100 miles of that of the other. As it happened, the Plymouth Company made little progress and did not become a serious competitor of the Virginia Company. It planted a short-lived colony on the Kennebec River in 1607 under the command of George Popham and Raleigh Gilbert, but Maine's bitter winter discouraged the settlers and they went home the following summer.

The first English colony to gain a permanent foothold in the New World was the result of private enterprise, not government effort, for the Virginia Company of London was a chartered company with the stock held by private investors. The Royal Council for Virginia, which served as a sort of midwife at the birth of the Virginia Company and the Plymouth Company, disappeared in 1609. In its place the king created a council that was expected to run the Virginia Company from London; for the rest of James's reign, colonial affairs remained the exclusive concern of the king and the Privy Council. Later, during the reign of Charles I and the rule of the Puritan regime that followed, various committees and commissions dealt with colonial affairs, and not until 1675 was there a well-organised body to oversee the colonies, a committee of the Privy Council generally known as the Lords of Trade.

The Virginia Company found enthusiastic investors ready to risk their money in shares of an enterprise that they hoped would return as rich a profit as the East India Company's early voyages. The shareholding base was broad and included all sorts of people from simple tradesmen to bishops and great lords. By late December 1606 the expedition, under command of Captain Christopher Newport, a seaman with a background of good luck, was ready to sail with three vessels and a complement of 144 men, only 105 of whom survived the voyage. Their route took them by way of the Canaries and the West Indies and thence up the American coast. Their instructions required them to find a river up which they could sail far enough inland to be safe from sea-marauders and to choose a site that would provide a good anchorage for ships.

On reaching Chesapeake Bay in late April they discovered one of the great rivers draining into that estuary, named it the James in honour of the king and sailed upstream as far as a peninsula where deep water permitted them to tie up to trees on shore. They landed on 14 May and named the site James Fort, later Jamestown. Unfortunately the terrain was marshy and unhealthy but the settlers took no note of this condition. They were glad to be ashore after a voyage of more than five months, and the scent of spring flowers and wild strawberries was sufficient to make them believe they had arrived in Elysium.

Sealed instructions which they now opened provided the names of seven resident councillors who were to govern the settlers in the name of the Virginia Company. Edward Maria Wingfield was elected by the Council to serve as president. Thus was the little colony organised. Captain John Smith, named in the instructions as one of the Council, was immediately expelled because he had been 'mutinous' on the outward voyage, but a month later he was allowed to take his place. In September 1608 he was elected president and served until July 1609. His vigorous efforts probably saved the colony from total collapse.

Captain Newport had orders to search for precious metals and to explore the interior as far as he could. He had also to supervise the erection of a fort and to supply it with a few guns from his vessels. After this he was to sail for home with such lading as he could find for his ships. As it turned out, his only cargo consisted of timber and sassafras, a shrub whose roots and bark were used to make an infusion believed to be a remedy for venereal and other diseases. Even now, sassafras is sold in many American grocery shops in the spring to make tea which, according to folklore, will 'purify the blood'.

Although the Spaniards for more than a century had been successful colonisers, the English had little experience and at first displayed an incredible lack of aptitude. Englishmen, it is true, had resettled portions of Ireland, but colonies in Ireland were a very different matter from colonies in the American wilderness teeming with murderous Indians. The group that Captain Newport left at Jamestown were singularly quarrelsome, lazy and inept at insuring their own survival. Later generations have wondered about their lack of initiative in procuring food on a river alive with fish and fowl, with woodlands filled with game and a soil fertile enough to grow almost any garden vegetable or field crop. It has been customary to dismiss these early colonists as a pack of ne'er-do-wells, unwilling to work for the company, even to save their own lives.

But Professor Edmund Morgan in an essay on 'The Labor Problem at Jamestown, 1607–18', in *The American Historical Review* for June 1971, analyses all the evidence and concludes that Englishmen of this time were accustomed to plying only specialised trades; indeed it was 'against the law for a man to practice more than one trade or one craft'. The early settlers simply were unable to adjust to the requirements of a raw frontier where later pioneers learned to be jacks-of-all-trades. A ploughman ploughed but found it difficult to apply himself to a bit of carpentry. Furthermore malnutrition and the diseases in its train left little energy to be expended. Gentlemen and soldiers in the group were not disposed to engage in the sweaty work of a day labourer. It took near-starvation—and the stern discipline of Captain John Smith, and later that of Sir Thomas Dale, who applied martial law—to whip the settlers into productive workers.

Other factors also help to explain the lack of enterprise and the fecklessness of the first settlers. Many of them had come merely for adventure and still believed that their main objective was to search for gold. Even Captain Newport had to look for precious metals. These first adventurers hoped to make a quick fortune and return home. Then too some of the emigrants were the off-scourings of the London docks, a crew about as effective as Falstaff's company of militia; they were both rebellious and lazy. Since as yet they were merely working for the profit of the company and were not clearing land for themselves as later settlers would do, the incentive of private enterprise was lacking. Furthermore most of the settlers were city-bred men, terrified of the woods and the savages therein. They had seen the Indians creeping through the brush, had heard the whizzing of their arrows and had seen a few of their number die at the hands of the natives. Small wonder that they dared not venture into the woods in search of game.

It was the Indians however who actually saved them from starvation, for by trading trinkets for maize the settlers managed to gain enough corn to keep alive. Captain John Smith proved a skilful and courageous trader, sometimes using diplomacy, sometimes appealing to the natives' cupidity and occasionally forcing them to trade at the muzzle of a gun.

On one of his trading expeditions Smith was captured by warriors of Powhatan, the ruling chief of the region, and according to Smith's own story was only saved from having his brains beaten out by the intercession of Powhatan's daughter, Pocahontas. This Indian maiden later married John Rolfe, came to London on a visit and died of smallpox. But she left a son from whom many Virginians claim descent and she became the subject of one of the most enduring of American legends.

When Smith was not dealing with the Indians for supplies or trying to get work out of his recalcitrant colleagues, he was exploring the rivers of the back country. With a small shallop he ventured up the Potomac River past the future site of Washington and up other great rivers of the Chesapeake Bay region. A map that he made and an account entitled *A Map of Virginia* (1612) provided a remarkably accurate concept of the country he traversed.

In the meantime the Virginia Company of London was seeking money and recruits to keep the colony going. The first 'supply' of emigrants, food, livestock and equipment reached the colony in January 1608, followed by a second 'supply' in October of the same year, both brought by Captain Newport. He had been told, said one report, not to return from the latter voyage without 'a lump of gold, a certainty of the South

Sea, or one of the lost company of Sir Walter Raleigh'. Thus the lure of gold still permeated English thinking as did the dream of finding a route to the riches of Asia by some water passage through the American land mass. The search for a North-west Passage became an obsession that lasted for generations.

Captain Newport also brought for 'King' Powhatan gifts believed suitable for an Indian potentate: a bedstead, a wash basin and pitcher, a fine scarlet cloak and a royal crown which Newport, much to Captain John Smith's disgust, was determined to present in a coronation ceremony. A contemporary narrative, included by Smith in his *Map of Virginia*, gives an account of this curious ceremony:

> All things being fit for the day of his coronation, the presents were brought, his basin, ewer, bed, and furniture set up, his scarlet cloak and apparel (with much ado) put on him (being persuaded by Namontack [his son who had been to England] they would do him no hurt). But a foul trouble there was to make him kneel to receive his crown. He, neither knowing the majesty nor meaning of a crown, nor bending of the knee, endured so many persuasions, examples, and instructions as tired them all. At last, by leaning hard on his shoulders, he a little stooped, and Newport put the crown on his head . . . then remembering himself to congratulate their kindness he [Powhatan] gave his old shoes and his mantle to Captain Newport.[3]

A mantle, supposed to be this one, is still preserved in the Ashmolean Museum.

As the Virginia colonists' experience proved, they had no firm notion of how to deal with the Indians, what to expect of them or what products of the country would be profitable. About all they could do was to survive if possible, and survival depended upon continued supplies from London. The officials of the company had ideas of productive industries in Virginia and sent out a few Polish and German glassmakers, who set up a furnace at Jamestown. The settlers were instructed to make soap ashes, hew out clapboards, cut cedar timber, and collect rosin and make tar. Naval stores, which England had previously obtained from the Baltic, were commodities much in demand.

In the meantime the Virginia Company in London had been studying the colonial problem and had concluded to ask for a new charter, which was granted in May 1609. Among other things it changed the form of government in Virginia from a Council and president to a governor appointed for life. He would be the sole authority and would be styled 'lord governor and captain general of Virginia'. Lest the public worry over the possibility of tyranny, the company appointed a high-minded member of its own body, Lord Delaware (generally spelled at this time Lord De La Warr). Since Delaware could not go out immediately, the company appointed Sir Thomas Gates deputy-governor and ordered him to proceed to Virginia with all dispatch.

To supply the colony the company prepared a fleet of nine vessels and recruited something over 600 men, women and children as emigrants. The flagship of the fleet, the *Sea Venture*, was commanded by the veteran Virginia skipper, Captain Newport; Sir Thomas Gates and Sir George Somers, who bore the title of admiral of the flotilla, were aboard the same vessel. The fleet encountered a terrific hurricane as it approached American waters and was scattered. One vessel was lost. *The Sea Venture*'s seams opened and the water poured in, but Newport managed to beach his vessel on one of the islands of the Bermudas. All the passengers got ashore and the vessel, lodged between rocks, though a wreck, did not sink.

During the next eleven months the castaways cut timber and made two pinnaces with tools and equipment salvaged from the wreck. The island provided wild hogs, crabs, fish and fruits, so that they did not suffer for food. Finally in their two little vessels, the *Deliverance* and the *Patience*, the survivors from the *Sea Venture* reached Jamestown on 23 May, 1610. They found the colony in a desperate state.

After the hurricane of the previous summer seven of the fleet had limped into Jamestown one by one with some 400 survivors. But their supplies were inadequate, and during the terrible winter of 1609–10 most had perished from disease and hunger. In Virginia history this period is known as the 'starving time'. Captain John Smith had been injured in a powder explosion and returned to England in one of the emigrant ships, leaving George Percy as president of the Council. Had Smith been able to remain in Jamestown, his skill in trading with the Indians and his capacity to enforce discipline might have saved the colony from the disasters of the winter.

When Gates arrived, he took over the command from Percy. Of all those who had come to Jamestown, only about sixty embittered settlers survived. These demanded to be taken away from a place they regarded as cursed. Gates did not have sufficient supplies or room in his pinnaces for a voyage across the Atlantic, but he agreed to take them to Newfoundland in the hope of finding shipping for England.

As the forlorn crew made their way down the James, they met a fleet under Lord Delaware headed upstream for Jamestown. He ordered them to return. Delaware showed a firm hand and soon brought order out of chaos. According to William Strachey, whom he appointed secretary, he condemned indolence and incompetence and warned that if the unruly did not mend their ways and put aside their vanities and idleness, he would 'be compelled to draw the sword of justice to cut off such delinquents'. Discipline had its effect, and though Virginia had many future crises, it never again reached a point of abandoning the settlements.

The propaganda of the Virginia Company had led investors to believe they could expect quick profits, but no profitable commodities had been found. Settlers could not be driven to exert themselves to prepare naval stores in sufficient quantities to show a profit. In 1612 however John Rolfe planted some tobacco seed that he had obtained from the West Indies or South America. The crop he raised was sweeter than the astringent variety of tobacco native to Virginia, and two years later he shipped his new product to London. It sold immediately, and within the next decade tobacco became a valued money crop. The future of Virginia's economy for the next two centuries was secure.

An equally momentous development occurred in 1613–14 when Governor Thomas Dale, remembered unfortunately for his harsh enforcement of martial law, permitted every old settler to claim three acres of arable land for his own use. In 1616 the Virginia Company gave to each subscriber of stock to the value of £12 10s. fifty acres of land in perpetuity, subject only to nominal rent. He could dispose of this land as he saw fit. The grant of fifty acres of land was extended two years later to everyone who transported himself to Virginia. An emigrant could expect fifty acres as a 'head right' for himself and every person he brought with him, whether a member of his family or a servant. At last the lure of land provided the incentive that Englishmen had previously lacked. The recruiting of emigrants was no longer a problem. The Virginia colony was laying the foundation for its future growth.

An important step in the government of the colony occurred on 30 July, 1619 when the first legislative assembly in English America met to make laws for the governance of the colony. Governor George Yeardley, his Council, and twenty-two burgesses (two elected from each of the eleven settlements) repealed the martial laws proclaimed by Governor Dale and enacted in their place statutes based an English common law. From this time forward Virginia was essentially self-governing, though the authorities in London had the right to veto any statute enacted in Virginia.

Although the Virginia Company exerted every effort to make its colony an economic success, it could never show a profit. Factions and quarrels within the company led to the replacement in 1619 of Sir Thomas Smith as treasurer (that is, head of the company) by Sir Edwin Sandys, but the change in management brought no improvement in conditions in Virginia. The colony was almost wiped out by an Indian massacre on Good Friday in March 1622. The company itself was virtually bankrupt and could do little to succour the colony. Finally on 24 May 1624, after careful legal investigation, the Court of King's Bench vacated the company's charter, and Virginia was taken over by the king as a royal colony, England's first.

The king's interest in the colony was more than nominal. He conceived of Virginia as a source of products that England bought from rival nations, particularly silk and wine. To that end James instructed John Bonoeil, a Frenchman in charge of the royal silk works, to compile a treatise telling how to manage silk worms, produce raw silk, plant vines, make wine and produce other commodities of value. To this treatise the king himself wrote a preface, and the book was published in 1622 as *His Majesty's Gracious Letter . . . Commanding the Present Setting Up of Silk Works and Planting of Vines in Virginia . . . Also a Treatise of the Art of Making Silk . . . and the Breeding . . . of Silkworms . . . Together with Instructions How to Plant and Dress Vines and to Make Wine, and How to Dry Raisins, Figs, and Other Fruits, &c. And in the End, a Conclusion, with Sundry Profitable Remonstrances to the Colonies. Set Forth for the Benefit of the Two Renowned and Most Hopeful Sisters, Virginia and the Somers Islands.*

Colonists in both Virginia and the Bermudas were to be supplied with this treatise, which would guide them to prosperity. King James did not favour tobacco, and Sir Edwin Sandys expressed a hope in Parliament in 1621 that the Virginia colonists could 'subsist by more solid commodities, silk and iron'. He was certain that the silk of Persia would not excel that of Virginia, which grew the best mulberry leaves in the world to nourish silkworms. Alas, silk production failed in Virginia, as it failed throughout the American colonies for the next century because of the lack of skilled labour. Not even the royal injunctions of King James could overcome that defect. In the end the king's hated tobacco saved Virginia from ruin and brought prosperity to its producers.

The colonisation of the Somers Islands, or the Bermudas, resulted from the shipwreck of the *Sea Venture* there in 1609 and the discovery of the ease of life in islands earlier believed to be the haunt of witches and devils. Shakespeare's *The Tempest* is thought to have been inspired by a letter sent back to England by William Strachey after the wreck; it was not published until 1625, when Samuel Purchas included it in his *Pilgrims* as 'A True Repertory of the Wreck and Redemption of Sir Thomas Gates, Knight, upon and from the Islands of the Bermudas', but it may have circulated in manuscript.

The Virginia Company received a grant of the islands in 1612, but in 1615 the Bermuda Company was organised with stockholders from the Virginia Company. Sir Thomas Smith was chosen governor. Bermuda is peculiar in colonial history because it remained under the control of the corporate body under which it was chartered for longer than any other colony. When King James took over Virginia, he left Bermua undisturbed, and the Bermuda Company was not dissolved until 1684.

Because of the wholesome climate and the abundance of food, Bermuda was spared the diseases and the starvation that so nearly ruined Virginia. Its promoters praised its prospects lavishly. Lewis Hughes, one of the first preachers to go to Bermuda, wrote back that God had kept the islands 'secret from all people of the world . . . till now that it hath pleased His Holy Majesty to discover and bestow them upon His people of England'. He declared that 'by the blessing of God men may in time live very comfortably here and grow rich if they will provide seeds of indigo, etc., and plants of currants, figs, raisins, and mulberry trees for the silkworms, and vines that they may have wine for their drinking. . . . For the present tobacco is the best commodity.' Tobacco and foodstuffs continued to be the mainstay of the Bermuda colony.

English colonisation in the Caribbean region had to wait for the next reign. Although an English and a French group settled on St Christopher (St Kitts) in 1624, nothing much came of this venture. Barbados, which was colonised in the reign of Charles I, became one of the richest of the sugar islands.

Several efforts were made during the reign of James to establish colonies in Newfoundland and Nova Scotia, but none of these had much success. In 1610 a group that included the earl of Northampton, Sir Francis Bacon and John Guy, a wealthy Bristol merchant, obtained a charter for a colony in Newfoundland. Guy as governor took out some forty colonists and settled on Avalon peninsula, but he had trouble with the fishermen and his venture never proved a success although it survived under the governorship of John Mason and later Robert Hayman until 1628. Sir George Calvert also received a charter for a colony in Newfoundland and landed men at Avalon in 1623. Since he wanted to make his colony a refuge for Catholics, he suffered from the hostility of Protestants in Newfoundland. The French from Canada also threatened the existence of the colony. Consequently Calvert in 1629 deserted Newfoundland for Maryland where he was more successful.

A Scot, Sir William Alexander of Stirling, in 1621 received a charter for a colony in Nova Scotia and drew up grandiose plans that included the establishment of a Nova Scotian hereditary nobility, but little came of his project and in 1632 Charles I by the Treaty of St Germain-en-Laye renounced claims to Nova Scotia in favour of France.

The fisheries of the northern region attracted English and other fishermen throughout the seventeenth century and made colonisation in Newfoundland and the mainland appear attractive. Captain John Smith, who continued to have an interest in America after leaving Jamestown, in the spring and summer of 1614 commanded two ships which cruised along a coast that he called New England, a name that stuck. Fishing and trading with the Indians for skins and furs, Smith concluded that these occupations would prove more profitable than the search for treasure that had been the will-o'-the-wisp of too many adventurers. On his return he published in 1616 *A Description of New England; or, The Observations and Discoveries of Captain John Smith (Admiral of that Country)*. His report of the abundance of fish and the profit from the fur trade helped to stimulate further interest in the region.

In the meantime an Englishman in the employ of the Dutch West India Company, Henry Hudson, in 1609 discovered the great river that now bears his name and gave the Dutch a claim to the region that later became New York and New Jersey. Since the French were also getting a foothold in Canada, the future of the English in the northern portions of the continent depended upon colonies in the region that Smith had given such a good report.

The Plymouth Company had done little to develop its claims since the abortive effort in 1607 of George Popham and Raleigh Gilbert to settle on the Kennebec. But in 1620 Sir Ferdinando Gorges, one of the leading spirits in the old Plymouth Company, contrived to reorganise the group and get a patent to the territory previously granted the Plymouth Company. The new organisation, composed of forty noblemen and landed gentry, was called the Council for New England. They were au'horised to serve as proprietors of the lands in New England and to settle colonies, make laws and organise a government for all of New England. Their grant also gave them exclusive fishing rights in New England waters, a provision that aroused intense animosity in the fishing industry. Despite Gorges' pretentious programme, little came of it, and in 1639 Gorges made another attempt under a new charter granting him the 'Province of Maine'.

The most enduring settlement after Jamestown was made at Plymouth in 1620–21 by the little band of religious separatists later known as the Pilgrims. Although they had very little economic impact in the colonial development, their heroism and dignity have given them a significant place in later history.

A congregation of separatists in 1609 had fled to Holland from Scrooby in Nottinghamshire and eventually had settled at Leiden. But by 1620 they were concerned about their future. The truce between Holland and Spain was about to expire, and they feared a renewal of the religious war. Their children were also drifting away and acquiring Dutch ways and Dutch wives. The time had come to move once more. Somewhere in the New World they believed they might find the peace and freedom they desired.

At first they had been attracted to Guiana, but in 1620 they received from the Virginia Company a grant of land on the north side of Delaware Bay. Since they had little capital, they made a deal with a syndicate of promoters headed by Thomas Weston to finance them—for a consideration. The emigrants agreed to cultivate all land in common for seven years for the benefit of the syndicate and to reserve all trading rights for the syndicate.

The separatists set out for Virginia in the late summer of 1620 in two ships, the *Speedwell* and the *Mayflower*, but the *Speedwell* sprang a leak and they turned back to Southampton, where the leaking vessel was abandoned. Some of the prospective emigrants decided against the voyage. Not until 16 September, 1620, did the *Mayflower* clear Southampton with 101 passengers. For reasons not entirely clear, the emigrants missed Virginia territory completely and made their first landfall on Cape Cod late in November. After exploring the region for nearly a month, they found Plymouth harbour and decided to land there, though they had no legal right to do so. Since the group had no charter, before going ashore they drew up a simple plan of government known as the 'Mayflower Compact'.

On Christmas Day 1620 they began work on their first house. The days that followed were difficult. Before the winter was over nearly half of the emigrants had died. Nevertheless when the *Mayflower* sailed for England in the spring none of the survivors chose to return. By the next autumn the little colony had prospered sufficiently to declare a day of Thanksgiving and to have a feast, a custom which long afterward, in 1863, resulted in the setting aside of a day in November as a national Thanksgiving Day.

The Council for New England, though it had given no permission for the Pilgrims to settle in their territory, made no objection. Gradually the little colony, under the governorship of William Bradford, became self-sustaining and gained a modest prosperity from farming and the fur trade. Bradford's own narrative of the colony, *Of Plymouth Plantation*, is a noble epic of settlement in the New World.

A small scattering of other settlers landed in New England during the reign of James but no colony except Plymouth attained any importance. The great migration of Puritans to New England occurred in 1628–9 during the reign of Charles I.

The reign of James I ended without the development of a well-thought-out colonial policy. Aside from the mercantilist view that colonies should supply raw materials and needed commodities to the mother country and become a market for the nation's manufactured products, England had no well-defined programme for colonial development. All the early efforts were carried out by joint-stock companies with only nominal support from the Government. Even after Virginia was made a Crown colony, other schemes for settlement continued to receive encouragement. It would take generations of trial and error for England to reach anything approaching a consistent policy towards colonial enterprise.

In 1624 a country parson in Somerset, Richard Eburne, published a treatise entitled *A Plain Pathway to Plantations* in which he argued that the Government should develop an orderly programme for colonial expansion. He insisted that the Crown should take responsibility for colonisation rather than leaving it to chance and private investment. Eburne however was ahead of his time, and King James contented himself with issuing charters, taking control of Virginia and advising the Virginians about the cultivation of silkworms.

8. English Politics and Administration 1603-1625

MENNA PRESTWICH

THE Great Rebellion of 1641 has cast its shadow back into the reign of Elizabeth I, so that some historians have seen the collapse of the monarchy as already determined when James I rode south into his Promised Land. However high his hopes, James's real legacy was a Crown weakened by inflation and by the costs of war with Spain, a Government undermined by faction and an administration polluted by corruption. Clientage wove bonds of association between nobles, ministers and civil servants who competed for the rewards of the Crown and the profits of office. Parliament, largely composed of the prosperous and educated gentry for whom court and county connections played the part that politics does in our modern society, had acquired strength and prestige. Puritan groups had taught sophisticated opposition tactics in Elizabeth's Parliaments, while James was to encounter formidable and learned antagonists in the common lawyers. Sir John Neale considered that towards the end of the sixteenth century 'the Tudor constitution was by now standing on uncertain foundations: on little more than the masterful nature and unique personality of an ageing Queen.' Professor Notestein tolled his passing bell when, emphasising the role of the common lawyers, he wrote that the reign of James I 'gave us in politics a new kind of Commons that was by and by to make inevitable a new constitution'.[1]

Professor Tawney, surveying the wider social scene, also saw the revolution of 1641 immanent in Elizabeth's reign, for the ascendant gentry, the beneficiaries of the land-sales of the Crown and of an indebted peerage, sought power. He was paying tribute to James Harrington, who, from the vantage-point of the Protectorate in the mid-century, held that tensions in society had caused the collapse of the monarchy which had been 'as natural and inevitable as the death of an individual'.[2] Mr J. E. C. Hill, whose books by reason of their learning, number and coherence of approach have added weight to this authorised version, has linked Puritanism with capitalism, stressing the

For Notes to Chapter 8, see pages 238–40; for Bibliography, see pages 222–3.

importance of the 'industrious sort of people' to whom Puritan asceticism appealed, just as in twentieth-century China the peasantry resented mandarin ostentation. Tracing the ideas at large in the Civil War, Mr Hill found obvious candidates in the Geneva Bible and 'honest John Calvin', and causally connected new secular and scientific thought with the Puritan Revolution.[3]

Yet to read that revolution back into Elizabeth's reign is analogous to seeing the reign of Edward the Confessor merely as a necessary prelude to the Norman Conquest. Mr J. E. A. Jolliffe warned us against tracing a receding perspective back and back 'until it encloses so small a sector of the past that the historian's perspective becomes gravely contracted'. He further observed that the facts to which a historian's lines of observation lead may by the process of their selection produce a distorted picture.[4] But period history can result in a landscape without contours and colour, and it is fair to test for seismic faults in government and society. Thus Professor Tawney gave the accolade to James Harrington, but with the warning that Harrington's interpretation had 'the weakness of all theories which rely on one key'.[5]

Seismic faults need not lead to volcanic eruptions. Yet when Professor Tawney, in the same year as he paid tribute to Harrington, wrote his seminal article on 'The Rise of the Gentry', he used the single explanation of social erosion to explain the Revolution of 1641. He soon received support from Professor Stone, who stressed the financial plight of the aristocracy. Battle was joined when Professor Trevor-Roper denied this and launched a direct assault on the view of the gentry as a prosperous and homogeneous class. He saw antagonisms between the rich gentry, the beneficiaries of office, law and trade, and the mere gentry, excluded from opportunity and thrust back upon landed incomes, projected on to the political stage.[6] In 1965 Professor Stone re-entered a comparatively deserted arena. Although still maintaining that statistical sampling proved that the peers owned proportionately less land in 1640 than in 1558, he disarmingly explained that he no longer wished to rely on 'the clumsy old Marxist bull-dozer' of his youth to push facts into place, but had added to his equipment the 'powerful tools' of psychology and sociology, and had thus detected a crisis of confidence in the peerage. Although this second crisis did not cause the Civil War it helped to make it possible, and he mistily conceded that the rise of the gentry was 'to some extent—though certainly not entirely—an optical illusion, resulting from the temporary weakness of the aristocracy'.[7]

However, when Professor Tawney in his last book partially abandoned the broad survey of society for the study of one individual,
Lionel Cranfield, a highly successful London merchant and an astute
land speculator, called in as business adviser to the inefficient and
corrupt administration of James I, he attributed the predicament of
the monarchy not to the operation of inexorable forces but to the king's
appetite for luxury and display and to the rapacity of those exploiting
his folly. James was not therefore 'the unoffending victim of impersonal
forces beyond human control', since the businessman's programme of
retrenchment and reform vigorously advocated and partially realised by
Cranfield offered the possibility of restoring both the royal finances and
public confidence. Cranfield, called into government service in 1612,
rose to be lord treasurer in 1621, but suddenly fell from power in 1624,
the victim of his own efficiency, hectoring disposition and disagreement
over war with Spain, which he saw ruining his careful financial calculations.[8] It may be argued that Cranfield's career need not weaken the
thesis of an inevitable erosion of royal power, since the forces he both
worked against and with made his fall predictable. Yet his achievement
in so short a space of time, together with his ambivalence, for he like
others looked to his own gains, calls for an inquiry into politics and
administration in the reign of James I, if the actual working of government and the play of personalities are to be justly weighed against
explanations of social forces and destiny.

When Cranfield was impeached in Parliament in 1624 as a result of
the intrigues of court faction, James reluctantly acquiesced in the fall of
a treasurer of whom it was said that 'in the general opinion, the White
Staff was as fit for his hand as if it had been made for it.'[9] James,
impelled by guilt to make some defence of Cranfield in Parliament,
stated with a shrewdness that contrasted with his weakness that 'All
Treasurers, if they do good service to their Master, must be generally
hated, as Monsieur Rosny was in France.'[10] He was referring to Sully,
compared by contemporaries to 'a great furnace', whose energy and
heat were applied to the finances of Henri IV.[11]

Comparative history can give a different vision to evolutionary history both by focusing a close-up lens on problems of policy and personality and also by using a wide-angle lens for the social scene. The
different fortunes of the Bourbon dynasty and the early Stuart
monarchy in the seventeenth century illustrate this. The Bourbons had
the advantage of being able to tax without recourse to the Estates-
General, yet Henri IV succeeded to a heavily-indebted Crown, which

had sold both royal and church lands extensively and to an administration corroded by corruption and lamed by inefficiency. In contrast to James I, Henri IV appreciated the link between the power of the Crown and its wealth. He called upon Sully, who, without making radical innovations, toned up the administration, curtailed court expenditure and achieved an annual surplus. The capital accumulated in the Bastille led the English ambassador to observe that Henri IV coming 'to a broken state, and much indebted, yet in few years hath gathered more treasure than perchance any other king of Europe possesseth to this day'.[12]

The strains in French society can be compared to those in England. The French nobles were suffering financially as a result of the civil wars and continued extravagance, and exhibited a crisis of confidence early in the seventeenth century when they complained that their power was evaporating by the sale of their lands to merchants, lawyers and office-holders. Office-holding was a dominant feature of the administration inherited by Henri IV, and the consequent seepage of revenue was a major problem for Sully. But the Jacobean administration suffered similarly. Henri IV and Sully gave their answer in a policy decision of 1604 when sale of office was organised through a government department. The *paulette* both ensured a direct revenue for the Crown and also created a body of vested interests, since the office-holders supported a regime in which they had invested. There were further political dividends. The Crown could—and did—use divisive tactics by playing off the nobility against the office-holders, and also whittled down the powers and political pretensions of the law courts by manipulating the terms on which offices were held. The revolt of the Fronde in 1648 reflects tensions in society, but there was no revolution in France where absolute monarchy triumphed.

In England sale of office was handled privately. Cranfield, when treasurer, suggested that office-holders should voluntarily renounce their profits for a year, but moral appeal was ineffective, while the French Government could enforce periodic bleeding. In both countries the financial losses were grave, but Richelieu's response to venal office-holding was to recruit an administrative elite by the intendants, drawn mainly from the central law court, the *Parlement* of Paris. The intendants, owing their appointments to their ability, were dedicated to the Crown to which they looked for future promotion, and stood apart both from the nobility and also from the venal bureaucracy. No minister of James I recruited such agents.

Yet in view of the resentment expressed in the Parliaments of James I towards an extravagant and scandalous Court, it is significant that similar animosity to the corrupt and rapacious ministry of Mazarin sparked off the Fronde. In 1661 the young king, Louis XIV, recognising the urgency of reform, appointed Colbert whose dynamic thrust would have appealed to Cranfield. Like Sully and Cranfield, Colbert made no radical administrative innovations, but the treasury was purged, office-holding was made less remunerative, while the intendants, closely supervised, governed the provinces. The budget showed a surplus within two years. It can be argued that more might have been achieved. Thus both the *taille* and the English subsidy were antiquated and inefficient land-taxes.* Colbert planned reform, but was defeated by the anomalies he encountered. But there was no attempt to grapple with the problem of the subsidy under James I, although Sir Walter Raleigh had said in Parliament in 1601 that the assessment of some mens' estates was not a hundredth part of their wealth.

But the French success shows how much could be achieved, provided that the support of the king was given. The seven-fold increase in the returns from crown lands and forests achieved by Colbert illustrates this. Under Elizabeth a third of the crown revenue had come from the royal demesne, and Robert Cecil, earl of Salisbury, made treasurer in 1608, recognised the importance of this source of income. He tried to stop James dissipating his inheritance by prodigal gifts and began a highly necessary survey. But reform slackened due to the complexities of tenures and to the inefficiency of those he employed. Faced by the mounting debt he raised immediate capital by huge land-sales. In 1613 Bacon urged a renewed attack on crown land administration, savagely emphasising that payments to bailiffs absorbed more than the profits of the manorial courts over which they presided. In his turn Cranfield, when treasurer, argued that the melting of crown land was the melting of power. He told the king that 'in selling land he did not only sell his rent, as other men did, but he sold his sovereignty.' It was Cranfield's negative boast—though what he had done was an achievement compared with what had gone before—that as treasurer he 'never sold one foot of land, never made any one lease, never felled a timber-tree'.[13] His refusal to run down capital dictated retrenchment, and the court parasites to whom James invariably capitulated, exacted retribution when they procured Cranfield's fall.

* Strictly speaking of course, the English subsidy was not a land-tax in the proper sense, but a tax on land or goods, according to which gave the higher yield. But generally, the subsidy operated as a form of land-tax.

There was faction and clientage at the Court of Louis XIV, but the king exercised control, supporting in Colbert a minister whose coldness to suitors earned him the name of *Le Nord*. Neither did Elizabeth allow factions to control her initiative, and Sir Robert Naunton wrote that 'the principal note of her reign will be, that she ruled much by faction and parties, which herself both made, upheld, and weakened, as her own great judgement advised.'[14] But in her last years Elizabeth had to contend with embattled faction, and Bacon commented tartly on court feuds when he wrote: 'Envious and malignant dispositions are the very errors of human nature, and yet they are the fittest natures to make politiques of.'

Faced by the blatant ambition of the earl of Essex, Elizabeth found an obvious counterpoise in strengthening the power of Burghley and his son, but she nevertheless avoided giving a monopoly to the *Regnum Cecilianum*. Robert Cecil was patiently trained by his father, and he more than any other secured James's peaceful accession. He did so in alliance with a new faction, the Howard family, in disgrace since the execution of the duke of Norfolk for treason in 1572. Lord Henry Howard, Norfolk's younger brother, a crypto-Catholic, rightly distrusted by Elizabeth for his malice and guile, was Cecil's intermediary with James. There were to be other factions at the Jacobean Court for the king had his emotional involvements. He had his Scottish followers, Lennox, Dunbar and Hay, and their appetite for gains, like their master's, was whetted by the rich English prospects. Lord Hay's jest 'Spend and God will send' was apt given a monarch ready to play the part of Providence. James's relationship with his favourites was delicately put by Bishop Hacket who wrote that 'the sweetness of this king's nature' led him to clasp from the age of fourteen 'someone *Gratioso* in the embraces of his great love ... that is, when the sun finds a cloud so fit to be illustrated by his beams, that it looks almost like another sun'.[15] These Scottish clouds, shrouding the royal rays, darkened the English scene, until even they were overshadowed by Robert Carr, created earl of Somerset in 1613.

The Howards and the Scots were initially content with honorific posts, basking in the tropical climate of a Court, presided over by a king who 'had no power to deny a man that was an importunate suitor'.[16] The tone was set for prodigal spending and Hacket chanted of the sumptuousness, the feasting, the gorgeous attire, the plate and the jewels. James, who hated business and loved hunting, called Salisbury 'the little beagle that lies by the fire when all the good hounds are dəily running in the fields'.[17] But Salisbury did not slumber; trained to public service, he worked attentively, recruiting a specialised secretarial [18] and having a sharp eye for his gains. He was master of the Court of Wards and secretary of state. When he became treasurer he achieved the pluralism which Elizabeth had denied him, and could enjoy the full delights of power, patronage and wealth.

The Howards garnered a rich harvest, aided by James's calamitous disregard for the mounting debt. Lord Henry Howard, created earl of Northampton, had complained to Elizabeth that he lived only in a 'little cell', but he now erected a mansion at Greenwich. His nephew Thomas Howard, made earl of Suffolk and appointed treasurer in 1614, two years after Salisbury's death, built Audley End, of which even James remarked that it was too big for a king, but fitting for a lord treasurer. Suffolk's gains were too blatant even for the Jacobean Court, and in 1619 he and his associates were brought to trial and found guilty of corruption. The countess of Suffolk and Sir John Bingley, a Howard creature strategically placed in the Exchequer, ran a system of bribery which Bacon, summing up for the prosecution, scornfully described, saying, 'my lady kept the shop, Bingley was the prentice that cried "What do you lack?", but all went into my lord's cash.' Audley End was alluded to in the accusation that 'the great foundations of the Exchequer must be subverted for the building of my lord's stables.' [19] Audley End is said to have cost twice as much as Salisbury's palace at Hatfield, which John Evelyn compared to a diadem 'by the decorations of the cupolas and other ornaments of the pavilions'.[20] Salisbury himself succeeded Thomas Sackville, earl of Dorset, called 'Lord Fill-Sack', for 'the greatest gettings were in Treasurer Dorset's time'.[21]

Laxity and corruption marked Dorset's years of office, but no treasurer was as incompetent and rapacious as Suffolk. But how does Salisbury's record stand? He carried preponderant influence even when Dorset was treasurer, and we have to ask why crown finance and administration deteriorated so fast between the death of Elizabeth and Salisbury's own death in 1612. Bacon was then asked by the king for his opinion of Salisbury and said, 'I do think he was no fit counsellor to make your affairs better; but yet he was fit to have kept them from growing worse.' [22] His edged reply is explicable, since Salisbury had blocked his cousin's advancement. But does it contain a kernel of truth? Modern historians have been kinder. Acridly as they dispute over the origins of the Civil War, they unite in paying homage to Salisbury, who although secretive, devious and complex, yet gave some coherence to policy and government and showed statesmanship in trying to bridge the gulf between the Court and the country. Salisbury has been described as reforming, bold, heroic and imaginative, trying to do more in four years than his father did in twenty-six.[23] To be fair, responsibility lay with the monarch in a period of personal government. Elizabeth had possessed a sense of practicalities and of conduct totally lacking in James. But did Salisbury try to prevent, acquiesce in or even aid the pollution of standards which James happily accepted? Did he restrain or condone the king's extravagance? And could he remonstrate with the king without jeopardising the Cecil inheritance, acquired so patiently but yet resting on uneasy financial foundations? Even with the opportunities of office, Salisbury before his death had agreed to the sale of some of his own lands, just as he had authorised the sale of crown lands.[24]

Official salaries were ludicrously low, so that perquisites, which at their worst meant bribes and peculation and at their best rewards and benefits, were a necessary adjunct of administration. The relation of salaries to responsibilities and to the price-rise was never considered and would have entailed an administrative revolution. The fungus of corruption had already attacked Elizabethan administration, but the queen, acting with Burghley and also alone, had checked the wet-rot by for example instituting inquiries into expenditure in the Royal Household and into profiteering in the army. Burghley wrote gloomily of corruption, but his own palace of Theobalds, the prototype of the ostentatious mansions of the age, advertised the rewards of great office. He had profited greatly as master of the Wards, and he bequeathed to his son Michael Hickes, his astute patronage secretary, who saw to the gains of the Cecils and did not neglect his own. Salisbury had been indoctrinated in the double standard, service to the State and to his family fortunes. But did he in the new reign stretch his opportunities unduly and so have to acquiesce in the gains of others? And how, faced by the king's prodigality, did he try to meet crown debts and deficits?

Elizabeth left a gross debt of £400,000, but there had been war with Spain and revolt in Ireland. Parliamentary grants between 1558 and 1603 had met only half the war expenditure. Crown lands to the value of £643,493 had been sold, while there was much administrative slack to take up. Yet this gives too sombre a picture, for £300,000 of the subsidy voted for the war in 1601 was still due to come in. The net debt was thus £100,000, while the ordinary accout had a surplus of £90,000, part of which had been used for the war. Elizabeth had inherited a debt twice this size from Mary. She left James, given the subsidy voted and the debts owed by the Dutch and the French, enough not only to cover the costs of her own funeral but also of his coronation, and to extinguish the outstanding debt. Besides, even when allowance is made for a married sovereign with a family, there should still have been a surplus of £40,000 on the ordinary account, which could even have been increased, since prices were rising less fast and James's reign was to be one of peace. Even so, proper supervision of the revenue and care over spending were imperative.[25]

James lacked royal presence, but a lavish Court with banquets and masques gave him compensation and a setting for his pretentious vapourings on monarchy. But within a year of James's accession the archbishop of York felt impelled to warn him that his extravagance and bounty would 'exhaust the treasure of the kingdom and bring many inconveniences'.[26] By 1608 the crown debt was nearly £600,000 after five years of peace, six times the net debt left by Elizabeth, which had been in part subsidied by the Crown, after fifteen years of war. In Parliament in 1610 Thomas Wentworth showed himself the radical son of a radical father, when he said that silver streams voted by the Commons would only run out by private cocks and by a pipe-line from London to Edinburgh.

What was Salisbury's role? He returned, as James did, a scornful answer to the archbishop of York and concurred in the royal largesse. Thus he told Sir David Murray, a Scottish gentleman of the Bedchamber, given a pension of £400 a year from an imposition on wines, that he was sorry that this was less than was merited, but that he would in future 'give my voice to any benefit you shall crave',[27] The earl of Dunbar, making a rich haul as master of the Wardrobe, was carefully cultivated by Salisbury, to whom James jested, as Elizabeth never would have done, 'ye as two knaves do recommend one another for cozening of me.'[28] But the debt forced Salisbury to resort to huge land-sales, though in alarm he also drew up in 1609 *The Book of Bounty*, which forbade pensions and grants made at the expense of the revenue. Yet when he also suggested to James's delight that Sir Walter Raleigh's estate of Sherborne should be given to the cherished favourite, Robert Carr, he demonstrated that rules were made to be broken.

Salisbury's public policy was as paradoxical as his private position was ambiguous. He had for instance obtained the farm of the silk duties from Elizabeth at a profit of £434 a year; by 1610 renewals of the lease and increased duties were bringing him £7000 a year. At James's accession full-scale customs farming was introduced. The Crown could borrow more easily, but Salisbury's shady dealings with the farmers meant that he could not extract stringent leases from them. Cranfield was alert to Salisbury's care for his public image when, as a young merchant scenting a lucrative government concession in dye-woods, he wrote to his business partner, Arthur Ingram, 'Assure my lord of Salisbury that there shall be no monopoly that shall cause any public clamour.'[29] He was wrong: there were angry protests in Parliament in 1610 against this and other grants sanctioned by Salisbury.

Apart from land-sales, did Salisbury have any solutions to the mounting debts and deficits? Retrenchment would imperil his position at Court, while an attack on administrative costs would entail unpopularity and labour. The axe of redundancy was never a weapon Salisbury cared to use. Thus when direct customs administration was abandoned, royal officials retained their posts and were paid by the Crown, though the interest in diminishing smuggling was transferred to the farmers.[30] The easiest revenue to tap lay in raising customs duties. In 1608 new duties were levied on 1400 articles, a 30 to 40 per cent increase, designed to produce up to £70,000 a year, with no pretence that this was a tariff reform in the interests of trade. In 1620 Bacon stigmatised Salisbury's impositions as 'an immature counsel and cause of much mischief following', and contrasted 'the work of one morning' with the labours in the past two years of the treasury commissioners—who included Cranfield —in imposing administrative cuts in various departments.[31] The mischief to which Bacon referred was the heated constitutional argument in Parliament over impositions.

The feudal revenues of the Crown were another possible source of increasing income, but tainted because of the resentment felt against wardships, often the cause of much human unhappiness. Feeling was exacerbated, since the courtiers and officials of the Court of Wards profiteered, while the country gentlemen paid. Shortly after becoming master of the Wards, Salisbury raised valuations on estates and exacted higher selling prices, but while he stepped up the burdens he still permitted unofficial profits. In 1606 he wrote ruefully on the margin of a paper which denounced the private gains and prophesied rebellion if there were not reform, 'this is part of my fault.' Yet in 1609 he pocketed £1400 from a wardship which brought £370 to the Crown. The returns from the Court rose by about £9000 a year during his mastership, but only about a quarter of the income from the Court came to the Crown, while the rest filtered into private hands.[32] Neither impositions nor wardships nor land-sales were enough to meet the debt and the deficits. In 1610 Parliament had to be summoned.

Salisbury's introduction of new impositions had evoked constitutional tension; his proposed renunciation of feudal revenues in 1610 was designed to produce harmony. But the political and financial consequences of the Great Contract were acrimoniously debated in Parliament and in the Court. Some in the Court criticised trading 'the flowers of the Crown for cash', considered the financial terms unrealistic and argued that elastic revenues were being exchanged for a fixed income when inflation was still feared. In the Commons the country gentlemen became nervous of a permanent land-tax and had no faith in a corrupt administration. There was too a hardening of views, the result of the king's flaunting of his powers and the consequent friction with the common law judges, who set restrictive definitions upon the prerogative.

Salisbury needed maximum political skill. But the Contract was only linked to a concession over impositions under pressure from the Commons, while inside the Court it was argued that solvency could be achieved by economy and administrative reform which would divert 'the current of private men's gains' and bring 'that benefit to the king's purse, which heretofore hath served to raise the fortunes of others'. Without retrenchment and sound administration, tension between the Crown and Commons would continue, for the revenue proposed in the bargaining over the Great Contract was insufficient to meet the king's spending at the level to which he had become accustomed.[33] There was thus a measure of agreement between Sir Julius Caesar, chancellor of the Exchequer, and the parliamentary opposition. Salisbury had put the cart before the horse in proposing the Contract before even palliative measures had been taken to stem the rampant extravagance and corruption.

The challenge of retrenchment and reform proposed by Caesar, which included the doubling of returns from crown lands, was not taken up by Salisbury, who, subjected to the ungraciousness of the king and worn down by his own ill-health, lost what grip he had after the failure of the Contract. He resorted to the device introduced under James of raising capital by selling honours, even though this seamy trade had already provoked scandal. When Salisbury died Hatfield in all its grandeur stood complete, but the Crown had a debt of £500,000 and a deficit of £160,000.

The Howards now rode to power, but the insolvency caused disquiet. Northampton, thought to be the most likely new treasurer, was said to have preferred that the revenues and debts 'should be thoroughly looked into, before he meddle withall'.[34] A treasury commission was therefore appointed, which called in Bacon, an indication that he could hope for preferment now that his cousin Salisbury was dead. The Commissioners laboured; the Howards enjoyed halcyon days. Their dominance seemed secured when Frances Howard, countess of Essex, after unedifying divorce proceedings, married the earl of Somerset. The king loaded the bride with jewels worth £10,000. The Parliament of 1614 summoned in the hope of a subsidy was wrecked both by the grievances of the Commons and also by one of the most dangerous of Jacobean developments, disagreement in the Council. Northampton's solution to the financial dilemma was a Spanish marriage and a dowry for the Prince of Wales. His insidious intrigues turned what it had been hoped would be a 'Parliament of Love' into the Addled Parliament. For those who see the Revolution of 1641 foreshadowed in the reign of James satisfaction can be found in Thomas Wentworth's baleful remarks that the Spaniards had lost the Netherlands through impositions, while French kings had 'died like calves upon the butcher's knife'. Such princes he said menacingly 'might read their destiny in the 45 Ezechiel verse 7 or thereabouts, but specially in Daniel, the 11 chap, verse 20'.[35] This looks forward to the language of the regicides and Fifth-Monarchy Men. But Wentworth was an extreme radical, and it can be argued that Northampton's sabotage was more important, both immediately and also for the precedent set for the later intrigues between court factions and oppositions in Parliament. Northampton's success in procuring the dissolution of Parliament within two months of its meeting establishes his claim to be the most dangerous of the ministers of James 1.

Death snatched the treasurership from Northampton, but it was given to his nephew Suffolk, called by James 'a plain, honest gentleman'.[36] Parliament had granted no subsidy and the hope of the Spanish dowry was illusory. Neither was there retrenchment. Lord Hay, the glass of fashion, presided over the Wardrobe, and standards generally sagged with the auction of offices and consequent graft. But how long could this continue? The king was faced with 'living like a shell-fish upon his own moisture'[37] and the treasury commissioners were scanning dry pools. The Howard edifice had to be attacked. Since ministerial and policy changes depended upon the king's emotional involvements, the anti-Howard party struck with three weapons: seduction, scandal and efficiency. An annulment was effected between James and Somerset with the help of the archbishop of Canterbury, who observed that the king 'began to cast his eye upon George Villiers', who seemed 'a modest and

courteous youth'. Bishop Hacket called Villiers, later duke of Buckingham, 'our English Alcibiades', since 'from the nails of his fingers, nay,
from the sole of his foot to the crown of his head, there was no blemish
in him.' The Puritan D'Ewes was more candid since, while conceding
that Villiers had delicate and handsome features, added that 'his hands
and face seemed to me especially effeminate.'[38] Secondly the scandal
was unleashed that the Somersets had instigated the murder in the
Tower in 1613 of Sir Thomas Overbury, a client who had been found
meddlesome and independent. Thirdly Suffolk's inefficiency and corruption came under fire.

Meanwhile the treasury commissioners, notably Bacon, pressed upon
the king the tough and energetic business consultant and administrator,
Cranfield. It is one of the paradoxes of Cranfield's career that he
crossed the frontier from the City to the Court under the auspices of
Northampton. He was first employed to investigate the laxity of customs
farming under Salisbury, but showed his wider vision when he seized
the opportunity to attack the policy of impositions, contending that the
word 'imposition' in itself had caused unnecessary trouble. He maintained that proper tariff reform, with duties levied on selected imports
and designed to protect trade, would have procured more revenue and
prevented constitutional repercussions. He also argued that English
merchants had not been given preferential treatment and that the customs officials, as a result of the policy of farming, were under-employed.
In 1613 he obtained his first government post as surveyor-general of the
customs.

By 1615 Cranfield felt that he had more to gain by abandoning the
Howards and operating under the flag of reform. Besides, Cranfield,
although intent on honours and wealth, had a concern for efficiency.
Alderman Cockayne's nefarious scheme for prohibiting the export of
white cloth, the traditional and main English export, in favour of the
dyed product, lacked capital backing, while, in contrast to the Dutch,
English manufacturers did not possess the necessary techniques. Cockayne, with Howard support, was jeopardising an established trade. His
camouflage of national interest was easily penetrated by Cranfield,
originally a member of the Company of Merchant Adventurers which
handled the old trade, and his telling statistics were singled out for
praise by Bacon. Simultaneously Cranfield again urged a protective
tariff instead of impositions, an idea acclaimed by Bacon, who with
unashamed snobbery said that 'this was more indeed than I could have
looked for from a man of his breeding.' Moreover, Cranfield adroitly

linked his tariff reform with the advice that the king should knock down
the second partition wall which separated him from Parliament by showing that the main cause of insolvency was not the royal bounty but
administrative corruption, as a result of which only a third of the revenue
reached the Exchequer, while the spending departments paid out a
third more than was necessary. The pill of reform was temptingly
sugared.[39]

But James himself, hating the admonishments of the Council, escaped
in 1617 to Scotland, saying that he had a salmon-like instinct to return
to the land of his birth. His expensive holiday was partially financed by
the sale of two earldoms, while the disposal of the Cautionary Towns to
the Dutch, a legacy from Elizabeth, helped his fondness for largesse.
Lord Hay, profiteering enough from the Wardrobe, received £10,000 as
a wedding present, the same sum as James had given to the countess of
Somerset. But on the king's return a desperate Council made James
swallow the medicine of administrative reform. Bacon urged the policy,
but, improvident himself, when faced by the details said, 'these things
are out of my element.' In contrast Cranfield wrote: 'The King's inclination to thrive. Great men are not fit for work of labour.' He was an
admirable executant of economy. In his private life he scrutinised his
wife's spending, sold his old clothes and supervised his rentals, declaring
that it was the course he was resolved to hold, 'for so I shall plainly see
my clear revenue and expense'.[40]

He applied the principle to the royal revenues. The first target was
the Household. Cranfield dominated the subcommission, triumphantly
discovering that 132¼ oxen were unaccounted for, ordering that there
should be fewer courses at meals and hangers-on dismissed, and that
'cast-off fish, bottles and jugs etc.' should be sold. A saving of £18,000
a year was effected. The crumpling of the household officials facilitated
attacks elsewhere. The inquiry into naval expenditure saw Cranfield
turning with zest from oxen to cables, deploring redundant officials and
declaring explosively that the carriage of timber from the royal forests
cost more than buying directly. A saving of £23,000 a year was proposed. Meanwhile a frontal assault was made on the Exchequer, resulting in the trial of Suffolk and the fall of the Howards.

The Treasury was now put into commission with strict orders for
assignment and audit. Cranfield had incurred unpopularity for his
ungentlemanly inquiries, but his reward came with his appointment as
master of the Wardrobe and of the Court of Wards. Lord Hay had been
spending in the Wardrobe around £42,000 a year; Cranfield offered to

keep expenditure down to £20,000 a year. Purchasing had been lavish, while long arrears entailing credit meant that prices double or triple the market rate were charged. Cranfield circumvented the officials by using his own servants, and by applying commercial standards and offering prompt payment 'damned the detestable name of Wardrobe prices'. His surgeon's knife operated more sharply on the spending departments, yet the returns from the Wards rose by a quarter when he was master, and again he operated through his own secretary.

In 1619 Cranfield became a member of the Treasury Commission. Redundancy had been attacked in the Household and the navy, and was a target in a renewed attempt at reform of crown land administration. But there could be no quick returns as a result of the absence of proper surveys and the problem of long leases. Increased revenue from customs was also difficult, since the effects of the Cockayne scheme, leading up to the depression of 1621, were already being felt. Cranfield himself told Villiers, now marquis of Buckingham and shortly to become duke, that 'the City is undone' and 'the trade of the kingdom lost'. No attack on customs administration was made, as Cranfield had earlier advocated, even though Sir William Garway, a prominent farmer, when asked for his views said bluntly that there were numerous officials 'without use or service as long as the customs were continued in farm'.[41] The windfalls from fines on new leases, together with the overdrafts and loans from the farmers, were too important. The commissioners hoped to gain revenue by recovering arrears owed to the Crown, half of which were due from Elizabeth's time, but over £1½ million were still extant in 1621. The French were more successful at investigations of this kind, although the English Government did possess machinery, as the trial of Suffolk in Star Chamber had shown.

Yet the treasury commissioners could congratulate themselves on a 25 per cent increase in the revenue, of which 70 per cent came from economies and 30 per cent from expansion. But impetus was slowing. The debt was still rising, while the balance on the annual account was fictitious, since anticipated revenue was included. Bacon wrote wearily that 'the King's state, if I should now die and were opened, would be found at my heart, as Queen Mary said of Calais.' He urged that the king must be told the truth and not betrayed with a kiss. Cranfield also tried to drive home to a king, fuddled with drink, the point that his bounty had prevented the reduction of the pension list and blunted reform. He, like Bacon, considered the position hopeless, saying at the end of a memorandum 'by this time your Majesty may judge me who am no scholar, to be of the disposition of the schoolmen who propound such questions as they are not able to answer.'[42]

The pessimism of Bacon and Cranfield suggests that focusing the close-up lens sharpens the picture of the doomed monarchy. Yet the figure of the king always dominated the foreground. The annual accounts came to be balanced by the treasury commissioners, but, as Cranfield said, the king's personal expenditure ruined all calculations. When the responsible members of the Council persuaded James to discard Somerset for Villiers, they obtained a total surrender, for James was to announce at a banquet that 'Christ had his John and I have my George.'[43] But when they gave James his George they also ensured financial defeat, since the Villiers tribe was as grasping and irresponsible as the Howard clan. The efficiency of Cranfield was cancelled by the rapacity of Villiers.

But Cranfield's career also illustrates not only the tensions but also the temptations of the times. Behind his public front lay concern with his private profits, natural enough given the minute official salaries and the gains of others. But how were his profits made and did they affect his public policies, as Salisbury's involvement with the customs farmers had done? And what were Cranfield's relations with Buckingham? Hacket paid tribute to the latter's power when he said that Bishop Williams 'had crept far, as I may say, for ground-ivy . . . but he must clasp upon this tree, or none, to trail and climb'.[44] Cranfield recognised this, but he was also arrogant, becoming more so with success. Would he ultimately try to disengage himself from Buckingham in the interests of his financial policies—and also of his ambition? Would that ambition lead him to play the game of court faction with noxious effects on council solidarity and relations with Parliament? And how did those intrigues rebound upon him, since his fall was to be engineered through Parliament?

It is revelatory of the decayed standards of the Jacobean Court that when Cranfield tried in 1618 to become chancellor of the Duchy of Lancaster he applied to Buckingham, stressing his services in the reform of the Household, but also offering £4000 in gold, though prudently asking that his letter should be burned. A saving of £3000 a year by bringing the duchy under Exchequer control was then under debate, but the chief executant of reform was ironically trying to bribe his way into a department considered redundant. Cranfield did not acquire the duchy, but he became master of the Wardrobe, both as a reward for his services and also as a result of his astute tender. When he offered to run the Wardrobe at £20,000 a year, he added the proviso that any savings under that figure should be his own. He netted over £7000 a year for himself, almost doubling the profits made by his grasping but inefficient predecessors. His profits in the Wards were discreetly shrouded, but he was said to have given £6000 for the mastership, and his personal secretary, blatantly corrupt, channelled gains to him—though crown returns rose. Again the investigation of arrears owed to the Crown offered him attractive opportunities, involving devious intrigues, of acquiring estates cheaply for himself.

When Cranfield became treasurer in 1621 he unctuously told Buckingham that he intended 'to pursue the course I have begun, which is not to make a fortune myself, but humbly leave it to the King to make me one, which is a new way of thriving at court'.[45] This is interesting in view of his own gains and of the king's record for bounty. When he became treasurer, he wished to be a pluralist and to continue as master of the Wardrobe, but Buckingham insisted that his brother-in-law should be installed. Cranfield was compensated by a lease of the sugar duties at a nominal rent of £2000, but in reality worth £6000 a year. Since his wardrobe profits had been more, he had to be soothed by getting his arrears of £6192 owed on his monopoly for the retail licensing of wines cancelled. Yet as treasurer he could look forward to rich opportunities for profit, and indeed during his two and a half years in office he more than trebled his landed wealth besides living more grandly.

Bacon wrote: 'Honour hath three things in it; the vantage ground to do good; the approach to kings and principal persons; and the raising of men's fortunes.' Neither he, the sponsor of the programme of administrative reform, nor Cranfield, its agent, saw flaws in this compendious definition. Pym, clearly with Cranfield in mind, was to say in the Parliament of 1626: 'He is accounted the wisest merchant that gains most; so that if such comes to offices and places of trust, he thinks it best to advance his profit.'[46] This is an interesting remark coming from the leader of the so-called bourgeois revolution, but it was true that Cranfield's training as a merchant had sharpened his acquisitiveness and his acumen. Yet it was that training combined with his drive and energy which made him so valuable a servant for an insolvent monarchy.

In 1620 James had three ministers of quality, Bacon, Cranfield and Sir Edward Coke, who in their differing ways could have served the Crown. Cranfield did not possess the vision or subtlety of Bacon, but as Ben Jonson said, 'My Lord Chancellor of England wringeth his speeches from the strings of his band and other Councillors from the picking of their teeth.'[47] Coke himself had been dismissed in 1616 from his position as chief justice of King's Bench, but ambition made him quickly make his peace with the Court, and he became a treasury commissioner. The public and personal antipathy between Coke, the protagonist of the common law, and Bacon, the champion of the prerogative, was notorious, though Bacon complimented Coke for his work on finance. But council solidarity, always fragile, splintered at the point when Parliament met in 1621. Coke had aimed to become treasurer. He was passed over for Montague, a double insult since the latter had succeeded him as chief justice, paying heavily for the office. In Parliament Coke, still a privy councillor, led the opposition, finding a platform in the burning grievance of monopolies. He was thus able to attack Bacon, who although he had advised the king that monopolies were inflammatory, had succumbed to Buckingham's pressure and, as chancellor, had signed the patents. Coke had an ally in Cranfield who believed that Bacon had stolen his ideas and appropriated the credit for them, while openly despising him for his merchant origins. Elizabeth in 1584 had threatened to dismiss councillors who used the leverage of Parliament,[48] but in 1621 Bacon was impeached with court backing. Yet to Coke's chagrin the triumph went to Cranfield who became treasurer.

Cranfield had solid administrative achievements behind him, while in a Parliament which met at the peak of the business depression, he had his facts and figures, and also commercial proposals. In the debates on trade one member said, 'The Master of Wards speaks upon knowledge' and another echoed approvingly, saying, 'as Sir Lionel can instruct us well, so doth he ever inform us faithfully.'[49] The Crown with a minister who had been a merchant seemed to be gaining the confidence of the Commons. But possible harmony was wrecked by James's foreign policy, when he sought to solve the crisis in the Palatinate by seeking to appease Spain through the marriage of his son to the Spanish Infanta. Protestant sympathy for James's son-in-law, the Elector Palatine, was roused. James's stand upon his prerogative forced a dissolution with no subsidy granted during the second session of Parliament.

Cranfield himself had climbed to the top of the winding stair and was created earl of Middlesex in 1622. But what did he accomplish as treasurer? He inherited a debt equal to almost two years' revenue and an income anticipated by a quarter. Further, as he told the king, trade was decayed and James could 'neither borrow in City nor country considering the great debts he owes both'. The treasury commissioners had tried and failed. What could Cranfield do alone? He attempted to freeze pensions and wanted office-holders, customs farmers and beneficiaries of land-grants to renounce their profits for a year 'by way of thankfulness'. He did not have the backing of the king nor the machinery of the *paulette*. His long-term plan, virtually an administrative revolution, was a gradual reduction of office-holding by refusing to renew 'new created offices and new charges after those in possession'. But paradoxically he sold offices as his predecessors had done.

Revenue was sought in Ireland, but here Cranfield was faced with reversing Salisbury's policies when he sought to recover crown lands. His attack on administrative costs, especially in the army, initially looked hopeful, but the obstruction of officials and landlords showed Cranfield's last Irish revenue account again showing a deficit. In England he had to continue Salisbury's policy of customs farming, since a loan, which he successfully negotiated, was imperative. His attempt to recover arrears owed to the Crown was defeated, though had two-thirds of these been paid the crown debt would have been extinguished. Total repayment was politically impossible, though collection by instalments through distraint on estates would have helped to meet the interest charges on the debt. The French Crown developed the powers of the intendants. Cranfield merely sighed for the old sheriffs, 'being not only great accountants, but having a great command over the county'. In all he raised the revenues slightly by squeezing the customs, but the deficit when he fell was just over £160,000.[50]

Forced back upon retrenchment at Court, he encountered the king, Buckingham and the office-holders. Hacket said of James that 'for thrift and saving he could never be brought to think of them', suspecting servants who 'were modest, as if they loved not him'.[51] Buckingham was not guilty on this score, and James worried over his favourite's debts while showing little concern for those of the Crown. The pension list rose however much Cranfield protested. Thus in 1622 a page of the Chamber received an annuity of £300; what services he had rendered to his sovereign we are not told. Cranfield buzzed ineffectively, ordering the use of old flags and that wine should not be wastefully served in bottles, infuriating the Court by his economies and self-righteousness. The courtiers, led by Buckingham, retaliated against the vulgar merchant.

The final break came over foreign policy. The proposed Spanish marriage involved the expensive visit of the Prince and Buckingham to Madrid, though Cranfield could hope for a dowry. On their failure the Prince and Buckingham demanded war against Spain, though they had no Bastille full of treasure and no Arsenal packed with arms, which Henri IV had boasted of to the English ambassador when they had walked in the alley which linked the two. When Cranfield opposed war Buckingham turned to the parliamentary opposition. Cranfield was impeached and his dubious private gains made the charges stick. The power of the Commons was enhanced, but this was preferable to Cranfield's austerity and insistence on balanced accounts. Again therefore the Parliament of 1624 shows that court faction was as much responsible as the ability of the opposition for increasing the strength of the Commons in the years that ended with the victory of king Pym over king Charles.

The close-up lens catches the interplay of personalities and intrigues at the Court, but we need a wide-angle lens to reveal the opportunities which James missed. Secure in his faith in the divine right of kings and preaching the doctrine of the prerogative, James had a major responsibility for driving a wedge between Court and country. Ben Jonson wrote:

> O! Your Parasite
> Is a most precious thing, dropt from above

James's parasites were his most precious possessions, and he was ruled by them rather than by his ministers. But he showed little discrimination in assessing the qualities of his ministers and he permitted quarrels in the Council to be injected into Parliament. The problems of an administration corroded by corruption were great but not insoluble, as the treasury commissioners had begun to demonstrate; nor was the weakening of the monarchy inevitable had not the king himself been financially irresponsible and contributed so largely to the polarisation of politics. It is after all worth remembering that when James acquiesced in the fall of a treasurer, who with all his faults had struggled for solvency as basic to the power of the Crown, in a moment of sanity he paid tribute to Cranfield whom he compared to Sully. Henri IV had chosen wisely, since both he and Sully appreciated the connection between power and finance, and on the broader front had conciliated rather than antagonised interests. Henri IV established the Bourbon monarchy; James's achievement was to endanger the Stuart dynasty.

9. Constitutional Ideas and Parliamentary Developments in England 1603-1625

ALAN G. R. SMITH

IN his last book, a massive study of *The House of Commons 1604–10*, published in 1971, Professor Wallace Notestein placed his great authority firmly behind the traditional view of Jacobean parliamentary history, drawing a stark contrast between Elizabeth, the 'great Queen' who handled the House of Commons skilfully, and James, 'a foolish man . . . wanting in common sense', who 'failed not only to understand English personalities but also to adjust himself to English codes and traditions. By 1614 he was a weary old potentate disinclined to effort.'[1] This view was not altogether accepted by Professor Robert Zaller, one of the younger generation of early seventeenth century parliamentary historians in his study, also published in 1971, of *The Parliament of 1621*.[2] He did not deny that James made errors, but also depicted the king as a man who sometimes showed considerable shrewdness in attempting to deal with a multitude of difficulties which were exploited by the members of an aggressive House of Commons to serve their individual and collective ambitions.

Historians also disagree about the nature and significance of the constitutional ideas which lay behind James's practical difficulties with his Parliaments. In 1949 Dr Margaret Judson argued that there was no basic ideological conflict between the Crown and the parliamentary opposition in James's reign; both agreed about the fundamentals of a balanced constitution and the difficulties which arose were due to disputes about the precise point of balance.[3] Professor G. L. Mosse, writing in 1950, produced a very different interpretation, arguing that by 1610 a 'struggle for sovereignty' had developed in England, with the clear statement by that date of rival theories of sovereignty for the king alone and for the king in parliament.[4]

Two general questions emerge from these debates. Firstly was there a fundamental conflict of constitutional ideas in James's reign? Secondly

For Notes to Chapter 9, see pages 240–1; for Bibliography, see pages 223–4.

were James's difficulties with Parliament essentially the result of his own actions, or were they due primarily to the growing ambitions of the House of Commons?

Evidence can be produced, particularly if it is taken out of context, which seems to support Mosse's view of an ideological conflict. In a speech to the assembled Lords and Commons at Whitehall in March 1610 James made one of his most famous pronouncements about the nature of royal power. 'Kings', he said, 'exercise a manner or resemblance of Divine power upon earth.' They can 'make and unmake their subjects: they have power of raising and casting down; of life and death; judges over all their subjects and in all causes, and yet accountable to none but God only. . . . Now a father may dispose of his inheritance to his children at his pleasure: yea, even disinherit the eldest upon just occasions, and prefer the youngest, according to his liking; make them beggars or rich at his pleasure . . .; so may the King deal with his subjects.'[5] This seems a categorical statement of complete royal supremacy, leaving no room for independent parliamentary authority.

In July of the same year the lawyer James Whitelocke made a notable speech in the House of Commons in which he explicitly discussed the source of supreme power in the State and came to conclusions which looked very different from those of James. In the course of this speech, Whitelocke said:

In the King is a twofold power, the one in Parliament, as he is assisted with the consent of the whole state; the other out of Parliament, as he is sole and singular, guided merely by his own will. And if of these two powers in the King, one is greater than the other and can direct and control the other, that is *suprema potestas*, the sovereign power, and the other is *subordinata*. It will then be easily proved that the power of the King in Parliament is greater than his power out of Parliament, and doth rule and control it. . . . If a judgment be given in the King's Bench by the King himself, as may be and by the law is intended, a writ of error to reverse this judgement may be sued before the King in Parliament. . . . So you see, the appeal is from the King out of Parliament to the King in Parliament . . . than which there can be no stronger evidence to prove that his power out of Parliament is subordinate to his power in Parliament; for in acts of Parliament . . . the act and power is the King's, but with the assent of the Lords and Commons, which maketh it the most sovereign and supreme power, above all and controllable by none. . . . The power to make laws, the power of naturalization, the power of erection of arbitrary government, the power to judge without appeal, the power to legitimate . . . all do belong to the King only in Parliament.[6]

This seems an unambiguous assertion of the supremacy of the king in Parliament over the king acting alone.

It has also been suggested that there was a third view of the source of ultimate authority in the state: the theory that it lay in the common law. This idea is usually associated with the pronouncements of that great seventeenth century legal oracle, Sir Edward Coke. In his celebrated judgement, in James's reign, on the case of Dr Thomas Bonham, Coke, then chief justice of King's Bench, stated: 'And it appears in our books that in many cases the common law will control acts of Parliament, and sometimes adjudge them to be utterly void: for when an act of Parliament is against common right and reason, or repugnant, or impossible to be performed, the common law will control it, and adjudge such act to be void.'[7] These words, if taken at their face value, seem to make the decisions of king, Lords and Commons, taken in Parliament in the most formal manner possible, subject to the overriding authority of the common law as interpreted by the judges.

It is important to insist however that none of the three statements just examined can properly be considered in isolation. James was notoriously fond of making exalted theoretical claims about his authority, but these must be set against the occasions when he quite explicitly recognised that there were specific limitations to his powers. For example on another occasion in 1610, in a message sent through lord treasurer Salisbury to a conference between members of the Lords and Commons, he acknowledged that 'he had no power to make laws of himself, or to exact subsidies *de jure* without the consent of his three estates.'[8]

As for Whitelocke, he qualified his seemingly clear words about the supremacy of the king in Parliament when, in the very same speech quoted above, he added: '[Other powers] there be of the same nature that the King may exercise out of Parliament, which right is grown unto him in them . . . by the use and practice of the commonwealth, as denization, coinage, making war, which power the King hath time out of mind practised without the gainsaying and murmuring of his subjects.'[9]

In other words, just as there were certain actions which the king could only take in Parliament, there were others which he could take by his own 'absolute' power, without the need for parliamentary discussion or consent.

It seems also that Coke's words in Bonham's case were not really an attempt to express a theory of a fundamental common law which empowered the courts to nullify statutes. It is much more probable that he was merely saying that courts could and should construe statutes strictly in order to see that they did not conflict with accepted principles of reason and equity which, it was assumed, underlay all legislation. In Bonham's Case the College of Physicians had levied a fine in a dispute in which it was itself a party, thus contravening a basic maxim of the common law, that no man could be judge in his own case. The College based its actions on statutes of the reign of Henry VIII and Mary; but Coke ruled that, if the officials of the College were allowed to take their share of the fine, 'they shall be judges in *propria causa*, and shall be summoners, sheriffs, judges and parties also, which is absurd; for if the King grant to one by his Letters Patent under the Great Seal that he may hold plea, although he be party, and if the King doth not appoint another judge than the grantee which is party, the grant is void, though that it be confirmed by Parliament.'

This reasoning certainly allowed the judges a discretionary power in the interpretation of statutes, but fell far short of a general theory of a fundamental common law which could override the powers of both Crown and Parliament. Coke indeed had the highest conception of the authority of the king in Parliament. In a famous passage in one of his writings he described the 'power and jurisdiction of the Parliament, for the making of laws, in proceeding by bill', as being 'so transcendant and absolute as it cannot be confined either for causes or persons within any bounds'.[10] This appears to contradict his statement about the common law and to exalt instead the authority of Parliament.

It seems then that James, Whitelocke and Coke did not claim absolute supremacy for the king, or for the king in Parliament or for the common law. This was essentially because in Jacobean England, although the word 'sovereignty' was frequently used in imprecise ways, there was no conception of sovereignty in the modern sense—no idea that an individual or institution in a state had final and supreme authority based on the possession of unrestricted legislative power. In the early seventeenth century the legislative capacity of *any* institution was believed to be limited by higher laws. Speaker Phelips made this point well in an address to the House of Commons in July 1604, when he stated that the common law of the realm was 'grounded or drawn from the law of God, the law of reason, and the law of nature'. These laws, superior to any made by men, were 'not mutable'.[11]

Coke in fact did not really contradict himself when he endowed both Parliament and the common law with very high authority. He did not ascribe true sovereignty to either, but regarded both as subject to divine and natural law and the law of reason, or—as we might put it today— to moral principles. In this situation both Crown and subjects had certain 'absolute' rights of which they could not legitimately be deprived. The king had his prerogative, which, as Chief Baron Fleming put it in Bates's case, 'is most properly named policy and government',[12] and which among other powers gave him the inalienable personal right to conduct foreign policy, regulate trade, make appointments to government offices and control the country's armed forces. Subjects on the other hand had the right to property, both in the sense of their material possessions and of their lives and liberties. It was for example a fundamental maxim of the common law that beasts of the plough could not be distrained: these were essential for a man's livelihood, necessary for the work which it was God's will that he should perform. Also direct taxes could not be taken by the Crown on its own authority but had to be granted freely by the people through their representatives in Parliament.

In Jacobean England then the dominant constitutional theory, accepted by king, Parliament and common lawyers alike, was of a balanced constitution which was founded on certain inalienable rights possessed by both Crown and subjects and safeguarded by the common law, with the law itself based on principles which could not properly be challenged by men: principles enshrined in the laws of God, nature and reason, however these might be defined. This idea of balance was very well expressed by Francis Bacon in a speech in the House of Commons in May 1610:

The King's sovereignty and the liberty of Parliament are as the two elements and principles of this estate; which, though the one be more active, the other more passive, yet they do not cross or destroy the one the other, but they strengthen and maintain the one the other. Take away liberty of Parliament, the griefs of the subject will bleed inwards: sharp and eager humours will not evaporate and then they must exulcerate, and so may endanger the sovereignty itself. On the other side, if the King's sovereignty receive diminution or any degree of contempt with us that are born under an hereditary monarchy . . .

it must follow that we shall be a meteor or *corpus imperfecte mistum*; which kind of bodies come speedily to confusion and dissolution.[13]

Granted that all agreed on the idea of a balanced constitution, the vital question was: where did the exact balance come, and who was to decide if Crown and Parliament differed? Differ they did, and James himself certainly contributed substantially to the conflicts. Many of his ideas and policies aroused the mistrust and dislike of the Commons. He had a passionate love of peace, which, he insisted in his first speech to Parliament in March 1604, 'is no small blessing to a Christian commonwealth'. He gave these words effective meaning in August of the same year, when he brought the long-drawn-out Elizabethan war with Spain to an end, and throughout the rest of his reign he set himself the task of acting as the peacemaker and peacekeeper of Europe. It was a noble aim and not unwelcome to war-weary England in 1604; but when it became clear to his subjects that his policies involved not only friendship with Spain but even the marriage of his heir, Prince Charles, to a Spanish infanta, they showed their profound disapproval and dismay. In December 1621 the Commons drew up a petition in which they asked that 'our noble prince may be timely and happily married to one of our own religion',[14] and in 1624, following the breakdown of the negotiations for the Spanish match, Parliament did its utmost to push James into war with Spain. He made his reluctance plain to a committee of Lords and Commons, saying that he had gloried 'to be styled *Rex Pacificus*', and had taken pride in the honour which he had obtained at home and abroad, 'in endeavouring to avoid the effusion of Christian blood'.[15] The outbreak of hostilities with Spain late in 1624 was therefore a tragedy for James as well as a triumph for the Commons, who had shown such persistent suspicions of his pro-Spanish policies.

James's attitude towards English Catholics aroused as much parliamentary opposition as his policy towards Spain, and indeed coloured that opposition. He disliked persecution as much as war. 'My mind', he told Parliament in 1604. 'was ever so free from . . . thralling of my subjects in matters of conscience, as I hope that those of that profession [i.e. the Catholics] within this kingdom have a proof since my coming, that I am so far from increasing their burdens . . . as I have so much as either time, occasion or law could permit, lightened them.' There were periods in the reign when he did order the full enforcement of the penal laws, but generally he preferred leniency. The Commons reacted with predictable disapproval. In 1610 they stated 'that the laws are not executed against the priests, who are the corrupters of the people in religion and loyalty' and asked that they be put into force 'without dread or delay'. In 1621 they returned to the attack. Because of the Spanish negotiations, they said, 'the Popish recusants have taken too much encouragement and are dangerously increased in their number and in their insolencies.' The remedy was 'to put in execution . . . the laws already and hereafter to be made for preventing of dangers by Popish recusants'.[16]

James's desire for a real as opposed to a merely personal union between England and Scotland also brought him into conflict with the House of Commons. In his opening speech to Parliament in 1604 he made an eloquent plea for such a union. 'What God hath conjoined,' he said 'let no man separate. I am the husband, and all the whole isle is my lawful wife. I am the head and it is the body. I am the shepherd and it is my flock. I hope, therefore, no man will be so unreasonable as to think that I, that am a Christian King under the Gospel, should be a polygamist and husband to two wives.' In November 1606, at the beginning of the third session of his first Parliament, he described the question of the union, as 'the greatest and weightiest matter of all', and asked Parliament to 'embrace it, that we may all enjoy it'.[17] To his dismay, the Commons, under the leadership of Sir Edwin Sandys, accepted only the repeal of hostile English laws against the Scots. The Government's other main suggestions; for mutual naturalisation, for a commercial treaty looking towards free trade, and for the improvement of justice along the Borders, were rejected, partly because of practical difficulties but principally because of the fears and suspicions of the Commons and their dislike and contempt for the Scots. James was both hurt and angry at this attitude towards his fellow countrymen and never really forgave the Commons for their rejection of what was undoubtedly his favourite parliamentary project.

In his hopes for a 'perfect' union with Scotland, in his reluctance to engage in religious persecution and in his desire for friendship with Spain, James was ahead of his times. His Parliaments took a narrower, or, as they would have argued, more realistic view of these problems. They just did not trust the king's policies and ultimately therefore the king himself.

Posterity might well sympathise with James's idealistic plans for peace, tolerance and a united kingdom of Great Britain, but there is little to be said for the financial extravagance which lay at the root of many of his most serious problems with Parliament. For most of his reign his financial difficulties arose from annual deficits on his ordinary revenue: he quite simply failed to live within his means, as the Crown was expected to do in times of peace. The frugal Elizabeth indeed in the years before the outbreak of war with Spain in 1585 had saved large sums each year from her regular income. James however spent money lavishly on the Royal Household and made huge cash gifts to favourites, mainly to Scots in the early years of the reign, and later on to Buckingham, who was an army in himself. In this situation he was constantly in need of extraordinary parliamentary grants, but the four subsidies, which were all that he obtained before 1621, were merely a drop in the ocean. The Commons were naturally reluctant to vote money to fill the pockets of worthless favourites, especially when they were Scotsmen! John Hoskyns, a prominent critic of the Government, voiced a general feeling when he stated in the House of Commons in 1610 that 'the royal cistern had a leak, which, till it were stopped, all our consultation to bring money unto it was of little use.' [18]

Lacking adequate subsidies, the king and his chief minister in the early years of the reign, Robert Cecil, earl of Salisbury, turned to other measures for raising revenue. Their two principal projects were the new Book of Rates issued in 1608 and the Great Contract of 1610. The Crown's claim to impose, on its own authority, duties on goods entering or leaving the country was upheld by the judges in Bate's case in 1606, principally on the grounds that such duties were designed to regulate trade, which was an aspect of foreign policy and thus within the 'absolute' prerogative of the Crown. On the basis of this decision Salisbury in 1608 issued a new Book of Rates which increased duties on a very large number of articles, and thus raised a substantially increased revenue. The new impositions provoked a storm in Parliament in 1610 and again in 1614. The issue seemed quite clear to many members of the Commons: it concerned the sanctity of private property, a field where, as we have seen, the subjects' rights were generally held to be beyond dispute. 'It is', said James Whitelocke, 'a question of our very essence... whether we shall have anything or nothing.' If the king's claims were admitted, 'we are but tenants at his will of that which we have.' [19] The Crown and its supporters on the other hand insisted that impositions belonged to the field of trade and foreign policy. Neither side would give way on the principle and the fears and bitterness engendered by the conflict were largely responsible for the failure of the sessions of 1610 and 1614 and for the angry royal dissolutions of Parliament which followed.

The Great Contract, Salisbury's most notable brainchild, was designed to add £200,000 a year to the royal revenue in return for a number of concessions to Parliament, including the abolition of purveyance —the right of the Crown to buy supplies for the Court at less than the market price—and some reforms in the system of wardship—the right of the Crown to control the marriages and lands of its minor tenants in chief until they came of age. The Commons however insisted on the total abolition of wardship, and by the summer of 1610 a provisional bargain had been struck by which the king was to receive a fixed annual revenue of £200,000 in return for the end of wardship and purveyance and other concessions. When Parliament resumed in the autumn of 1610 however, both sides were having second thoughts, and at the beginning of November James raised his terms, demanding immediate supply of £500,000 in addition to the annual £200,000, and insisting that this provision had been implicit in the Contract from the beginning. In this situation the Commons, already resentful at the Crown's attitude over impositions, refused to proceed with the discussions, and the following month Parliament came to an end, with Crown and Commons at loggerheads.

Such failures were partly due to James's ineffective management of Parliament. Elizabeth had intervened in Commons debates only occasionally, but usually with decisive effect. James on the other hand bombarded the Lower House with a multitude of tactless messages in which he often strayed from the strict point at issue to indulge in general remarks about his own power and the nature of the Commons privileges. For example in March 1604 he told the Commons that 'they derived all matters of privilege from him and by his grant',[20] a constitutional doctrine which they were not prepared to accept. They felt that the king was trying to deprive them of their birthright, and James, aware of his good intentions and used before 1603 to dealing with the subservient Scottish Parliament, resented their constant criticisms. His own style of life did not help matters. His passion for hunting took him into the country for long spells at a time, and he was frequently absent from London when Parliament was discussing important business. Even when his pet project, the union with Scotland, was being debated in 1607, he was away from the capital. 'The Lords of Council', wrote the Venetian ambassador, 'have with great justice pointed out to his Majesty that his continued absence from the city, especially while the question of the union is on, is very injurious to the negotiations.'[21]

The speakers in James's Parliaments did little to make up for the king's defects. The speaker was at this time a government nominee, and the extensive control which he traditionally exercised over Commons procedure made him an important asset to the Crown in the task of controlling the House. In the very first Parliament of the reign however there was obvious lack of enthusiasm for the official candidate, Sir Edward Phelips, and some members even suggested an alternative name—a grave slight to the Crown. The speaker in 1614, Ranulph Crew, was an undistinguished choice. He had sat in only one previous Parliament, in 1597, and his lack of experience may help to explain the notorious rowdiness of the 1614 House of Commons. Thomas Richardson, speaker in 1621, had a very unhappy time, being constantly rebuked by members. The speaker in 1624, Sir Thomas Crew, was a better nominee. He had been a member of the opposition in previous Parliaments and his selection seems to have been a concession to popular opinion. Quite apart from the personal qualities of the speakers however there was less opportunity for them to intervene decisively in debates as James's reign went on. This was partly due to the increasing importance of committees, where the speaker did not preside, partly to the restrictions which the Commons explicitly imposed on his authority. In February 1621 it was resolved that no bill under consideration in the House should be read a second time before 9 o'clock in the morning, and that a day's notice must be given before bills were put up for a third and final reading.[22] These orders deprived speakers of important opportunities, which they had previously exploited, of pushing government measures through the Commons.

The Crown's ability to control the Lower House was also weakened by the changing situation in the House of Lords. Under Elizabeth the Upper House had been almost completely subservient to the Crown and the Queen had frequently used it to reject measures which she disliked but which had got through the Commons. In James's first Parliament Salisbury tried to manage the Lower House from the Lords through an extension of the already established system of conferences between Lords and Commons committees. At these meetings he explained government policies and used his considerable dialectical powers to try and persuade the Commons to accept them. The system was not a success, largely because the Lower House insisted on strictly limiting the powers and terms of reference of their committees—with inevitable limitations on the usefulness of the debates.

In James's reign the Lords grew greatly in size. Its membership, eighty-one at Elizabeth's death, had increased to 128 by 1625. As the number of spiritual lords remained constant at twenty-six the increase was due to James's lavish creations of new hereditary peerages, a policy which had almost doubled the number of secular lords by the time of his death. The holders of older peerages disliked this flood of new titles, and there were undignified squabbles between old and new peers in the Parliament of 1621, when a group of 'opposition lords', led by the earl of Southampton, emerged, the first example of such a phenomenon since pre-Elizabethan days. Many members of the Lords also disliked the complete dominance at Court of James's prime favourite, Buckingham, and the changed atmosphere in the Upper House can be gauged by the increasing difficulties of Lord Chancellor Bacon in controlling debate.[23] In this Parliament the Lords co-operated willingly with the Commons in reviving the procedure of impeachment, which could be used with decisive effect against the king's ministers, and Southampton held meetings with members of the Commons opposition in order to co-ordinate tactics—a practice which led to his arrest in the summer of 1621.

The most important instruments of all for controlling the House were traditionally those privy councillors who were also members of the Commons, and Elizabeth throughout her reign made use of a succession of distinguished councillors to guide and influence debates in the House. In the early years of his reign James did not grasp the need to keep a sufficient number of able councillors in the Commons. In Elizabeth's last Parliament, in 1601, there had been five privy councillors in the House. For the first three sessions of James's crucial first Parliament of 1604–10 there were never more than two in the Commons at any one time, and in the fourth and fifth sessions there were only three. None of them had remarkable abilities: in fact only one, Sir Julius Caesar, rose above mediocrity. In 1614 there were four councillors in the Commons, but none of them was really fitted to lead the House; indeed one, Sir Thomas Parry, was ignominiously expelled for corrupt electioneering practices—a severe blow to the prestige of the councillors as a body. The leading government spokesman was Sir Ralph Winwood, an honest and worthy man who had been appointed secretary of state just before Parliament met, but the burdens of his new office and the fact that he was sitting in the Commons for the first time hardly augured well for his success, and he was distracted by overwork throughout the session. After the failures of 1610 and 1614 James at last became aware of the need to secure adequate Privy Council representation in the Lower House, and no fewer than nine councillors secured election in 1621. Two of them, Sir Lionel Cranfield and Sir Edward Coke, were men of outstanding ability. Not all of the councillors however were effective members of the Commons throughout the two sessions of 1621 and the practical strength of the Council in the House was usually only four or five. The two most notable losses were Coke, who openly joined the opposition, and Cranfield, who became lord treasurer and was raised to the peerage during the course of the Parliament. In the last Parliament of the reign in 1624, there were six councillors in the Commons, none of outstanding ability, and not all of them attended regularly.[24] Jacobean councillors moreover were never as well prepared as their Elizabethan predecessors with a programme of business to lay before the Commons, and it is a striking and important fact that it was *private* members who seized the initiative in proposing topics for discussion at the beginning of each of the Parliaments of 1604, 1614 and 1621.

The declining influence of the Privy Council in the Commons was greatly exacerbated by James's failure to prevent faction struggles at Court from spilling over into the parliamentary arena, where they weakened the Crown's position in both the Upper and Lower Houses. In 1614 the pro-Spanish earl of Northampton, who had been opposed to the calling of Parliament, worked behind the scenes to ruin the session, encouraging rumours about government attempts to pack the Lower House and eventually advising a dissolution when king and Commons were at loggerheads. In 1621, though there was no equivalent to Northampton's wrecking tactics of 1614, the bitter rivalries and jealousies which existed among Bacon, Coke and Cranfield had important repercussions in Parliament. Coke and Cranfield were united in their desire to secure the downfall of Bacon, the king's principal minister in the Upper House, despite the damage which this would do to the prestige of the Crown, but they were united in that alone. Otherwise they were rivals for the leadership of the Commons, and there was no real co-operation between them in the House even before it became plain that Coke had thrown in his lot with the opposition. Moreover Cranfield did not hesitate to contradict openly other councillors, such as Sir Humphrey May, Sir Thomas Edmondes and Sir George Calvert. In the 1621 Parliament in fact the Crown's principal servants were in almost complete disarray. Three years later, in 1624, Buckingham set out to exploit the warlike fervour of the Commons against Spain to secure the ruin of Cranfield, then in the Upper House. Cranfield, as lord treasurer, was opposed to the idea of war, with all the expense which it would entail, and he had obtained considerable support in the Council for his views. Buckingham's enmity secured his impeachment, and the Crown lost the services of a remarkably able servant.[25]

James's failures in managing Paliament were however by no means due only to his own lack of skill. The increasing political maturity and growing aggressiveness of the Commons, combined with important procedural developments in the House, go far to explaining the conflicts of his reign. In the Elizabethan period the Commons had grown in numbers—from 400 to 462 (it grew still further to 489 in James's reign)—and members, who came predominantly from the increasingly wealthy country gentry, had in their capacity as J.P.s played an ever greater role in local administration as the queen's reign progressed. At the same time more and more of them had been going on to some form of higher education at university or inn of court—well over half of the House by the Parliament of 1593. This significant increase in the size and improvement in the 'quality' of the Commons meant that any successor to Elizabeth was bound to have difficulties in controlling it, especially as by the 1590s more and more of the detailed work of the House was being done in committees which showed a distinct desire to free themselves from the influence of privy councillors. The important section of the House of Commons which drew up the 'Apology and Satisfaction', a justification of the House's actions in 1604, made their aggressive intentions plain when they stated that, in the later years of Elizabeth, 'in regard of her sex and age . . . and much more upon care to avoid all trouble which by wicked practice might have been drawn to impeach the quiet of Your Majesty's right in the succession, those actions were then passed over which we hoped in succeeding times of freer access to Your Highness of renowned grace and justice, to redress, restore, and rectify.'[26]

The implication was clear. If the king did not make the desired concessions, he could expect trouble.

Trouble came, and it was made possible partly by procedural changes in the House. Besides the important limitations by the Commons in 1621 on the speaker's right to control the business of the House, there were developments of fundamental importance in the committee system. During the later Elizabethan period committees increased rapidly in numbers and size until by the 1590s they might include nearly half the House. In 1607 however there appeared, almost by accident, the committee of the Whole House, where, as the speaker was not in the chair, the usual rules of debate were suspended and members could speak much more freely—for example they could wander at will from topic to topic, a practice not allowed at formal sittings. By 1610 it was becoming customary to refer many important matters to such committees of the Whole, and in the 1620s nearly all significant business came before them. By then, these committees and the various subcommittees which proliferated from them were dominated by men who were usually critical of the king's actions. The opposition had in effect seized control of Commons procedure.[27] In this situation privy councillors found it almost impossible to get a fair hearing for Crown policies.

Throughout James's reign there is evidence of co-operation and consultation among opposition leaders in the Commons, and, as we have seen, in 1621 there were discussions between prominent opponents of the Crown in the Lower House and the earl of Southampton, the leader of opposition in the Lords. Lord Chancellor Ellesmere commented on the organisation of the Commons opposition as early as 1610 when he noted that in that year 'some [members] . . . did single them from the others and kept secret and privy conventicles and conferences, wherein they devised and set down special plots for the carrying of business in the House according to their own humour and drifts, and that in the weightiest and most important causes.'[28] This does not mean of course that there was an opposition 'party' in anything like a modern sense; it is difficult to find a single Jacobean M.P. who stuck rigidly to an 'opposition line' on all important matters throughout the reign. It simply means that individual members who strongly disliked specific government measures or actions came together to decide the best ways of opposing them. There was a considerable turnover of members who opposed the Crown. Of some sixty who took a definite opposition line on at least one issue in the Parliament of 1604–10, only about ten remained by the 1620s,[29] though by then others had come forward as leading critics of the king, including those great parliamentarians Sir Robert Phelips, Sir John Eliot, Sir Edward Coke and John Pym.

If opposition members did not form a coherently organised party, they were nevertheless sufficiently determined and aggressive to carry the House as a whole with them in a number of actions and statements which taken together formed a serious challenge to the authority of the Crown. The Commons were obsessed with questions of privilege. In 1604 in the case of Goodwin versus Fortescue, after a prolonged wrangle with the king in which James made one concession after another, they obtained the right to decide disputed elections to the House themselves, although traditionally this task belonged to Chancery. In a petition of right, drawn up in 1610, they asserted that it was the 'ancient, general and undoubted right of Parliament to debate freely all matters which do properly concern the subject and his right or state',[30] a claim which could be used to cover virtually every issue; and in their famous Protestation of 1621 they stated quite unambiguously 'that the arduous and urgent affairs concerning the King, state and defence of the realm and of the Church of England, and the maintenance and making of laws, and redress of mischiefs and grievances which daily happen within this realm, are proper subjects and matter of counsel and debate in Parliament . . . and that the Commons in Parliament have . . . liberty and freedom of speech to propound, treat, reason and conclude the same.'

The Protestation arose from James's command that the Commons must not discuss high matters of state, and specifically foreign policy, without his permission. This was the position which both Elizabeth and he had always adopted, and the Commons' claim had no historical basis. By the 1620s however they insisted on making it on the grounds that they were the representatives of the nation. The issue had in fact ceased to be one of historical precedent; it had become a question of political power, though the Commons themselves refused to recognise the fact. They still admitted in theory the king's absolute right to *conduct* foreign policy as he saw fit, only asserting their own absolute right to *discuss* it. James however saw very clearly the implications of the Commons claims. In reply to their petition of December 1621, protesting against the proposed Spanish match, he asked, 'What have you left unattempted in the highest points of sovereignty in that petition of yours except the striking of coin? For it contains the violation of leagues, the particular way how to govern a war, and the marriage of our dearest son.' To have admitted an unfettered right in the Commons to discuss such matters would in effect have given them a voice in government, which to James was unthinkable. Foreign policy, he said, was not a matter for parliamentary discussion, 'except your King should require it of you'.[31] In 1624, under pressure from Prince Charles and Buckingham, who were by then clamouring for war with Spain, James did give the Commons explicit permission to discuss foreign affairs. In return they voted supply, but insisted in the Subsidy Act that the money should be appropriated to certain specific aspects of the expected war, and that it should be collected and disbursed by treasurers appointed by Parliament and responsible to the House of Commons.[32] This was a sign of lack of trust in the king and as such a damaging attack on his prestige and authority.

In other ways too the Commons of 1621 and 1624 showed their aggressive spirit. They discussed patents and monopolies—economic and fiscal privileges which the Crown granted to individuals or corporate bodies—and condemned many of them as illegal, though they had no right to reach such conclusions. James protested at their actions. 'It is not enough for me', he told the House in 1624, 'if some of your doctors of law stand up and say this patent is against the law. I must for the law rely upon my learned counsel and upon my judges, whether the patent be in itself good by law or not.'[33] The upshot of the debates was the Act of Monopolies of 1624,[34] the first statutory limitation of the royal prerogative and as such a landmark in constitutional history.

The 1621 and 1624 Parliaments also saw the impeachments of two of the Crown's principal ministers, Lord Chancellor Bacon in 1621 and Lord Treasurer Middlesex in 1624. The revival of the ancient judicial process of impeachment, last used in 1449, in which the Commons laid charges of crimes or oppressions before the Lords, was made possible by the antiquarian researches of members of the Lower House and the forceful advocacy of Coke. Bacon and Middlesex were both condemned by the Upper House for taking bribes, but the effect of the proceedings was to put a powerful political weapon into the hands of the Commons, who in future were always able to think up 'criminal' charges against ministers and courtiers whom they disliked.[35]

The apparent harmony between Government and Parliament which was so notable in 1624 was founded solely on the desire of Prince Charles, Buckingham and the Commons for war with Spain. It was an alliance to secure a single end, and prince, favourite and Parliament succeeded in bullying an ill and protesting James into granting their wishes. In this situation Charles and Buckingham were prepared to accept with equanimity such invasions of the royal prerogative as those enshrined in the Subsidy and Monopolies Acts. 'It is very strange', wrote an old Scottish courtier, 'to see the Prince go on so in applauding all or the most part' of the actions of a Parliament, 'which does every day grate upon the King's prerogative so much.'[36]

James was wiser than his son. He rightly sensed that throughout his reign the Commons had been making claims which were historically unjustifiable. He condemned the Protestation of 1621 as a direct challenge to his royal authority, and made his feelings crystal clear at the solemn meeting of the Privy Council at which he declared it 'invalid, annulled, void and of no effect', and tore it out of the Commons Journal with his own hand.[37] In 1624 he warned his son and favourite of the dangers of their intrigues with the Commons. 'You are a fool,' he said to Buckingham, 'and will shortly repent this folly, and will find that in this fit of popularity you are making a rod with which you will be scourged yourself.' Then, turning to the prince, he told him 'that he would live to have his bellyful of Parliaments, and that . . . he would have too much cause to remember how much he had contributed to the weakening of the Crown by this precedent he was now so fond of . . . as well the engaging the Parliament in the war, as the prosecution of the earl of Middlesex.'[38]

These were prophetic words. James may have been losing his grip on affairs by 1624 but he was still capable at times of considerable shrewdness, and two years later, in the second Parliament of the new reign, both Charles and Buckingham had cause to reflect upon the wisdom of his words.

Throughout James's reign both king and Parliament adhered to the theory of a balanced constitution. James's errors in his dealings with the Commons certainly contributed to the practical difficulties which arose in determining the exact point of balance, but his mistakes must not be allowed to conceal the fundamental fact that the Lower House was in truculent and aggressive mood throughout the reign: by the 1620s it was making claims in practice, though not in theory, to an effective share in the making of policy and thus in the government of the country. It seems fair to conclude with Professor Wormuth that James's difficulties arose primarily 'because there was a new spirit in Parliament, rather than in the Crown'.[39]

10. The Crown and the Courts in England 1603-1625

W. J. JONES

THE attention traditionally paid to James I's dealings with courts, judges, and lawyers is not altogether without merit although writers no longer concentrate instinctively upon theories of divine right of kings and unlikely extensions of prerogatives. James was not an original thinker but he did have a practical and theoretical interest in various kinds of law. Often irritated by common lawyers, whom he once likened to wind instruments, he probably had doubts about their education and he certainly enjoyed jokes made at their expense. Unlike Elizabeth he became involved in legal and jurisdictional disputes. His difficulties with Sir Edward Coke are a fact, but the nature of their 'confrontation' should not be distorted. Notions that the king was 'opposed' by judges or common lawyers lack credibility. Indeed it can be suggested that both he and his son placed too much reliance upon common lawyers and the common law.

The pitfall which historians may traverse but not evade is provided by the rhetoric and grandiose statments of the age. Kings were gods, but then so were judges although this might be explained away by reference to delegation. One inclines towards Plucknett's view that in deciding for the Crown judges who relied upon available historical evidence often spoiled the effect by 'gratuitously introducing a good deal of dogma on divine right'. An exercise of the prerogative, quite acceptable on strict legal grounds, might be defended on the more debatable ground of 'absolute power'.[1] An appeal by Lord Chancellor Ellesmere to the law of God has been interpreted as 'an elegant allusion rather than an integral part of his argument'.[2] There was never any question that the highest law of the land, statute law, could only be made in Parliament, but it has been argued that James accepted this 'grudgingly' and trouble arose because the prerogative 'was supreme where the law had not insinuated itself'.[3] Some judicial opinions must have worried the king, and Coke's assertion that 'Magna Carta is such a fellow that he will have no sovereign' has been read as a blow against the prerog-

For Notes to Chapter 10, see pages 241–3; for Bibliography, see page 224.

ative.[4] Coke's constant stand on the sovereignty of law however has too often been interpreted as a rebuttal of James whereas it seems equally appropriate to view it as a constraint on the sovereignty of Parliament. In 1607, producing a stream of precedents to support the doctrine of naturalisation by allegiance, he treated the arguments of Commons spokesmen with contempt. He can be grouped with Sir John Davies and others in that they emphasised the common law to the point of confining statute. It was, writes Dr Hinton, 'a plain contradiction of parliamentary legislative sovereignty . . .; the effect of this was to elevate the status of the King in relation to the status of Parliament.'[5]

There is a danger that the pendulum of interpretation might swing too far. Professor Kenyon's assessment of James reflects our current understanding: 'he was careful always to operate within the framework of the common law; he never imprisoned anyone without trial, he never levied money from his subjects without authorisation from Parliament or the courts of common law, he never promulgated law of his own accord, even if he believed he could, and he was certainly more moderate and 'constitutional' than Queen Elizabeth.'[6] This is more to the point than many previous verdicts although the contrast drawn with respect to his predecessor needs justification. However something else needs to be said. With respect to the levy of money there was an increasing demand for the authorisation of both Parliament and the courts. As an M.P. asked in 1610: 'shall all other courts be at liberty . . . to dispute the law and shall this court [Parliament] be barred and tied not to dispute it? Is not the King's prerogative disputable?'[7] He was referring to the Exchequer decision of 1606 with respect to impositions and the attempt to restrict parliamentary discussion of the same subject. Actually the prerogative—a legal exercise of royal authority—was hardly ever denied. At various times some wondered about its rightful exercise, perhaps thinking that favourites manipulated the situation to their own advantage, or questioning if some particular area was really within the prerogative. With respect to impositions, the point was made by Coke in 1614: 'if it be a prerogative it is warranted by law, for the King hath no prerogative to impose that the law giveth him not power to do.' Ellesmere expressed the same sentiment: 'the King hath no prerogative but that that is warranted by law and the law hath given him.'[8]

The ability of modern historians to recognise their ignorance about many of the forums and institutions which provide the essential context for an interpretation of the rights of Crown and subject has led to a new picture, one which is slowly being built out of minute details. We are becoming better acquainted with borough and manorial courts, petty and quarter sessions, and the general world of local officialdom. There is a good book on the Elizabethan Council in the Marches of Wales and its author has provided some telling papers on the early Stuart situation. Old books on the Council in the North—although supplemented by a modern pamphlet—and on the Palatine of Durham are hardly adequate. Ecclesiastical courts in the diocese of York have been surveyed by Dr Marchant, who provides detail without avoiding debate.[9] The *Victoria County History* is valuable, articles proliferate and graduate theses multiply. However little has been put together. Insubstantial generalisations about the great courts have been shattered, but there is little to put in their place. Major works are expected on the Admiralty and the Star Chamber, the latter court already having been exposed by Professor Barnes.[10] My book on the Elizabethan Chancery deals with the administrative and political background to jurisdiction and procedures, but much remains to be done on fees, rolls and writs. Certainly there is no warrant to suggest that we know very much about the Marian or Jacobean institution.[11] Our knowledge of Common Pleas and Exchequer is even more minimal. King's Bench provides almost as sad a picture, but here the gloom is parted by work such as Dr Blatcher's piece on *latitat*. Much of England's legal heritage had become outmoded. This was inevitable, but lawyers and officials were unable to comprehend change. Their attempts at rectification, shrouded in traditional assumptions, must call to mind Plucknett's warning about the perennial trouble of casual reform which did not make a clean sweep of the past. This must be understood if we are to grasp the effort of King's Bench to free itself from medieval bonds. 'Although the motive was self-interested and the means a fiction, those who employed the writ of *latitat* to achieve that end were serving the cause of necessary change.' Dr Blatcher has provided a classic exposition of the role played by resort to fiction.[12]

How then should future work be constructed? One possibility is provided by Dr Blatcher's essay. Another is suggested by work done on the Court of Wards. Dr Bell wrote a solid study of particular interest to the early Stuart period, but Professor Hurstfield's Elizabethan analysis is outstanding because it blends the institution into the realities of society.[13] A similar ambition should be applied to other areas. We cannot understand the history of criminal law without studying criminals and crimes, and it is hopeless to write about debt without studying debtors.

A little has been said on equity but any serious study must collate work on the provincial councils, the palatine courts, the rewarding records of the Exchequer and many other tribunals. Equity would become synonymous with Chancery but this was not the situation in James's reign although that institution's preponderant role had been acknowledged. Above all it is pointless to write about the land law without studying the land and hence all that such a massive theme entails.

What is a court? Certainly it is not just a series of law reports or manuscript legal proceedings although too many works have been constructed upon this basis—as though a cow could be described in terms of its milk. Courts were institutions with a physical location, departments, officials, records and rooms, all of which might be dispersed. There was a greater distance between the Chancery bench and its administrative heart, the Rolls in Chancery Lane, than there was between the benches of Chancery, Common Pleas and King's Bench, separated as they were by a few feet and some partitions in Westminster Hall. Coke's removal from Common Pleas to King's Bench meant that he had to walk a distance of perhaps eighty yards. Not surprisingly it was said that 'there are not two such acres in all the country as the Exchange and Westminster Hall.'[14] Yet the remarkable activity which this edifice housed represented only one aspect. Chancery was an institution which issued over 10,000 subpoenas annually in the early years of Elizabeth and twice that number in the last years of James—figures which can become insignificant when compared with the number of judicial writs it issued returnable to Common Pleas and King's Bench. Courts gave employment to elevated seniors, burdened hacks and service officials—the Exchequer at Chester had a carpenter and mason. The six clerks of Chancery had fine plate and table linen; the lowlier cursitors had a society which dined regularly, the meal followed by the reading of writs. Competition and selection for office, apparent at all levels, was just one element which confirmed that all institutions were part of the general political picture.[15]

Thomas Powell wrote about the 'great courts at Westminster, to whose motion all other courts . . . are diurnally moved'.[16] He was referring to the shadow of regulation which Chancery, Common Pleas, Exchequer, King's Bench and Star Chamber had thrown over minor, provincial and specialised jurisdictions. The eminence and power of these central and national courts was underlined by Coke's acknowledgement that there were different kinds of jurisdiction: 'the bounds of all and every several courts being most necessary to be known'.[17] A major theme of James's reign is to be discerned in principles of regulation and supervision adopted by judges of the major courts. Delivery by habeas corpus of those committed, injunctions and prohibitions were the major weapons. Process of this nature—really the standard means of communication between courts—was in exceptional demand, and we must not ignore the multitude of instances in which writs were refused or quashed. The judges of Westminster courts were clearly asserting their claim to decide the limits of other jurisdictions, but the real issue was that of finding lines of demarcation between all courts. There was debate between Common Pleas and King's Bench, between common law and ecclesiastical courts, between diocesan courts and the Arches. The hardest task of all was that of distinguishing between the proper jurisdictions of courts which exercised a similar procedure or which avowed a similar competence. Across this tangle swept the demands of great Westminster courts, aided by superior procedures and record requirements. Amid many issues, the arrogant assertion of these national courts is most obvious. Yet a sense of context is still all important. Common Pleas did deny the right of High Commission to define its own jurisdiction but it and other courts adopted the same attitude towards many tribunals. In 1598 the power of the Court of Requests to imprison was cut to pieces by the chief justice of the Common Pleas—it was said that an action of false imprisonment might be had—but in that same year the power of the Requests to commit to prison was vindicated against the lord mayor's court.[18] England was a network, a jig-saw puzzle, of courts constructed on different levels. At every stage there was a struggle to assert authority. Provincial courts, scrutinised from Westminster, were themselves supervising lesser units. The Exchequer at Chester demanded acceptance of its supremacy from the courts of the city of Chester and elsewhere in the palatinate. Despite resistance and complaints—Berwick, Beverley, Carlisle, Heddon, Hull and York struggled to avoid the mesh—the Council in the North established control over lesser courts from the Trent to the Scottish Border. There was trouble over the jurisdictional boundaries of the Tower and the City of London. Surrey J.P.s questioned London's authority over Southwark.[19] A myriad of examples could be given and perhaps the manorial courts were the most obvious victims of this process of regulation and record superiority. However the bigger courts—whether it was the Common Pleas surveying the nation or the Exchequer at Chester surveying the palatine—had no wish to embark upon a course of destruction. All jurisdictions, lay and ecclesiastical, provincial or specialised, were valued and often supported.

Courts which claimed the power of supervision had neither the wish nor the ability to handle all kinds of suit. There was a trend towards excluding small cases, personal actions and actions not involving title to land from Westminster. There are limits to the thesis that competition provides an explanation of the difficulties between courts, and it must be recognised that great courts did not want to be swamped by small cases which, if heard at Westminster, would entail costs, expenses and time out of all proportion to the matter in dispute. Local, provincial and specialised courts would still attract considerable business but in the long run their area of ability was defined and this invited extinction. Courts which could not change or expand in accordance with the fluctuating needs of society had little future even if they continued into the nineteenth century. Only the great courts of Westminster Hall, excepting Star Chamber which was felled amid curious political turmoil, adapted themselves. Tudor government had been based upon the centralisation of authority and the decentralisation of its administration. In later times both would be centralised and this was not always conducive to efficiency. One has only to look at the hideous monstrosity that was the eighteenth-century Chancery.

The great courts at Westminster had their differences, but they maintained a common front. The appearance of justices on the benches of Chancery and Star Chamber was only the most superficial expression of this accord. This does not imply that disputes can be taken lightly, and in the contest for fees Exchequer and King's Bench raids upon the lucrative area of Common Pleas civil jurisdiction has justifiably been called shabby.[20] There was none the less a trend towards deleting the possibility that different courts might offer different remedies. Initially Common Pleas played the most independent role; subsequently Chancery was to occasion difficulty; finally King's Bench seemed inclined to run a course of its own and Thomas Powell found that his pen was excluded from 'meddling' in the crown office side of that court.[21] Definition was still the essential problem. The Westminster courts supervised other tribunals but it was wondered if they also should not be supervised. Those who asked this question looked to Crown or Parliament.

Judges were government employees active in administration. Justices of assize for example oversaw most aspects of local life and without them early Stuart government is inconceivable. A clear distinction between judicial and administrative authority would only be grasped in later years. Yet there was an apparent contradiction. It might make sense to place limits upon lesser and provincial jurisdictions, or for that matter the Privy Council, but this meant that the justices were regulating the structure of government as established under the Tudors. They were an integral part of the system and yet seemed to be assuming the role of a *deus ex machina*. They owed their exceptional position to the Crown, the fount of the law and the source of all their authority. The king appointed them, paid them and used them.[22] It is hardly surprising therefore that James, who was not enamoured of ideas which drew too sharp a distinction between the personality and function of the sovereign, felt sometimes called upon to intervene. James being James was fascinated and puzzled by theoretical implications. Being the source of jurisdiction, he wondered how he could give a *praemunire* against himself.[23] He was after all the linchpin of justice and he represented the idea of enforceable arbitration. The practical justification for his interference—he was the most interested person—called in question the value of his attempts. His particular legal rights, or prerogatives, with respect to proceedings before the courts made him an unlikely arbitrator.[24]

No one is more rightly associated with the questioning of jurisdictions than Coke. Furthermore he was outstanding among the many lawyers who contributed to the current emphasis on historiography. Many myths were unearthed—Coke once described thirty-three martyr popes of a former Protestant Rome [25]—but he and others cannot be judged by modern ideas of historical scholarship. Even so it is clear that his reputation is no longer accorded its former respect. His *Reports* have been justifiably criticised,[26] but Coke, even at his most bombastic, might have been perplexed by some later dependence upon his authority. That he was headstrong was clear before he joined the bench as chief justice of the Common Pleas in 1606, but he was no more arrogant than others. Indeed he deserves sympathy in that he had to deal with Thomas Walmsley, a Common Pleas justice since 1589, and Peter Warburton, a justice since 1600. These Cheshire men, associates of Ellesmere, were renowned for their scathing tongues. Often they agreed, but when genuine points of legal difference arose the debate was fierce. During these years the Common Pleas bench was an exciting place. Similar difficulties doubtless afflicted the King's Bench, and for a time the number of justices in both courts was increased from four to five in the hope that ties could be avoided.[27] A necessary appreciation of personal and political circumstances helps to explain how great constitutional and legal issues came to be raised. There was also a struggle for influence and office which in the mid-period of the reign had its roots in the fragmented interests of those who opposed Howard dominance at Court. Coke's difficulties in 1616 are crucial to an understanding of the success of the new favourite, Villiers, and Bacon's story forms part of the same picture. Once political battle was joined however it was natural that dissension would prompt serious analysis and disagreement with respect to affairs of jurisdiction and judicial performance.

Amongst instruments of regulation, the writ of prohibition, issued to forbid inferior courts from further proceedings in a cause, is perhaps best known. It had long been used to restrain ecclesiastical courts, but in the second part of Elizabeth's reign it seemed to attract a novel demand. Initially High Commission and Requests were the most worried, but around the time of James's accession major provincial courts became targets. Prohibitions to the Council of the Marches of Wales had previously been rare, although English proceedings before the Council had of course been confined by Chancery to cases within the geographic boundaries of the Council's jurisdiction. This done, it was almost inevitable that these boundaries would be challenged. Disagreement over the status of the four Marcher shires was apparent in the 1597 Parliament, and it is possible that dissident border gentry were already making their voices heard. Under James, the matter was repeatedly before the House of Commons and it has been suggested that the king's personal intervention played some part in the Council's retrenchment of authority over these shires. Even so it was the early years of James which marked the greatest flow of prohibitions to the Council. The Council in the North experienced more or less the same thing. In the course of one term Common Pleas could issue over fifty prohibitions to York. In 1605, before Coke reached the bench, Archbishop Bancroft complained about 'the over frequent and undue granting of prohibitions', and Sir Henry Townshend fumed over the issue of this writ to the chamberlain of Chester. In the second half of James's reign the pressure slackened and by 1617 the Welsh Council had recovered from a difficult decade. Prohibitions still issued, it would have been revolutionary if they had ceased, but many problems which had occasioned their grant had been resolved for the time being. Even so Wentworth, on becoming president of the Council in the North, would describe them in 1628 as 'the bleeding evil'.[28]

Courts and judges did not act in a vacuum. Prohibitions, like injunctions and other process, were only issued in response to individual request. It is not therefore surprising that the most serious complaint was that prohibitions were granted on surmise. However Bancroft's suggestion that prohibitions, although returnable elsewhere, should only be issued from Chancery was unrealistic. The archbishop subsequently tried to invoke royal power as a means to reform abuses in the use of writs but the judges retorted that 'what the law doth warrant in cases of prohibitions to keep every jurisdiction in his true limits is not to be said an abuse, nor can be altered but by Parliament.'[29] Far more serious was argument over the right of a court which did not have a suit before it or which did not claim jurisdiction to issue a prohibition. If this could not be done, it meant that the ability of a court such as Common Pleas to regulate other jurisdictions was seriously circumscribed. Common Pleas justices themselves were divided on the matter. Coke supported the issue of a prohibition against a court which did not have jurisdiction, but Walmsley said that this was only justifiable if some court had jurisdiction and the dispute, or something material to it, should already be 'hanging' in Common Pleas.[30]

The difficulties of supervision were most apparent with respect to the hierarchy of ecclesiastical courts. These had authority over clergy and laity in matters of heresy, matrimony, morality, testaments, tithes and so on. Obscurity between spiritual and temporal jurisdictions was enhanced by the inadequacy of church legislation. Church courts, the troublesome canons of 1604 notwithstanding, had to rely mostly on old canon law and some statutes. Tudor Parliaments had allowed clerical marriage, governed clerical discipline and regulated degrees of consanguinity, tithes, grants of administration and other matters. Justices of the great courts viewed statute as just one of the lines of authority which enabled them to provide supervision. Thus it was declared that the opening of shops on Sunday was forbidden by statute and outside the scope of the High Commission. However the essence of supervision is to be found in the concern expressed by the justices that a proper order of doing things should be followed. A prohibition was issued because the plaintiff had sued for tithes in the wrong diocese. Above all there seems to have been much interest in maintaining a line of appeal from the archdeacon to the diocesan court and thence to the provincial court of the archbishop—the Arches for Canterbury or the chancery court for York. If licensed by the bishop, the Arches or its fellow could act as a court of first instance. Otherwise Common Pleas would grant a prohibition on the grounds that evasion of the diocesan court robbed men of their statutory right of appeal. The archdeacon should not remit cases to the archbishop; instead he should remit to the bishop and only the latter could remit to the archbishop. The principle was that all courts had a proper jurisdiction and procedure. Ecclesiastical tribunals, surveyed by the great central courts, were not alone in their predicament but they were singularly trapped within the enforced web of their own rules. It was the confinement of church courts within set limits, not the prohibitions debate as such, which in the long run sapped their strength.[31]

In granting or refusing a prohibition the justices sometimes explained their understanding of jurisdictions. The Welsh Council was authorised by its instructions to hold plea where there was no common law remedy but this did not allow it to poach on ecclesiastical courts and so a 'prohibition may be granted to reduce that to its proper court'. The Council was also rebuffed when, during a minority, it tried to take account of an administrator. This responsibility belonged to the ecclesiastical court. Coke had no objection to the High Commission exercising jurisdiction over polygamy and the Common Pleas refused to interfere in an accessory matter, as when an acquitted defendant was required to pay costs. Late in James's reign it was declared that a 'legacy is a thing merely which is determinable in the spiritual court, and no other court may have conusance of that'. Supervision of legacies was a matter of spiritual jurisdiction, but payment of the testator's debts concerned the temporal courts. Acquisition of business was always important, but the great courts were also nudging ecclesiastical tribunals into alignment with common law rules. Coke once argued that if the spiritual court found itself faced with a collateral temporal issue there need be no difficulty so long as common law rules of evidence and law were used. Common Pleas later ruled that an executor should be able to prove a full administration by the same rules as those which applied in actions of debt.[32]

Some idea of the nature of supervision and other themes can be gained by a glance at the Courts of Admiralty and Requests. The Admiralty was valued: its proceedings were relatively speedy, its system of direct written examinations was advantageous, and it could employ commissions to examine abroad. The judges of this court had an unrivalled grasp of foreign agreements, contracts and techniques. Yet it lacked authority in some areas and hence the necessary aura of command. Early in Elizabeth's reign contracts made abroad became a matter of common law jurisdiction through the fiction of describing the place as being 'in the parish of St Mary-le-Bow in the ward of Cheap'. In the reign of James the Admiralty's power to enforce appearance or to imprison was questioned. It was denied jurisdiction over offences committed on land or over contracts made in England or abroad, irrespective of whether they were to be performed on the high seas. It was once declared that the Admiralty was only competent to handle contracts arising on the sea: otherwise 'though it arise upon any continent, port or haven in the world out of the King's dominions . . . the courts of common law have unlimited power in causes transitory.' If a bond was clearly made *super altum mare* the Admiralty had jurisdiction, but if these words were omitted a different situation would prevail. Some found this ridiculous, and they noted that contracts entered abroad were governed by the civil law. Coke responded by observing that there was nothing to prevent the justices from seeking the advice of civilians. It is fair to note that these experts were often invited to speak before the Common Pleas bench when Coke was chief justice. Certainly there was a struggle for business and there were particular complications, instanced by the Spanish ambassador's complaint against prohibitions and commissions of appeal granted after a decree for possession. Holdsworth suggested that Coke and his fellow justices were unscrupulous, but perhaps it is better to give them the benefit of the doubt and suppose that they were trying to make sense of a disordered situation. In the reign of Charles I a settlement, framed in a set of King's Bench resolutions, was achieved. There would still be difficulties, but the Admiralty would be singularly undisturbed by revolutionary episodes.[33]

The flow of prohibitions to the Court of Requests became noticeable in the 1580s, but Common Pleas also referred cases to it and the chief justice of that court warned against ignoring its injunctions. In the 1590s the number of prohibitions increased, 'the like whereof is not remembered to have been done in former times'. Denial of its right to stay suits before the great courts of Westminster or to issue injunctions after judgement was only natural and therefore not very significant. More serious was the claim that it could not imprison and that it could not take bonds with condition to appear. Its ambition to be a court of record was thus denied. Sir Julius Caesar would emerge as an indignant champion of this court, but in truth the number of prohibitions was small in comparison with the litigation entertained. Every so often there were gleams of encouragement. In 1599 Walmsley recommended a suit to the Requests: 'God be thanked,' it was noted, 'that court which woundeth can heal some times.' In retrospect the challenge posed by prohibitions appears to have been a flurry of shots which was not backed by any great will to direct a destructive charge. The authority of the court was damaged but it remained popular. Coke appreciated this ar⁴ he advocated that it should be recognised by statute. Certainly the volume of business handled by the Requests could not be ignored, and in 1627 it was reported to have as many suits and clients as the Chancery. Envisaged by Chancery as a convenient disposal unit for small matters and poor plaintiffs, the Requests acquired the reputation of being an 'alms basket' for the greater court.[34]

The commissioners of ecclesiastical causes are now seen as having their origin not in the royal supremacy so much as in the Crown's traditional duty to guard the Church. The commissioners—those at York enjoyed an active existence independent of Canterbury—enforced the Statutes of Supremacy and Uniformity, suppressed movements dangerous to the Church and handled ecclesiastical offences. In 1613 they were empowered to enforce the rules of censorship. The High Commission was not unpopular and its disputed habits of fining and imprisonment were as much an attraction to confident litigants as they were an offence to others. These powers, together with the *ex officio* oath, attracted most criticism. The issue however was whether Common Pleas and King's Bench had the right to supervise the procedural ability of the commissioners. In pointing out that a person could not be bound to appear in another court, the Common Pleas justices explained that they themselves for example could not take an obligation binding a man to appear before the Council in the North. With respect to appearance before the High Commission itself, the judges repeatedly said that the only proper procedure was citation—those arrested might have an action of false imprisonment—and the commissioners were constantly told that they could not impose 'pecuniary or corporal' penalties. Above all there was a feeling that the High Commission often encroached on other jurisdictions. With respect to cases between party and party, Coke and Walmsley agreed that jurisdiction in the first instance lay with the ordinary ecclesiastical courts unless the matter was 'enormous', but they differed on the meaning of this word. One man, sentenced before the ordinary for adultery, had refused maintenance to his wife, and consorted with two other women, fathering two bastards. Walmsley agreed with Serjeant Doddridge that the man was so 'incorrigible' that the matter became 'enormous', but Coke, Foster and Warburton did not see it this way.[35]

Imprisonment was the issue which more than any other exposed the possibility of debate over the royal authority. Bancroft, Coke and James conspired to open this Pandora's box. Walmsley accepted that the Statute of Supremacy did not give power to imprison, but he emphasised that the sovereign's discretion had been mentioned and he argued that the exercise of imprisonment across two decades could not be ignored. Coke disagreed: the 'King is the supreme head by the common law, as to the coercive power, and ... the letters patent of the King cannot give power to imprison where they cannot imprison by the common law.'[36] Bancroft had complained about prohibitions before Coke became chief justice but the hardening attitude of Common Pleas prompted him to renew his efforts in 1607. This time he made reference to the king's right to hear cases personally, a theme which was to cause embarrassment as when Coke argued that although James had the right to sit on a bench he could not reassume the judicial power which had been delegated. As a matter of academic debate points could be made for both positions, but Coke hit the nail on the head when he suggested that anyhow James lacked the proper expertise and learning.[37]

Westminster justices, confident that there was a proper jurisdiction for every court, would have been astounded by the suggestion that they were attacking the king's authority. Their reliance upon this authority was fundamental to the grant of prohibitions. Coke, in justification of the issue of a prohibition, said that the admiral and his officers 'have without all colour encroached and intruded upon a right and prerogative due to the Crown'. James however felt that he must intervene. He urged all courts to define their jurisdiction, and he encouraged Common Pleas and King's Bench to be less 'prodigal' in granting prohibitions. He thought that this writ should be granted in open court and not by one judge or in the vacation. By no means opposed to prohibitions as such, he wanted to do all that he could to 'keep every river within his own banks and channels'. Conferences were arranged but the king muddled his role as arbitrator, as when he solicited opinions from the King's Bench justices to the effect that Common Pleas should only issue a prohibition when it was in 'first possession'. In March 1610 he spoke against both sides but he was most severe on the Common Pleas justices. The situation was not improved by objection to the High Commission in a Commons petition and by a brief from the lord admiral. There was the appearance of a truce but nothing had been settled, and in 1611 Walmsley provided Ellesmere with his own particular views.[38]

Bancroft's death provided an opportunity for compromise, and it was apparently hoped that new letters patent issued in 1611 would clarify the powers of the High Commission. Coke, already enraged by having had to present a defence of past prohibitions, was annoyed to find that he had been named in the Commission and that the justices of King's Bench unlike those of Common Pleas, had advance knowledge of it. In any case, the letters patent contained 'divers points against the laws and statutes of England'. The King's Bench justices were not very happy with the course of events even though they had not always agreed in the past with their colleagues of Common Pleas. During the ceremony of tending the oath, said Coke, 'I stood, and would not sit as I was requested . . . and so by my example did all the rest of the Justices.' [39]

The new letters patent named the lord chancellor, the chief justices, the chief baron, six justices and the attorney and solicitor generals. Earlier commissions had included leading judges and lawyers, but the real question was the degree to which these would participate. There were some changes in response to objection: jurisdiction over alimony disputes was barred, it was stipulated that at least five commissioners were necessary for a final sentence and there was provision for a commission of review. All this did nothing to dampen Coke's indignation. His opponents were happy to point out the former collaboration of common lawyers and they cited a warrant for arrest signed by Coke when he was attorney general. Argument continued, but a new period in the history of the Commission had been inaugurated and subsequent letters patent would both clarify and establish some aspects of its ability. [40]

With respect to both the High Commission and the ordinary ecclesiastical courts a change of emphasis can be discerned in the second half of the reign. This would appear to coincide with the refreshed confidence of the Council in the Marches of Wales. Plenty of prohibitions still issued, this was only natural, but, perhaps Coke's departure from the bench had something to do with the less acrimonious tone. It may also be suggested that the solution of problems and the formulation of rough sets of acceptable rules was also a factor. It is probable that some points had been conceded by the central justices, but flexibility was easier as the supreme power of supervision claimed by the Westminster courts came to be accepted.

Coke could still unite his fellow justices in 1611, but this did not erase antagonisms, and doubts were expressed as to the veracity of his reports and recollections. The undercurrent of criticism was apparent in 1612. After two men had been convicted by the High Commission, Abbott requested writs of *de haeretico comburendo*. Coke denied the legality of this proceeding. The archbishop, after consultation with James, asked Ellesmere to take the opinion of the judges, preferably those of the King's Bench. These had experience in capital cases and anyhow the king did not want Coke to be involved 'lest by his singularity in opinion he should give stay to the business'. Justice Williams took the opportunity to report that he and Baron Altham 'did once very roundly let the Lord Coke know their minds, that he was not such a master of the law as he did take on him, to deliver what he list for law and to despise all other'.[41]

Coke probably guessed that his intractability was a factor which determined the king's behaviour, and James knew that Coke did not command unanimous support even from his own bench. Hence during the height of the prohibitions dispute James had already begun to employ devious if legitimate practices in dividing the judges when he sought opinions. Coke was translated to King's Bench in the judicial reshuffle of 1613, and in 1614 he was admitted to the Council. In 1615 with Peacham's case and in 1616 with the case of Commendams James solicited separate opinions from the judges. In the latter instance he made it clear that he wished to participate in discussions. This time the judges refused, but in the end all save Coke recanted. The affair hastened Coke's dismissal. Coke and Ellesmere were in dispute over the jurisdictions of King's Bench and Chancery, and the chief justice had enraged the old lord chancellor by striking when the latter was mistakenly supposed to be at death's door. Attorney General Bacon, imbued with his own hopes, fanned the flames. That this was very much the stuff of politics does not diminish the genuine nature of debate over legal issues. Yet the dominant feature of the enmity between Coke and Ellesmere was that it revealed a rift among those who opposed the powerful Howard faction. Bacon's arbitration cruelly disguised his involvement with the rising star of George Villiers. Coke for his part had become saddled with the consequences of his aptitude for histrionics. In the trial of Somerset, the king's former favourite, he had seemed to invite too much exposure of the Court's dirty linen. Now, in his dispute with Ellesmere, he was trapped by his own reliance upon some dubious, perhaps fraudulent, litigants. His detractors moved in and his ability to blunt an attack upon his *Reports* had little immediate significance. Humiliating dismissal followed but he was still a man of consequence and he was by no means out of favour. In 1620 he was again offended when Montague, the graceless person who had replaced him on King's Bench, was made lord treasurer and in the following year he cannot have liked the selection of Williams as lord keeper of the great seal to succeed the fallen Bacon. Coke was over seventy by this time. Despite some petulant remarks by James, he never conceived himself to be a critic of Crown or prerogative.

It was a world of paradox.[42] There was a cry for reform but this always seemed to threaten vested interests. More officials were needed, but this meant more offices to sell. Established clerks were happy to increase the number of their subordinates but they did not wish more of their own kind and status. They complained bitterly against new offices created by patent and the noise of their objection may have done something to encourage popular criticism of offices in general. On another level it is apparent that lawyers were associated with greed and incompetence, but even so their services were in constant demand. Attorneys, clerks and counsel were held responsible for all the ails of a system which rested upon the backs of laymen. Great courts established their authority on the basis of an expanding complexity of procedures which required expense and time. Chancery and Star Chamber spawned an extraordinary machinery of evidence. With respect to one set of Star Chamber depositions, Walmsley said that a man might just as well have paid four subsidies or provided twenty horses for defence of the realm.[43] The circumstances of debtors illustrate another aspect. Their treatment was recognised as a social wrong but every attempt to alleviate their burden or to avoid senseless imprisonment aroused objection. This was the quagmire which lured Bacon towards destruction. He fastened upon the notion that a minority of creditors might be coerced by the majority into allowing the debtor more time or even a composition. The idea was not new, but Bacon was exploiting the reaffirmation of chancery powers obtained in 1616. In 1621, amid a storm of parliamentary objection, he was cut down, and there was general criticism of administrative practices in Chancery and other great courts.

Some aspects of the Parliament of 1621 are only understandable if the performance of previous assemblies is appreciated. James's ministers had to find more money and patronage. Trade and the structure of office provided most opportunity to crown lawyers who were happy to employ conventional legality. The Crown forced the pace with respect to impositions, and James could confront Parliament with the judgement of the Exchequer in Bate's case. This was basic to Salisbury's extension of trade taxes in 1608, but the Crown did not rely solely upon the limited decision expressed in Bate's case. Opponents, who employed lawyers to construct a counter-argument, questioned the right to impose but they also tried to distinguish between different commodities or challenged the amount of the tax. In 1610 this issue helped to disrupt consideration of Salisbury's proposals with respect to feudal incidents. In 1614 dissent over impositions was even more important. The House of Lords refused a conference with the Commons. Coke and his fellow judges declined to pronounce upon the legality of the tax. They had good reasons, but the episode underlined the fact that the judges as assistants to the Upper Chamber could only be of minimal help. This Parliament was dissolved without legislation being passed and so there was a problem about statutes which, it might be supposed, should have been renewed. An eventual solution was discerned in the theory that an assembly which failed to pass legislation was only a convention and not a parliament. It followed that statutes needing renewal continued in force until the next Parliament. There was embarrassment after the Parliament of 1621–2, which in mid-session passed a subsidy act and an act confirming the clerical subsidy but no other legislation— at times neither the justices nor the justices of the peace seemed to know what to do—but the Parliaments of 1624 and 1625 more or less cleaned up the mess. This little episode is important because it indicates that legitimate legal interpretations of Parliament were outmoded. Activity in the House of Commons made it impossible to interpret Parliament solely according to the established principles of traditional legal analysis. In terms of political reality, the Lower Chamber was a strident debating forum in which the grievances and ideas of the upper crust of society were presented.[44]

Traditional legal attitudes did not accord with the political role of the Commons but they were extremely relevant to the judicial revival of the Upper Chamber in 1621, one of the most striking occurrences of James's reign. The trials of Bacon and Mompesson are renowned, but in retrospect the most interesting factor was provided by a mass of petitions some of which invited supervision of proceedings in the great courts of law. The House of Lords, somewhat aided by Coke's explanations of its authority, seized the opportunity. By the end of the decade its specialised committee had developed recognised procedures and powers. Beneath the king the House of Lords made arrangements which matched its claim to be the summit of the legal structure.[45]

The reign of James was part of a period renowned for litigation, but often this means no more than that a great number of people were involved in the machinery of the law. In a large county, jury service could touch over a thousand men in a year.[46] The theme of dependence upon laymen is vital but so is the notion that distinctions between law and administration cannot be drawn too easily, and this was as true for the village as for great affairs of state. That there were many faults, acutely apparent to contemporaries, cannot be denied. The primitive nature of common law criminal proceedings was made more objectionable by the increasing severity of the criminal law. Civil procedures were protracted and sometimes destructive to parties with a good case. Obstreperous litigants were matched by fee-hunting attorneys, clerks, lawyers and solicitors. Disputes between courts, whether justified as part of a natural process of regulation or condemned as poaching, confused and embittered the citizen. The modern attitude towards case law can hardly be said to have existed, and Coke has been described as wandering at random over the cases in question.[47] Yet in the years that lay ahead a greater reliance on precedent, particularly when it seemed to buttress the financial claims of the Crown, aroused an even greater popular antagonism. Bate's case, as an M.P. had feared in 1614, did indeed become a precedent.[48] It was very easy to criticise the courts, their behaviour and officials, but there was an insufficient appreciation of real problems and real endeavours. James merely had to suffer a constant ebb and flow of difficulty and grievance but the climax would come in the reign of Charles. Oliver Cromwell, really a 'moderate' on this subject, would express the accumulated frustration of several decades. 'There is one general grievance in the nation. It is the law. Not that the laws are a grievance; but there are laws that are. And the great grievance lies in the execution and administration.'[49]

11. The English Local Community and Local Government 1603-1625

G. C. F. FORSTER

ENGLAND in the early seventeenth century has been described as 'a union of partially independent county states, each with its own ethos and loyalty'.[1] At this time the life of the vast majority of Englishmen, even of the wealthier sort, was lived almost wholly within the confines of their own county, or 'country' as they usually called it. During the sixteenth century the sense of county identity had been growing: 'local concerns and obligations', wrote Tawney, 'were the common stuff of life, and affairs of wider import an intermittent addition to them.'[2] County society was dominated by landowning families, groups of country gentry, sometimes distinct but often connected by ties of kinship and marriage. They formed what it is now fashionable to call the 'community of the county' or more explicitly 'the community of county gentry', characterised by insularity of outlook, provincial and family pride, localised preoccupations. These characteristics were also displayed by merchant families and other leading inhabitants of the more important chartered towns. The public and social positions of these men became much closer from the later fifteenth century as Governments made increasing use of the power of local families to manage affairs in counties and towns, which ultimately became important units of administration. Few people ever came into direct contact with the central Government. Instead it was the governors of the local communities who punished their wrong-doings, maintained order and organised such help as was available in time of trouble. The duties of officers and courts have formed the subject of several accounts drawn from statutes and legal manuals, but rather less attention has been paid to the work they actually did. Surviving records of local government in different parts of the country enable some conclusions to be drawn however and while this essay cannot claim to be the comprehensive survey which is needed, it tries to answer certain questions. What new responsibilities

For Notes to Chapter 11, see pages 243–5; for Bibliography, see page 225.

accrued to the authorities, and how were they discharged? What were the central Government's orders and how were they executed? What do the records reveal about the way local officers went about their public duties? To what extent did they try to make the existing administrative machinery work? How far were they equal to their responsibilities? The answers to these questions will tell us something about the local communities of Jacobean England and something too about the problems of an age when government meant, for most people, local government.

I

Many of the older courts and officers had lost power as a result of changes during the fifteenth and sixteenth centuries, and by the beginning of James's reign the principal agencies of local government were the justices of the peace, the sheriffs, the lords lieutenant, the provincial councils, the town corporations and the officers of hundreds (or wapentakes) and parishes.[3] With a jurisdiction dating from the fourteenth century, the J.P.s became in Tudor times key figures in the country's judicial and administrative system; their duties and powers were derived from the commission of the peace and from the statutes, which charged them with a multitude of judicial and administrative tasks. In contrast the sheriffs had lost many of their powers but they still had important legal duties and electoral responsibilities. To some extent the sheriff's place in the county hierarchy had been taken by the principal new officer, the lord lieutenant who, with deputies, was charged with organising the county's militia forces. In the five northern counties and in the Welsh Marches there were important provincial councils with wide civil and criminal powers, while for the security of the Scottish Border there was a military and judicial system under the wardens of the Marches. The corporate towns were also outside the ordinary structure of county administration: their rights of self-government were based on charters which provided for a variety of borough courts and councils. The counties had long been divided into hundreds (or wapentakes) which, with their high constables, retained administrative importance for taxation, police and the militia. High constables linked the county with the parish which after the Reformation had become the basic unit of secular administration, with its constable, churchwardens, surveyors of the highways and overseers of the poor, who formed the 'working staff' of local government.

In addition there were the ecclesiastical courts, coroners and other royal officials, and commissions for special purposes. Plainly the country was much governed, at least in theory. Yet each county was not, as is sometimes said, an organ of local self-government; J.P.s, sheriffs and lieutenants were accountable, even removable, for neglecting or abusing office. In many respects towns enjoyed more independence. On the other hand it would be wrong to suppose that the commands of the central Government or the provisions of statutes were always carried out. It would be equally wrong to suppose that either the long-established J.P.s or the newly emergent lords lieutenant had necessarily developed any sort of routine, let alone momentum, in the pursuit of their duties: much depended on the circumstances and on the men.

II

The lieutenancy and the militia still showed in James's reign some of the uncertainty and experiment usually discernible in a new institution, but some aspects were gradually settled. Of these the most notable was the permanence of the lieutenancy itself.[4] The tendency of Elizabeth's reign to allow the office to lapse was reversed under her successor, the first five years of whose reign were of decisive importance in establishing the lieutenancy as a permanent part of the system of local government. Existing lieutenants were either reappointed or replaced, and new appointments were made in twelve of the sixteen counties which lacked a lord lieutenant in 1603, although the process was not completed until 1626. It was not yet normal for each county to have its own lord lieutenant: two or more neighbouring counties were often associated, among them Lancashire and Cheshire, and the three Border counties. The lord lieutenant's authority usually extended over all corporate towns except London and the Cinque Ports. There were some lieutenants *ex officio* including the bishop of Durham and the presidents of the Councils of the North and of the Marches of Wales—an obviously sensible arrangement in view of the problems posed by those troubled areas. Elsewhere the lords lieutenant were nearly always magnates, in the nomination of whom there was sometimes a strong hereditary element: a Cecil in Hertfordshire, a Stanley in Lancashire and Cheshire, a Howard in Surrey. In Somerset and Wiltshire however the lord lieutenant until 1621 was the earl of Hertford, a choice which probably aroused the jealousy of the Herberts who might fairly have regarded the office as family property.[5]

At the same time as the Government settled the lieutenancy it made changes in the provisions for deputy lieutenants, introducing them into the eight counties where the office had not previously existed. Moreover the power of appointment was gradually transferred to the lords lieutenant themselves, who were given discretion in the number appointed. The result was that by 1623 the Government controlled the nomination of deputy lieutenants in only four counties; certain corporations, including Bristol and Exeter, chose their own deputies. In 1623 however the Government resumed the power of nomination, as part of its attempt to tighten up the lieutenancy. The change was naturally unpopular with the lords lieutenant and lasted no longer than the end of the reign. Clearly the county officer who chose his own deputies was in a stronger position than the one who did not, and he enjoyed thereby useful patronage, which was as usual alloyed by the risk of faction. Undoubtedly the office of deputy lieutenant was a desirable one and much sought after because of its prestige and local power. The number of deputies rose therefore and they were usually drawn from the ranks of the upper gentry.

Military tasks predominated in the obligations of the lieutenants and their deputies. They raised volunteers to fight for the Danish king and from time to time they pressed levies in various places for service oversea. Above all they were responsible for the militia.[6] They selected men for the 'trained bands' to meet the county quota of horse and foot. They organised twice-yearly general musters for the inspection of the trained bands as well as more frequent special musters for training the men, unit by unit. They commanded the militia and supervised its equipment; they appointed officers from among the gentry and were responsible for enforcing military assessments under the statute of 1558. The intention was that by these means the country would have a fully-armed force for its defence: the reality was rather different.

After the peaceful accession of James, the need for such a force did not seem urgent: the foreign situation was less menacing, the king himself was of a pacific temperament. Almost immediately the Government repealed the legislation of 1558 which gave the musters and assessment scales a statutory basis. Henceforth the lieutenancy, as part of the country's defences, depended on the royal prerogative.[7] At first the Government saw no need to exact regular military taxes or to enforce frequent observance of musters and training, which were costly and unpopular. Instead therefore for nine years the full mustering system was replaced by informal inspection. The response varied: slackness was widespread and deficiencies multiplied. But there were exceptions. In Northamptonshire the lord lieutenant, Lord Exeter, gave detailed orders and expected full reports; he inspected the horse himself and exceeded his instructions by ordering training; he tried hard to make a reality of the general muster in 1608, but had little success because of the reluctance of his deputies to carry out orders.[8]

Serious defects were laid bare during these years, but there were no good prospects of remedy. Accordingly the council decided in 1612 to re-establish the full system of musters, which were held regularly until the end of the reign, no doubt at first because of anxiety over Spain's intentions. Lord Exeter again responded with vigour, especially in the matter of training, but his absence from Northamptonshire nullified many of his efforts, and elsewhere the picture was less encouraging. In Northumberland and Durham the lieutenancy officers were loath to act. The trained bands of Staffordshire had forgotten how to use their weapons. Deficiencies in Lancashire and Cheshire delayed the completion of muster certificates. Gentry refused to serve as officers, equipment was borrowed to conceal shortages and some counties earned a conciliar rebuke as well as an order to repeat their musters.

Fortunately the picture was not wholly one of failure. There was for example some enthusiasm for drill in certain towns which followed the example of London in establishing artillery grounds for military exercises. Moreover the notebook of Sir Edward Montagu, a deputy lieutenant in Northamptonshire, provides impressive evidence of training there.[9] The Privy Council seems to have enjoyed a measure of success in improving the standard of weapons and securing the replacement of calivers with muskets. Here and there lieutenants made strenuous efforts to organise a system of reserves and to ensure that substantial farmers and householders were enrolled in the trained bands rather than the 'poorer sort'.

The attainment of better standards cost money and therefore proved to be a fruitful source of trouble. One difficulty was that the repeal of the 1558 acts gave rise to genuine confusion about military obligations and offered a loophole for evasion, for there was no longer any official scale of assessment. The result was that instead of money there was a spate of excuses which carried different degrees of conviction. In the absence of a recognised scale, the lieutenants had to rely on the customary obligations of landownership, but again they met obstruction, especially by absentee landlords who successfully played off one set of county authorities against another. There was also bickering in many dioceses between ecclesiastical officers and the lieutenants about the contributions of the clergy. All this evidence explains only too clearly the failure of the lieutenancy to raise anything like the full amount of money and equipment needed.

But the lieutenants' difficulties did not end with inadequate financial administration. During the years 1603–6 there was a bitter controversy in Lord Hertford's lieutenancy district about the county muster-master, the professional soldier who assisted the officers with inspection and training; similar disputes later broke out elsewhere.[10] Part of the antagonism to the muster-masters arose because their standards were usually higher than those of the deputy lieutenants. The hostility also had a financial aspect for muster-masters' salaries were fixed by the lieutenants but paid out of the normal militia funds; they were therefore entangled in the dispute about county obligations, and in the rivalry in some areas between the lieutenancy and the J.P.s for control of this part of local taxation. The widespread resentment against the muster-master was exacerbated by the fact that the lord lieutenant enjoyed the patronage of the office, for which the county was expected to pay. There were fears too that the muster-master would be the first of a number of paid officials and while the disputes included elements of personal feuds, as in Wiltshire, they were also a sign of the growing antagonism towards prerogative government and taxation.

In addition to the muster-master, the horse became a focus of controversy. It is clear that long neglect had made the horse troops the least satisfactory part of the militia. Wherever possible the gentry and richer yeomen evaded their obligations and bitterly resented attempts to coerce them. There were the usual excuses, and defaulters were encouraged by the bad example set by the deputy lieutenants anxious to avoid their share of the burden. Too often for the good of the militia the lord lieutenant and his deputies pulled against each other and deputy lieutenants quarrelled among themselves. Not surprisingly the J.P.s too did not always co-operate, fearing loss of authority to the lieutenant and trying therefore to find loopholes in his powers.[11]

Inefficiency and disaffection were only likely to be remedied by strong and urgent pressure from the central Government which acted in 1618 when the outbreak of the Thirty Years War aroused both alarm and determination. A strict general muster was ordered, and the trained bands were to be ready at ten days' notice. At last the Privy Council, and with its encouragement the lieutenancy, began to deal firmly with opposition by punishing defaulters including recalcitrant landowners. Where their former bad example had encouraged others in evasion, now their punishment was a useful deterrent and probably helped to raise the standard of the trained bands. Evidence from Sussex, Essex and Kent (all vulnerable counties) shows efforts to improve training. In various places muskets were rapidly introduced, while even the horse was brought up to the mark, for the moment. By 1621 there were discussions among lieutenants and in Parliament about standardising arms and training, and the Government included in its own orders provisions aimed at uniformity. Within two years there was official stress on the need for modern weapons, as well as an attempt to attain more 'exact' training by means of a new book of military orders based on continental methods.

Such measures had only limited success, as the deficiencies uncovered in Charles's reign show: there was too much to be done. For most of the period the Government had been content with a minimal amount of organisation and training, and the spread of slackness was the natural consequence. True the lieutenancy was never a sinecure but it lost vigour and a sense of purpose in these years. As the repeal of the 1558 statutes left the militia dependent ultimately on the prerogative, the Government could not shirk its responsibilities, and indeed it eventually recognized the need for military reform. The measures it adopted during the king's last years anticipated to some extent Charles's attempt to introduce the 'exact militia' at his subjects' expense, a fruitful source of opposition to his methods.[12]

III

The uncertainties of the lieutenancy contrast in many ways with the recognised, regular duties of the J.P.s, holders of a long-established office, with a legally-trained clerk of the peace and up-to-date handbooks to help them. The justices acted in two ways, either in general quarterly sessions, or out of them, singly or in small groups, but the main focus of their activities was at quarter sessions. There they could exercise all their judicial and administrative powers, much of the work being done through formal judicial process. Things were different in the towns where the courts confined themselves to the administration of justice, while other aspects of local government were the concern of the town council. The responsibilities of town and county magistrates alike fell under two main heads: criminal and administrative. The latter included the maintenance of the rudimentary 'social services', the regulation of economic activity and social life, the provision of certain public services, the supervision of subordinate officials and the collection of public monies. But the overriding consideration was the upholding of law and order.

Among the large number of criminal offences which came before the J.P.s with monotonous regularity, the most common were larceny, assault, brawling, poaching and riot. Disturbances were often the result of antagonism aroused by enclosure which indeed caused the Midland Revolt of 1607, the most serious breach of public order during the reign. Punishments imposed on convicted criminals included whipping, fines or bonds for good behaviour, but there were few executions at sessions because since 1590 all felonies save grand larceny had been reserved to Assizes. About half of those indicted were convicted and Professor Hurstfield had concluded that J.P.s meted out 'rough justice' in face of endemic lawlessness.[13]

Much of the threat to order arose from hunger, poverty and unemployment. The alleviation of these evils became one of the main duties of local government under Tudor legislation, which distinguished between the deserving (or impotent) poor and the undeserving (or ablebodied, work-shy) poor. Children, the old and infirm, the unemployed and the vagrants were treated in different ways by the parish officers, supervised by the J.P.s.

Repression was often easier than relief and bulks larger in the records. Quarter sessions regularly ordered the parents of bastard children to be whipped, and imposed a maintenance charge on the father. Later bastard and other pauper children were apprenticed compulsorily to local craftsmen who sometimes had to be forced to accept them. The harshest treatment was reserved for vagrants. Every bench periodically ordered county-wide repression and 'sturdy beggars' were discouraged by whipping and branding, but such punishments did little to prevent further offences. In one way the authorities made the problem bigger by evicting 'undersettlers' from rural hovels and urban slums.[14] The J.P.s therefore fell back on a notion of 'settlement': vagrants were returned to their birthplace or to wherever they had been settled for a year. When that failed, the only possibility was imprisonment in a house of correction.

Such an institution existed in some places before 1603, but a statute of 1610 obliged each county to provide at least one 'to set rogues or such other idle persons on work'. Houses of correction multiplied slowly. There were for example delays in Lancashire and the North Riding while the J.P.s argued about the location and the apportionment of expenses.[15] When completed, houses of correction were used for vagrants and suspected criminals, as well as for providing work for the able-bodied.

Relief for the deserving poor took several forms: pensions from a specially-raised county fund for lame soldiers and sailors; the provision in each parish of tools and raw materials on which the unemployed could work; doles or accommodation for the old and sick, paid for by the parish poor rate. But there is debate about the extent to which poor rates were regularly raised in the parishes. Professor Jordan has asserted that a regular rate was not common except in emergencies, and that private charities bore the burden of relief. Charities were certainly important, but there is much evidence for the activity of public authorities, as the example of Yorkshire shows. At York and Hull the corporations supervised parish relief and sought to provide work for the poor. The North Riding justices maintained almshouses and insisted on the provision of cottages and doles for the poor. After a slow start in both the West and North Ridings, the poor law was enforced during James's reign, and these instances could be paralleled elsewhere. Professor Jordan himself admits that recourse to parochial poor rates was more sustained after 1620. True the law did not work smoothly: parishioners refused to pay; parish officers neglected their duty; few stocks of materials existed until Charles's time; the Privy Council repeatedly urged better administration of the poor laws. Yet inefficiency is not surprising, for the poor law was only codified in 1598 and the execution of all its complex requirements was unlikely to be achieved quickly. Such relief as was offered was mainly a palliative; but rigorous enforcement of the law depended on local circumstances and usually fell short of the objectives.[16]

A host of economic controls were, like poor relief, related to social stability and public order. The great majority of 115 penal statutes in force in the middle of the reign concerned economic affairs and gave J.P.s formidable powers of interference.[17] The regulations were intended to prevent disturbance to trade or peace as a result of profiteering, unlawful wages, declining standards of quality, inadequate workmanship or new methods.

Innovation was generally suspect as is shown by the attitude to agrarian changes and by the attempts of J.P.s to discourage enclosure in many areas, including Norfolk, the North Riding and the West Country. The same suspicion of new methods lay behind regulation in industry, though here it was allied to a determination to maintain the standard of goods produced. But the J.P.s' attitude could be ambivalent.

Thus in both Witshire and the West Riding they appointed searchers who inspected the cloth, but they showed little enthusiasm for the official attempt to ban the use of the hot press and, despite much pressure from the Privy Council, the West Riding justices supported the tentering methods used by local clothiers. The Yorkshire J.P.s also objected to the Government's attempt to discourage wool-dealers—they considered they were necessary to the industry—but local influence did not prevent the Wiltshire justices from punishing some important clothiers, who had offered faulty cloth for sale. More successful was the official insistence on a seven-year apprenticeship for craftsmen. Quarter sessions fined a considerable number of unqualified craftsmen, who were especially common in textiles, retailing and the food trades. In Wiltshire the J.P.s began by issuing a code for the enforcement of the apprenticeship laws, while in York and other large towns the corporation and the guilds maintained steady pressure on unqualified traders. Prosecutions at quarter sessions reflected trading difficulties, especially in the cloth industry, for in bad times craftsmen tried to reduce competition by exposing unlawful competitors. Where there was slackness, or a temporary waiving of the law, it seems that the J.P.s were using their discretion in order to prevent unemployment and vagrancy.[18] Apart from their concern with apprenticeship, the J.P.s were involved in the relations between masters and men about wages and contracts, under the act of 1563. A few wage assessments issued at quarter sessions survive from the period and there is evidence of attempts to enforce them in some counties, notably Wiltshire, Hertfordshire, Lincolnshire and the North Riding; in the two last-named areas, justices seem to have been trying to prevent wage-labourers from taking advantage of a shortage of labour during the early years of the reign. For the same reason J.P.s sometimes enforced contracts of service.[19] But negative evidence suggests that there was no sustained effort anywhere to administer the statute, which was more usually held in reserve for emergencies.

The justices were concerned with marketing as well as manufacture and had detailed powers for protecting consumers against those who engrossed supplies, used faulty measures or sold goods of low quality. Town corporations tried unceasingly to detect and punish marketing offences which might threaten supplies to the townsmen, but the regulations were probably too complicated for the machinery available in the counties, where parochial officers were not specifically charged with market duties, and the laws seem to have been feebly executed.

If effort be the criterion the same could hardly be said of the regulation of alehouses, those 'nurseries of naughtiness' as Lambarde called them. Strengthened by legislation in 1604, 1606 and 1610, the J.P.s had ample powers to suppress or licence alehouses, in order to discourage gaming, idleness, crime and pauperism, and to foster godliness. Quarter sessional records abound in lengthy lists of offenders—450 unlicensed alehouse-keepers were presented at one North Riding sessions[20] —and in repeated orders for the suppression of unnecessary alehouses. There was emphasis on annual licensing and on the acceptance of articles of good behaviour. Stimulated by the Privy Council the justices in many areas had special or divisional meetings to deal with the problem. Another expedient tried by the Government was the grant in 1617 and 1618 to patentees, including Sir Giles Mompesson, of the right to license inns and alehouses, charging an annual rent for the licence and sharing the proceeds with the Exchequer. However complaints were made about the patent by irate members of the Parliament of 1621 (many of them J.P.s, no doubt angry at being circumvented). It was said for example that of sixty-seven 'inns' now licensed by Mompesson in Hampshire, seventeen had previously been suppressed as disorderly alehouses. As a result the patent was cancelled, and the J.P.s regained their sole authority over inns and alehouses. But it is clear that achievement fell short of intention: the J.P.s had very limited success in the enforcement of licensing obligations and did not find it easy to carry out orders for the suppression of alehouses in the face of local wishes. One difficulty was that the power to grant a licence lay not only with quarter sessions but also with the single justice who, because of pressure in his own neighbourhood, sometimes acted contrary to the decisions of his colleagues.[21]

Sessions records show that some economic regulations were administered in a halting and half-hearted way, others remained a dead letter. To achieve more regularity in local government, the Privy Council called in 1605 for divisional meetings of J.P.s to be held between quarter sessions.[22] One aim of this order was, as we have seen, the closer control of alehouses, but those divisional meetings were also enjoined to supervise the due execution of the laws concerning poor relief, vagrants, apprentices and other matters. In some counties such arrangements only formalised a practice which had survived since Tudor times. It is impossible to say whether divisional meetings were adopted universally, and in some places they were evidently short-lived, but it is clear that where they existed they were concerned with the business originally assigned and no doubt buttressed the efforts of quarter sessions.

Moreover emergencies stimulated the J.P.s into more activity. The plague for example produced a greater sense of urgency about precautions and relief; there was a severe outbreak in 1603, but plague occurred sporadically throughout the period, and the close communities of the towns were badly affected. Precautions included the restraint of vagrants, suspension of fairs and markets, and in towns like Chester, York and Hull the removal of infected people and their contacts to pest-houses specially built outside the walls. Special relief measures taken by the J.P.s in many places included the strict levying of poor rates and, by the act of 1604, the raising of a special rate-in-aid in parishes adjacent to the worst-affected places.

The Midland Revolt and the harvest failure of 1608 had temporarily an invigorating effect on local government. Scarcity orders, similar to those of 1587 and 1594, were issued by the Council. The J.P.s were called upon to conserve supplies of grain by limiting the number of brewers and alehouses, and to ensure that markets were served; to arrange selling to the poor at reduced prices; and to see that poor relief was fully administered in the parishes. Reports from the counties show a satisfactory response by the J.P.s: pressure on farmers to take corn to market; a halt to grain exports; persuasion used to secure reductions in prices; special purchases of corn in districts where it was not plentiful; orders for parochial relief. Even so, thought Miss Leonard, there was nothing to suggest that the orders were executed any better than under Elizabeth.[23]

Another test came towards the end of the reign, for the harvest failed in 1622, but by then the problem was complicated by a deep depression in the cloth trade, beginning in 1620. The threat of starvation therefore accompanied that of unemployment. In addition to the scarcity orders the Privy Council adopted more elaborate methods to relieve, and where possible to prevent, distress. Country gentlemen were ordered home from London to carry out their public duties as magistrates and their social duties as landowners. J.P.s tried to persuade clothiers to continue employing their men, and if that were not enough they made an effort to ensure that parish stocks of raw material were available for setting the jobless to work. Whatever success they had at first was much diminished as the depression continued and coincided with the bad harvest. In response to pressure from the Council the J.P.s tried hard to relieve privation. Corn-banks were established for selling at reduced prices, funds were raised to set the poor to work, alehouses were closed, there was a whipping campaign to deter vagrants. Steps were taken to prevent the hoarding of wool, and cloth was carefully inspected to maintain quality in the interests of trade. The scarcity measures were probably well executed and helped both to relieve distress and to preserve peace.

The same comment applies in a more limited way to the attempted improvement of poor law administration, although in Wiltshire for instance—a county particularly hard hit by the trading depression—it seems unlikely that the J.P.s were able to carry out all their tasks 'with real thoroughness'. They were besieged with complaints from weavers about their desperate plight but the poor law was unequal to the emergency: hence threats and rioting. Elsewhere too local relief fell short of its objectives, and the J.P.s were adamant that their powers alone could not solve the problem because of the numbers involved. As a result partly of local pleas the Privy Council then began to pursue a different and more promising solution by means of freer trade, and before James died the situation in most areas had improved. Nevertheless the work of the J.P.s had clearly shown what could be achieved by concerted and vigorous local action under strong central pressure, and the lesson was acted upon by Charles I's Government in the early 1630s.[24]

The truth was that the J.P.s were overburdened, being heavily involved not only in punishing criminals but also in other administrative tasks, some of them of as much importance to the well-being of the local community as those already discussed. Thus each county was charged with the repair of bridges unless the duty undoubtedly lay elsewhere. Bridge repairs were an insistent burden on the county and could easily be a source of dispute between the magistrates of different counties when, as at Yarm and Ripon, bridges spanned a boundary river. Responsibility for road repairs rested squarely on the parishes but J.P.s had to enforce their obligations. They had little initiative in the matter, but acted on complaints. The records show that the J.P.s had short bursts of activity, rather than regular inspection and repair. Neither the system nor the result was satisfactory, as the king himself discovered when the state of the Hertfordshire roads impeded his hunting journeys. In addition to their duties relating to communications some J.P.s served also as commissioners of sewers, charged with the maintenance of embankments and drains in low-lying areas, but in most counties roads, bridges, the gaol and the house of correction were the only public services. The position was different in large towns where there were guildhalls, market houses, water-pumps and conduits to maintain.

One major difficulty underlay all the aspects of the justices' work which we have considered: shortage of money. There was no general county or town rate. Instead the arrangements for raising money were 'makeshift and unco-ordinated': the sums required for bridges, gaols or social relief had to be raised *ad hoc*. All too often the record is one of evasion, delay and argument about the equity of the assessment—these rather than downright dishonesty. Moreover, although the J.P.s had some responsibility for levying rates, the collection of them, and in the all important case of poor relief the disbursement of them, lay with the parish officers, and that was another source of weakness in local government. Many subordinate officers were unreliable and too sensitive to the pressure of neighbours.[25] Even the sheriff, a social equal of the J.P.s, could cause trouble: some neglected their legal duties, one Yorkshire sheriff was gaoled by Star Chamber for exceeding his powers.[26] The need to supervise other officers thus added to the justices' already considerable problems.

The inadequate machinery at the J.P.s disposal meant that although they made efforts to enforce statutory obligations, their supervision was generally less close than the law intended. Criminal business occupied a good deal of the time which might have been devoted to administrative matters, while the quality of local government also suffered from slow communications, inadequate funds and wilful obstruction. These considerations often persuaded the J.P.s to narrow their interests and to leave things alone. Quarter sessions therefore concentrated on the most pressing problems: crime, vagrancy, the poor, alehouses, roads and bridges. Such matters were dealt with piecemeal, and the J.P.s' frequent need to reiterate their orders indicates that performance fell short of what was prescribed. Still even temporary palliatives were of some importance to the local community. In order to safeguard its peace and livelihood, and to secure some degree of continuity in local government, the J.P.s' responsibilities therefore extended, as we have seen, 'widely and deeply into the whole fabric of the county'.[27]

IV

Because of the local influence of the J.P.s, membership of the commission of the peace, prized as a social asset and a mark of prestige, was much sought after. In response to the demand, the size of commissions was increased in some counties to as many as sixty justices, but there were probably still more aspirants than places. The commission was dominated by the leading families, men like the Stanleys, Molyneux, Traffords and Heskeths in Lancashire, the Thynnes, Hungerfords and

Penruddocks in Wiltshire. The magistracy was often simply a concomit-
ant of gentle birth, but many of the J.P.s by this time had attended a
university or an inn of court, lawyers were strongly entrenched in the
commissions and the number of clerical J.P.s grew, perhaps in the hope
that they would stand outside local jealousies and faction. These had
multiplied during the previous half century, partly because of competition, partly because of antagonism between the older county families
and the newer men who challenged their place in the local hierarchy.

Such rivalries are admirably illustrated by North and West Yorkshire.
There the commissions included a considerable number of comparatively
new men, including Sir Thomas Posthumous Hoby, a recent arrival in
the North Riding who was anxious to establish his standing there in the
face of local rivals, namely the Eures and the Cholmleys, older families
with Roman Catholic connections. Accordingly he launched a series of
law-suits against them: the ingredients of these included a claim to
property, charges of slander, riot and nonco-operation in magisterial
duties, assertions of sympathy for both the Essex revolt and Gunpowder
Plot, together with the alleged fraudulent use of judicial powers to protect recusants, an accusation which Hoby rashly extended later against
several more of his fellow J.P.s. Meanwhile in Nidderdale Sir Stephen
Proctor, one of Hoby's associates and a fellow Puritan, assailed Sir
John Yorke, Sir John Mallory and Sir William Ingleby, members of
well-established families, again with Catholic connections. Here too
there was rivalry about property, this time concerning rights over common land, but Proctor's complaints included partiality to recusants, the
ridiculing of the Anglican Church and abuse of magisterial authority.
The outcome was defeat for both Hoby and Proctor, and the latter was
ruined by his failure. In each quarrel similar considerations were involved: personal dislike (Hoby had a reputation as a busybody and his
presence in Yorkshire was resented by some); a struggle for local esteem
and for recognition of magisterial authority; religious antipathies and
cross-currents; ambitions for parliamentary seats.[28] Factional strife
could spread into other aspects of county affairs. Thus in Somerset the
rivalry between Sir Robert Phelips and John Poulett originated in the
election of 1614 but was later carried on to the bench and into the
militia.[29] Again the quarrel between Sir Thomas Wentworth and Sir
John Savile about the office of *custos rotulorum* in the West Riding re-
appeared in parliamentary politics and was carried in to the Council
of the North, already racked by the machinations and financial disputes
of Sir Arthur Ingram.[30] The effects of feuds on local government is un-

fortunately hard to gauge, but it is probable that the Yorkshire J.P.s accused of misconduct by Hoby found it difficult to co-operate with him afterwards.

Factional rivalry was one of those local concerns which distracted the attention of local governors from wider public duties. Nowhere was localism stronger than among the oligarchies of towns like York, Exeter, Hull and Newcastle, where the dominant groups showed a spirit of municipal independence and pride, asserting their rights against the authorities of Church and State alike. For example York clashed with the Council of the North over the exercise of its jurisdiction, Exeter sported with Bishop Cary over episcopal powers and Newcastle eventually succeeded in upholding its rights over the Tyne against the J.P.s of the counties on Tyneside and the bishop of Durham.[31]

In the eyes of the central government, localism had disadvantages, for efficiency could suffer when local concerns had priority. Some J.P.s pursued their private interests at the expense of their public duties. In places they were unresponsive to legislation about cloth manufacturing or the provision of houses of correction. There were squabbles about expenditure and lack of purpose in collecting financial dues. Religious sympathies played their part: the presence of members of Catholic families on the North Riding bench weakened its will to convict recusants for example, while the religious opinions of J.P.s affected their reception of the Book of Sports in Lancashire and their attitude to the laws about Sunday observance elsewhere. Finally in the parishes officials were too often the object of resentment and suspicion; here government was often impaired by collusive obstruction, grudges, threats and strained relations over the reporting of misdeeds. Yet localism also ensured an understanding of provincial needs which could serve the ends of government. The justices' appreciation of local problems and knowledge of their neighbours shows in their endowment of charities to meet particular needs and in their attitude to laws affecting the cloth industry. Above all a sense of community and a general interest in a locality produced a certain pressure on justices to co-operate and conform.

Many of the J.P.s were undoubtedly conscientious and tried to inculcate a similar outlook in others. True the numbers attending quarter sessions fluctuated considerably from three or four to twenty or more; some attended regularly, some never appeared at quarter sessions, others seem to have been present only at the sessions town nearest their homes. But the labours of J.P.s out of sessions helped to share the burdens and brought the twin benefits of accessibility and speed to local government.

Divisional sessions possibly commanded more confidence than one or two J.P.s working separately, but the evidence shows that the single justice too was fully employed, dealing with vagrants, examining witnesses and absentees from church, and taking sureties. Even Hoby was later described as, 'the most understanding, able and industrious justice of the peace in this kingdom.'[32] Compensation for these burdens lay in prestige, a sense of service and the sort of influence and power which allowed for the indulgence of self-interest. Armed with a thorough knowledge of local conditions, the J.P.s were sharply aware of common needs, and this awareness led them to temper the statutes and orders of the central Government in the interests of their own localities.

V

The J.P.s inevitably saw themselves as to some extent representatives of the counties against the Government, a danger which the central authorities tried to prevent by using the several links in the chain of authority from Privy Council to parish. In their own areas the Councils of the North and of Wales reported to the Government and transmitted its instructions back to the counties, although neither body seems to have been working very efficiently in James's reign, partly because of challenges to their jurisdiction. On the Borders James had quickly established a new commission of English and Scots to form a united administration, but after a good start, the commission was torn with faction, the quality of government suffered and by the end of the reign the experiment had clearly failed.[33] The sheriffs were used to transmit conciliar orders to justices, who in turn passed them to high constables and parish officers. The lords lieutenant were charged with more than military duties, being called upon to detect recusants, collect loans, supervise local officials—in short, 'representing the Crown to the county and the county to the Crown'.[34]

The gap between the Privy Council and local authorities could also be bridged by the judges on circuit. Their prestige and powers gave them an authority far superior to that of the local benches. They dealt effectively with disputes involving local interests and important figures, a task which would have put a severe strain on the county justices, who usually took heed of Assize orders and observations. These included the charge given by the judges at Assizes and based on the charge they themselves received (except from 1609 to 1615) from the lord chancellor. The latter recommended certain measures to the attention of the judges who, in their Assize charges, were careful to express the Council's exhortations and demands.[35]

As the Jacobean Council was gradually excluded from national policy it devoted itself more and more to the innumerable details of local government, sending out orders, inquiries and rebukes to all parts of the country. Sometimes such official missives took the form of general proclamations, but the Privy Council registers show that more often they concerned the affairs of a particular district or individual, ranging from drainage works in Marshland to a complaint from a long-haired parson whose hair had been cut on the order of the Council of the North.[36] Moreover in 1609, to ensure some response to its messages, the Council ordered that a small group of J.P.s in each county should be responsible for circulating them to fellow-justices and for sending replies, an experiment which seems to have petered out.[37]

Other means of coercion included the Star Chamber which heard many cases involving negligence and malpractice by local governors. But perhaps the main method open to the Privy Council of minimising opposition was the threat of dismissal, which involved for a J.P. both loss of his own position and the possible inclusion of a rival. Probably only a few men were willing to risk such a penalty, and only a small number of justices was actually dismissed for misbehaviour. On the other hand the Council seems to have restored most of them to the commission fairly quickly; they could be a nuisance out of office, and in any case their services were usually needed in their own 'country'.

The small number of dismissals does not imply that the Privy Council was necessarily satisfied with the J.P.s, about whom damaging complaints were sometimes made. Lord Chancellor Egerton said that too many justices went to court 'in their braveries and stand there like an idol to be gazed upon and do nothing', interested as they were only in 'place, countenance and estimation'.[38] His remedy was a greater influence for the judges on the selection of J.P.s, at the expense of magnate patronage. The king himself spoke of 'good' justices and 'bad', 'idle slow-bellies' and 'busy-bodies', and he too looked to judicial supervision for an improvement.[39] There were even complaints in the Parliament of 1621 and the beginnings later of a purge.

The great trouble was lack of general direction. Paternalism had waned since Elizabeth's time, and with it the scope of local government had narrowed; the main emphasis was now on order, otherwise much of of the law was a dead letter, to be executed only in times of great difficulty or when the Council found it expedient. Thus the administration

of the recusancy laws during the entire reign reflects the wavering policy
of the Government. For much of James's reign directions and sanctions
were spasmodic and barely disturbed the routine of county administration. But during the king's last years, there are signs that the Government realised the need for a greater sense of purpose. At that time there
came the first uncertain moves towards an 'exact militia'; there was the
use of patents which sought to put the administration of certain laws
(including those on tillage, alehouse offences, recusancy and apprenticeship) into the hands of persons specially commissioned; there were the
scarcity orders and the other emergency measures, with their emphasis
on regular divisional meetings and reports. These experiments in cen-
tralism undoubtedly threatened the high degree of independence enjoyed by Jacobean local government, and they heralded the more sustained pressure of the reign of Charles I.

List of Abbreviations

(for Bibliography, and Notes and References)

Add.MS	British Museum Additional Manuscript
AgricHR	*Agricultural History Review*
AJLH	*American Journal of Legal History*
AHR	*American Historical Review*
APC	*Acts of the Privy Council of England*
APS	*Acts of the Parliament of Scotland*
BIHR	*Bulletin of the Institute of Historical Research*
BMJ	*British Medical Journal*
CHJ	*Cambridge Historical Journal*
CJ	*Journals of the House of Commons*
CMH	*Cambridge Modern History*
CSP Dom	*Calendar of State Papers Domestic*
CSP Scot	*Calendar of State Papers Scotland*
EcHR	*Economic History Review*
EHR	*English Historical Review*
HEH El	Henry E. Huntington Library, Bridgewater and Ellesmere Manuscript
HJ	*Historical Journal*
HLQ	*Huntington Library Quarterly*
HMC	Historical Manuscripts Commission
LJ	*Journals of the House of Lords*
PBA	*Proceedings of the British Academy*
PRO	Public Record Office
RO	Record Office
RPC	*Register of the Privy Council of Scotland*
SHR	*Scottish Historical Review*
State Trials	*Complete Collection of State Trials . . .*, ed. T. B. Howell, W. Cobbett and others (34 volumes, 1809–28)
THSC	*Transactions of the Honourable Society of Cymmrodorion*
TRHS	*Transactions of the Royal Historical Society*
VCH	*Victoria History of the Counties of England*
WHR	*Welsh History Review*

References to law reports follow the standard style given in Sweet and Maxwell's *Guide to Law Reports, Statutes and Regnal Years* (2nd ed., 1948); Brownl. = Brownlow's and Goldesborough's Reports, C.P. 1569–1624; Win. = Winch's Common Pleas Reports, 1621–5.

Bibliography, and Guides to Further Reading

GENERAL

This includes books and articles mentioned in the footnotes to the Introduction and items cited in more than one of the bibliographies of the other chapters.

R. Ashton (ed.), *James I by his Contemporaries* (London 1969).
S. B. Babbage, *Puritanism and Richard Bancroft* (London 1962).
P. J. Bowden, 'Agricultural Prices, Farm Profits and Rents', *The Agrarian History of England and Wales*, IV, ed. J. Thirsk (Cambridge 1967).
E. Cardwell, *Synodalia*, I (London 1842).
C. H. Carter, 'Gondomar: Ambassador to James I', *HJ*, VII (1964).
C. H. Carter, *The Secret Diplomacy of the Habsburgs 1598–1625* (New York 1964).
L. A. Clarkson, *The Pre-Industrial Economy in England 1500–1750* (London 1971).
D. C. Coleman, 'Industrial Growth and Industrial Revolutions', *Economica*, New Series, XXIII (1956).
P. Collinson, *The Elizabethan Puritan Movement* (London 1967).
J. P. Cooper, 'The Fall of the Stuart Monarchy', *New CMH*, IV (Cambridge 1970).
M. H. Curtis, 'The Hampton Court Conference and its Aftermath', *History* (Feb. 1961).
G. Davies, 'English Political Sermons, 1603–40', *HLQ*, III (1939–40).
G. Davies, 'The Character of James VI & I', *HLQ*, V (1941–2).
G. Donaldson, *Scotland James V–James VII* (Edinburgh 1965).
G. Donaldson, *The Scottish Reformation* (Cambridge 1960).
A. Everitt, 'Farm Labourers', *The Agrarian History of England and Wales*, IV, ed. J. Thirsk (Cambridge 1967).
F. J. Fisher, 'Tawney's Century', *Essays in the Economic and Social History of Tudor and Stuart England*, ed. F. J. Fisher (Cambridge 1961).
B. Ford (ed.), *From Donne to Marvel* (London 1960).
S. R. Gardiner, *History of England 1603–42*, vols I–V (London 1883).
C. Hill, *Economic Problems of the Church from Archbishop Whitgift to the Long Parliament* (Oxford 1956).
W. G. Hoskins, 'Harvest Fluctuations and English Economic History, 1480–1619', *Agric HR*, XII (1964).
W. G. Hoskins, 'Harvest Fluctuations and English Economic History, 1620–1759', *Agric HR*, XVI (1968).
W. G. Hoskins, 'The Rebuilding of Rural England 1570–1640', *Past and Present*, No. 4 (1953).
D. Hume, *The History of Great Britain, the reigns of James I and Charles I* (Pelican edn, Harmondsworth 1970).
W. K. Jordan, *Philanthropy in England* (London 1959).
Margaret A. Judson, *The Crisis of the Constitution* (New Brunswick 1949).
J. P. Kenyon, *The Stuart Constitution* (Cambridge 1966).

E. Kerridge, 'The Movement of Rent, 1540–1640', *EcHR*, 2nd ser. VI (1953–4).

W. Lamont, *Godly Rule, Politics and Religion 1603–1660* (London 1969).

P. Laslett, *The World We Have Lost* (London 1965).

Maurice Lee Jr, *James I and Henry IV* (Urbana 1970).

S. G. E. Lythe, *The Economy of Scotland 1550–1625* (Edinburgh 1960).

I. Macalpine and R. Hunter, *George III and the Mad Business* (London 1969).

I. Macalpine, R. Hunter and C. Rimington, 'Porphyria in the Royal Houses of Stuart, Hanover and Prussia', *BMJ* (6 Jan. 1968).

P. McGrath, *Papists and Puritans under Elizabeth I* (London 1967).

W. E. Minchinton (ed.), *The Growth of English Overseas Trade in the 17th and 18th Centuries* (London 1969).

J. U. Nef, 'Prices and Industrial Capitalism in France and England, 1540–1640', *EcHR*, VII (1936–7).

J. U. Nef, 'The progress of Technology and the growth of Large-Scale industry in Great Britain, 1540–1640', *EcHR*, V (1934–5).

J. U. Nef, *The Rise of the British Coal Industry*, 2 vols (London 1932).

J. U. Nef, *War and Human Progress* (Cambridge, Mass. 1950).

R. B. Outhwaite, *Inflation in Tudor and Early Stuart England* (London 1969).

S. Pollard and D. W. Crossley, *The Wealth of Britain* (London 1968).

J. Pound, *Poverty and Vagrancy in Tudor England* (London 1971).

M. Prestwich, *Cranfield: Politics and Profits under the Early Stuarts* (Oxford 1966).

T. K. Rabb, *Enterprise and Empire: Merchant and Gentry Investment in the Expansion of England, 1575–1630* (Cambridge, Mass. 1967).

R. E. Ruigh, *The Parliament of 1624* (Cambridge, Mass. 1971).

C. Russell, *The Crisis of Parliaments* (London 1971).

W. B. Rye, *England as seen by foreigners in the days of Elizabeth and James I* (London 1865).

W. R. Scott, *The Constitution and Finance of English, Scottish and Irish Joint Stock Companies*, 3 vols (Cambridge 1910–12).

T. C. Smout, *A History of the Scottish People 1560–1830* (London 1969).

L. Stone, *The Crisis of the Aristocracy 1558–1641* (Oxford 1965).

J. Summerson, *Architecture in Britain 1530 to 1830* (London 1953).

B. E. Supple, *Commercial Crisis and Change in England 1600–1642* (Cambridge 1959).

J. R. Tanner (ed.), *Constitutional Documents of the Reign of James I* (Cambridge 1930).

K. Thomas, *Religion and the Decline of Magic* (London 1971).

H. R. Trevor-Roper, *Archbishop Laud* (2nd edn, London 1965).

C. V. Wedgwood, 'Anglo-Scottish relations, 1603–40', *TRHS*, 4th ser. XXXII (1950).

D. H. Willson, 'James I and his Literary Assistants', *HLQ*, VIII (1944).

D. H. Willson, *King James VI & I* (London 1956).

C. Wilson, *England's Apprenticeship 1603–1763* (London 1965).

L. B. Wright, 'Propaganda against James I's "Appeasement" of Spain', *HLQ*, VI (1942–3).

R. Zaller, *The Parliament of 1621* (Berkeley 1971).

I. SCOTTISH POLITICS 1567–1625

The best starting point for politics in the reign of James VI is James's own works. There is an excellent edition of *Basilikon Doron* by J. Craigie, 2 vols

(Scottish Text Society, 1944–50); and this and James's other major works are now readily available with the welcome reprint of C. H. McIlwain, *The Political Works of James I* (New York 1965), in which the *Trew Law of Free Monarchies* and the 1607 speech to the English Parliament are of particular relevance to Scotland. Other contemporary sources include *The Historie and Life of King James the Sext*, ed. T. Thomson (Bannatyne Club, 1825); David Moysie, *Memoirs of the affairs of Scotland . . . from 1577 . . . to . . . 1603*, ed. J. Dennistoun (Bannatyne and Maitland Clubs, 1830); and David Calderwood, *The History of the Kirk of Scotland*, 8 vols (Wodrow Society, 1842–9), which is indispensable to the political as well as to the ecclesiastical historian. State papers and letters on both internal and foreign affairs are printed in *The Warrender Papers*, ed. A. I. Cameron, 2 vols (Scottish History Society, 1932); and on relations with England in *Letters of Queen Elizabeth and King James VI* and *Correspondence of King James VI of Scotland with Sir Robert Cecil and others*, both ed. J. Bruce (Camden Society, 1849 and 1861).

Of modern works the best and most balanced account is that by Gordon Donaldson, who devotes a third of his book *Scotland: James V–VII* (Edinburgh 1965) to the reign; and the shorter chapter on the king in the same author's *Scottish Kings* (London, 1967) is also valuable, as a more general statement of Professor Donaldson's interpretation of the most successful Stewart king. D. H. Willson's *King James VI and I* (London 1956; paperback edn 1963 and 1966) is the standard biography. His account of James in Scotland is full of intolerable magnates, and he is less than favourable to James personally; but his book is of value to Scottish historians, partly because it is a complete biography of James as king of both countries, and also because of its emphasis on James's education, and its picture of a cultured king in a cultured court in Scotland—which is something worth stressing. The other major political biography is Maurice Lee, *John Maitland of Thirlstane and the foundation of the Stewart Despotism in Scotland* (Princeton 1959). This is a well-informed book which gives a wealth of detail about the early years of the reign, but it is the most extreme statement of the theory that James sought to break the power of the nobility; and its central thesis that Maitland, the very able secretary and chancellor whom James overworked and ennobled, taught this policy to the king is an obviously strained interpretation of the facts.

Anglo-Scottish relations are dealt with by Douglas Nobbs, *England and Scotland, 1560–1707* (London 1952); and by a useful and detailed book which deserves more attention than it has recently received, in spite of its rather heavy-going narrative style, Helen G. Stafford, *James VI of Scotland and the throne of England* (New York 1940). For the period after 1603 there is an excellent article by D. H. Willson, 'Relations between Scotland and England in the Early Seventeenth Century', in *Scottish Colloquium Proceedings*, I (University of Guelph 1968); and an interesting but sometimes unreliable one by Dame Veronica Wedgwood, 'Anglo-Scottish Relations, 1603–40' in *TRHS*, 4th ser. XXXII (1950).

On the Borders before 1603, the best work is T. I. Rae, *The Administration of the Scottish Frontier, 1513–1603* (Edinburgh 1966); and after 1603, Penry Williams, 'The Northern Borderland under the Early Stuarts', in *Historical Essays presented to David Ogg*, ed. H. E. Bell and R. L. Ollard (London 1963), which shows how disastrous was any relaxation by the Government of the new and successful policy made possible by better relations and by union. Two works on the Highlands deserve mention: D. Gregory, *History of the Western Highlands and Isles of Scotland from . . . 1493 to . . . 1625* (Edinburgh 1836; 1881) which is still well worth reading; and A. Cunningham, *The Loyal Clans* (Cambridge 1932) which discusses the Highlands in the context of government policy.

The many articles on the reign include those by W. Taylor, 'The King's Mails, 1603–25' in *SHR*, XLII (1963), and the most recent attempt to make sense of the Gowrie Conspiracy, W. F. Arbuckle, 'The Gowrie Conspiracy', in *SHR*, XXXVI (1957). The recent book by R. Ashton, *James I by his Contemporaries* (London 1969) is a convenient and pleasant way of gaining a quick impression of the king and his reign.

This short note is necessarily highly selective; and it is therefore worth drawing attention to the invaluable and comprehensive list of works, both contemporary and secondary, on this period compiled by G. Donaldson in the *Bibliography of British History, Tudor Period, 1485–1603*, ed. Conyers Read (2nd ed. Oxford 1959), ch. XII.

2. THE SCOTTISH CHURCH 1567–1625

A period in which there originated the controversy between presbytery and episcopacy which has vexed Scotland ever since has inevitably attracted much partisan writing. But partisanship was in earlier times often combined with scholarship, notably in the Presbyterian Thomas McCrie, whose *Andrew Melville*, 2 vols (Edinburgh 1819, and later editions) is a work of meticulous research and a quarry of factual information. In the present century, while lightweight publications often ignore the findings of research, works with any pretensions to substantial scholarship have ceased to reflect sectarian attitudes. The fullest account of the subject is William Law Mathieson, *Politics and Religion in Scotland*, 2 vols (Glasgow 1902), which undermined the idea that Presbyterian concepts on church government and Church-State relations were introduced by the reformers, and showed that King James's preference for episcopacy was less indefensible than Presbyterian controversialists had allowed. The latest work covering the whole field, more briefly than Mathieson but putting James's relations with the Church in the context of his whole policy, is Gordon Donaldson, *Scotland: James V to James VII* (Edinburgh 1965). Another recent account, from a more purely ecclesiastical angle, is in J. H. S. Burleigh, *Church History of Scotland* (Oxford 1960). In *The Scottish Reformation* (Cambridge 1960), Donaldson examines in detail the development of ecclesiastical polity down to 1600, and in 'Scotland's Conservative North in the sixteenth and seventeenth centuries' (*TRHS*, 5th ser. XVI) he speculates about the reasons for the geographical division of opinion. Duncan Shaw, in *The General Assemblies of the Church of Scotland* (Edinburgh 1964), discusses Church-State relations in theory and practice.

3. THE ECONOMY OF SCOTLAND UNDER JAMES VI AND I

General economic studies of Scotland before the eighteenth century are still relatively few, but there is useful material on the reign of James VI down to the Union of the Crowns in I. F. Grant, *Social and Economic Development of Scotland before 1603* (Edinburgh 1930) and the whole reign is covered in S. G. E. Lythe, *The Economy of Scotland in its European Setting 1550–1625* (Edinburgh 1960). Agricultural history is thin though there is relevant material in J. A. Symon, *Scottish Farming Past and Present* (Edinburgh 1959) and in T. B. Franklin, *A History of Scottish Farming* (Edinburgh 1952). W. C. Mackenzie, *The Highlands and Isles of Scotland* (Edinburgh 1949 edn) provides a good introduction to the special problems of the highland economy. On the whole however the serious student must still depend heavily on such primary sources as *The Register of the Privy Council of Scotland; The Records of the Convention of Royal Burghs*; contemporary observers' comments on Scotland, of which valuable extracts appear in P. Hume Brown, *Early Travellers in Scotland* (Edinburgh 1891) and *A Source Book of Scottish History*, ed. W. C. Dickinson et al. 3 vols, (Edinburgh 1958–61), and in the records of individual burghs, many of which are in print.

On particular themes attention can be drawn to A. Davidson and A. Gray, *The Scottish Staple at Veere* (London 1909); G. Donaldson, *The Scot Overseas* (London 1966); J. Warrack, *Domestic Life in Scotland 1488–1688* (London 1920); R. W. Cochran-Patrick, *The Coinage of Scotland*, 2 vols, (Edinburgh 1876); T. Keith, *Commercial Relations of England and Scotland 1603–1707* (Cambridge 1910) and T. Pagan, *The Convention of the Royal Burghs* (Glasgow 1926). The economic impact of the Scottish Reformation is explored in G. Donaldson, *The Scottish Reformation* (Cambridge 1960) and in articles in the *Scottish Historical Review* which, especially in recent years, has published valuable contributions to social and economic history.

4. JAMES VI AND I AND WITCHCRAFT

1 *General*. The most interesting general works in English which set the subject of Jacobean witchcraft in its European setting are: (as a nineteenth-century sample) Sir Walter Scott, *Letters on Demonology and Witchcraft* (London 1830); Charles Williams, *Witchcraft* (London 1941); Pennethorne Hughes, *Witchcraft* (London 1952); H. R. Trevor-Roper, *The European Witch-Craze of the 16th and 17th Centuries* (Harmondsworth 1969).

2 *Scotland*. No serious account of Scottish witchcraft has been published this century. The only book on the subject remains C. Kirkpatrick Sharpe's *Historical Account of the Belief in Witchcraft in Scotland* (Glasgow 1884), which was first published in Edinburgh in 1818 as an introduction to an edition of Robert Law's *Memorialls*. This is still worth reading. The article by F. Legge, 'Witchcraft in Scotland', *Scottish Review*, XVIII (Oct. 1891), remains an important contribution; and John Ferguson's 'Bibliographical Notes on the Witchcraft Literature of Scotland' in *Proceedings of the Edinburgh Bibliographical Society* (Edinburgh 1899), are useful to the researcher. More recently G. F. Black's *Calendar of Cases of Witchcraft in Scotland 1510–1727* (New York 1938), is an important work of reference. It is the only statistical work so far done on Scottish witchcraft, and draws extensively, but exclusively, on references to witchcraft cases in printed books. Helen Stafford, 'Notes on Scottish Witchcraft Cases 1590–1591', in *Essays in Honor of Conyers Read*, edited Norton Downes (Chicago 1953), is essential for the North Berwick trials. The references to Scottish witchcraft in the widely known works of Dr Margaret Murray are entirely fanciful. Her contribution to the subject is adequately disposed of by G. Parrinder, *Witchcraft* (London 1958), pp. 105–12, and by E. Rose, *A Razor for a Goat* (London 1962) pp. 14–18.

3 *England*. English witchcraft has been better covered. There is Wallace Notestein's *History of Witchcraft in England* (Washington 1911); G. L. Kittredge, 'English Witchcraft and James I', in *Studies in the History of Religions* (New York 1912), and *Witchcraft in Old and New England* (Cambridge, Mass. 1929). C. L'Estrange Ewen, *Witch-hunting and Witch Trials* (London, 1929), worked on the records of the Home Circuit and established statistically the general pattern and intensity of witch-hunting in the area over the period in

which it was a criminal offence. His work has been built on and the general picture substantiated and enlarged by Alan Macfarlane, *Witchcraft in Tudor and Stuart England* (London 1970). A more general coverage from a sociological viewpoint is given by Keith Thomas in *Religion and the Decline of Magic* (London 1971).

5. THE ENGLISH CATHOLIC COMMUNITY 1603–1625

There is no full-scale study of Jacobean Catholicism. Three brief general accounts written from various points of view, are: David Mathew, *The Jacobean Age* (London 1938), pp. 230 ff.; W. K. Jordan, *The Development of Religious Toleration in England*, II (London 1936), pp. 54 ff., 492 ff.; Philip Hughes, *Rome and the Counter-Reformation in England* (London 1942), pp. 306 ff. Mathew's is much the most promising point of departure, as may be gathered from the use made of it in Lawrence Stone, *The Crisis of the Aristocracy* (Oxford 1965). Jordan reports on much otherwise inaccessible literary material; his discussion of it combines genuine insight with some confusion and *parti pris*. Hughes's range of interest and material is rather narrow; his book is more valuable for events after 1625. A new solidity, as well as a long-term perspective otherwise lacking, has been brought to the investigation of seventeenth-century English Catholicism by Hugh (J. C. H.) Aveling, notably in a series of systematic studies of Yorkshire: *Post-Reformation Catholicism in East Yorkshire, 1558–1790* (East Yorks Local History Society, 1960); *The Catholic Recusants of the West Riding of Yorkshire* (Proceedings of the Leeds Philosophical and Literary Society, 1963); *Northern Catholics: the Catholic Recusants of the North Riding of Yorkshire* (London 1966). The uninitiated may find these difficult to handle, and they are probably best approached through Aveling's paper, 'Some Aspects of Yorkshire Catholic Recusant History, 1558–1791', cited below, n. 31 to chapter 5. His Introduction to the 'Documents relating to the Northern Commissions for Compounding with Recusants' (Catholic Record Society, LIII, 1961, pp. 291 ff.), though it deals mainly with the following reign, is an indispensable guide to the workings of recusancy administration during the early seventeenth century, a subject not dealt with here.

Three collections of sources may be mentioned. The documentary appendices to M. A. Tierney (ed.), *Dodd's Church History of England*, IV–V (London 1843) [cited as Tierney-Dodd, *Church History*] are essential for ecclesiastical politics. H. Foley (ed.), *Records of the English Province of the Society of Jesus*, 7 vols (London 1875–83) contains in particular extracts and abstracts from the Jesuit annual letters, or missionary reports. Those for the country as a whole, to 1625, are in vols VII, part 2, pp. 976 ff.; V, pp. 987–99; VII, part 2, pp. 1098–121; those of the local districts are scattered through vols I–IV. The peculiarities of this source, and of Foley's presentation of it, have deterred historians from using it; used with discretion, as by Keith Thomas (see Note 41 to chapter 5, below), it may prove extremely valuable. *The Responsa Scholarum of the English College, Rome*, I (1598–1621), II (1622–85), ed. Anthony Kenny (Catholic Record Society, LIV–LV, 1962–3), is an admirably edited collection of several hundred replies (in Latin, with translated abstracts) given by students entering the college to a questionnaire devised by Robert Parsons about their background and upbringing; it is a remarkable and practically unexploited source of quantifiable information about family relations, social status and related matters, which may be recommended to historians whose interests transcend the Catholic community.

6. ENGLISH OVERSEAS TRADE IN THE REIGN OF JAMES I

Historians usually prefer to study long-term commercial trends which extend beyond the often narrow and arbitrary limits of a single reign. Astrid Friis, *Alderman Cockayne's Project and the Cloth Trade* (Copenhagen and London 1927) is exceptional in concentrating, as the subtitle suggests, on 'the commercial policy of England in its main aspects, 1603–25'. Although it is still useful for its considerable detail, a more stimulating and comprehensive survey of trade, policy and economic ideas is B. E. Supple, *Commercial Crisis and Change in England 1600–1642* (Cambridge 1959). Jacobean trade is put into a yet wider context in W. E. Minchinton's introduction to *The Growth of English Overseas Trade in the Seventeenth and Eighteenth Centuries* (London 1969), Charles Wilson, *England's Apprenticeship, 1603–1763* (London 1965) and *The Cambridge Economic History of Europe*, IV (Cambridge 1967). Ralph Davis, *The Rise of the English Shipping Industry* (London 1962) is indispensable on shipping and valuable too for the commercial background.

W. R. Scott, *The Constitution and Finance . . . Joint Stock Companies*, 3 vols (Cambridge 1910–12) can still be used with profit for the study of short-run fluctuations and particular companies, especially those like the Russia Company that still await a historian for the early Stuart period. T. K. Rabb, *Enterprise and Empire* (Cambridge, Mass. 1967) is an even more detailed account of company investment in these years. Recent studies of particular companies and markets include excellent monographs by R. W. K. Hinton, *The Eastland Trade and the Common Weal in the Seventeenth Century* (Cambridge 1959), and K. N. Chaudhuri, *The English East India Company: The Study of an Early Joint Stock Company 1600–1640* (London 1965). The historian's tendency to concentrate on north or extra-European trade is corrected by R. Davis on 'England and the Mediterranean, 1570–1670', in *Essays in the Economic and Social History of Tudor and Stuart England*, ed. F. J. Fisher (Cambridge 1961); and Harland Taylor, 'Price Revolution or Price Revision? The English and Spanish Trade after 1604', *Renaissance and Modern Studies*, XII (1968). For particular English ports there is still little available in print on the most important, London. Many historians, including the present author, have a considerable debt to A. M. Millard's unpublished London Ph.D. thesis (1956) on 'The Import Trade of London, 1600–1640', which complements F. J. Fisher's noted study of 'London's Export Trade in the early Seventeenth Century', *EcHR*, 2nd ser. III (1950). On the provincial cloth trade see W. B. Stephens, 'Cloth Exports of the Provincial Ports, 1600–1640', ibid. XXII (1969) and for particular outports see the same author's *Seventeenth Century Exeter, a study of Industrial and Commercial Development* (Exeter 1958), R. Davis, *The Trade and Shipping of Hull 1500–1700* (East Yorks Local History Society, 1964), and for Bristol the two volumes edited by P. V. McGrath for the Bristol Record Society XVIII (1951) and XIX (1955).

7. COLONIAL DEVELOPMENTS IN THE REIGN OF JAMES I

A concise and accurate appraisal of the development of overseas enterprise will be found in J. A. Williamson, *A Short History of British Expansion: The Old Colonial Empire* (London 1930).

For the history of the early development of colonies in North America, the most detailed and authoritative work is Charles M. Andrews, *The Colonial Period of American History*, 4 vols (New Haven, Conn. 1934–8). Also useful is an older work, H. L. Osgood, *American Colonies in the Seventeenth Century*,

3 vols (New York 1926–30). For a briefer treatment see Louis B. Wright, *The Atlantic Frontier* (New York 1947; paperback edn, Ithaca, N.Y. 1963).

An excellent summary of Raleigh's colonising activities will be found in David B. Quinn, *Raleigh and the British Empire* (London 1947; paperback edn, New York 1962). J. A. Williamson, *The Age of Drake* (London 1938; paperback edn, New York 1965) is also useful for the Elizabethan background. A variety of information about both exploration and settlement is given in J. H. Parry, *The Age of Reconnaissance: Discovery, Exploration, and Settlement, 1450–1650* (New York 1963; paperback edn 1964).

The involved history of the Virginia Company is explained in detail by Wesley F. Craven, *Dissolution of the Virginia Company of London: The Failure of a Colonial Experiment* (New York 1932). The documents concerning the early settlement of Virginia have been published by Susan M. Kingsbury, *The Records of the Virginia Company of London*, 4 vols (Washington 1906–35). The introduction to Miss Kingsbury's work provides a careful outline of the policies of the Virginia Company as well as an analysis of the difficulties and problems affecting the development of the colony.

Special aspects of colonial enterprise in the reign of James I, particularly the motives influencing expansionists, will be found in the following brief works by Louis B. Wright: *Religion and Empire: The Alliance between Piety and Commerce in English Expansion, 1558–1625* (Chapel Hill, N.C. 1943; reprint edition, New York 1965); *The Colonial Search for a Southern Eden* (University of Alabama Press [no place given] 1953); and *The Dream of Prosperity in Colonial America* (New York 1965). A concise bibliography compiled by the same author and published in pamphlet form by the American Historical Association may be useful, *New Interpretations of American Colonial History* (New York and London 1959; 3rd edn 1969).

A significant Jacobean discussion of colonisation, its purposes and its benefits, is provided by Richard Eburne, *A Plain Pathway to Plantations* (1624), edited by L. B. Wright (Ithaca, N.Y. 1962).

For a provocative discussion of the reasons behind the apparent indolence and lack of initiative on the part of the early settlers at Jamestown, see Edmund S. Morgan, 'The Labor Problem at Jamestown, 1607–18', *AHR*, LXXVI (June 1971), 595–611. Readable, informative and provocative is Howard M. Jones, *O Strange New World* (New York 1964). Recent scholarship concerned with certain aspects of Jacobean expansion is assessed in Theodore K. Rabb, *Enterprise and Empire: Merchant and Gentry Investment in the Expansion of England, 1575–1630* (Cambridge, Mass. 1967).

8. ENGLISH POLITICS AND ADMINISTRATION 1603–1625

S. R. Gardiner, *History of England 1603–42*, vols I–IV (London 1883), gives the magisterial political account of the reign. D. H. Willson, *James VI and I* (London 1956) is a lively biography of a king whose financial irresponsibility and political ineptitude have been generally conceded. The controversy over the role of the gentry and of the position of the nobility is best summarised by J. H. Hexter, 'Storm over the Gentry', with a full bibliography, in his *Reappraisals in History* (Evanston 1961). W. R. Scott, *The Constitution and Finances of English, Scottish and Irish Joint-Stock Companies*, 3 vols (Cambridge 1912) suggests by its title a limited subject, but gives the most succinct, penetrating and authoritative analysis of Elizabethan and Jacobean finance and aspects of the economy, especially in the first volume. F. C. Dietz, *English Public Finance 1558–1641* (New York and London 1932) combines liveliness with massive detail, drawn largely from manuscript sources, on every aspect of the administration.

Robert Cecil, first earl of Salisbury, awaits his biographer. Professor Hurst-field dealt with Cecil's work in the Wards in his concluding chapters of *The Queen's Wards* (London 1958), and Professor Stone has investigated his profits as a minister in 'The Fruits of Office: The Case of Robert Cecil, First Earl of Salisbury', in *Essays In The Economic And Social History Of Tudor And Stuart England*, ed. F. J. Fisher (Cambridge 1961). Menna Prestwich in *Cranfield: Politics and Profits under the Early Stuarts* (Oxford 1966) gives a critical account of Salisbury's administration. The best biography of Bacon is that by E. A. Abbott, *Francis Bacon* (London 1885), which covers both his political career and also his writings. Cranfield, who left a mass of papers dealing with his private affairs and public career, has had two books, separate and independent studies, devoted to him, neither of which is strictly a biography. Professor Tawney in his *Business And Politics Under James I: Lionel Cranfield As Merchant And Minister* (London 1958) presented a triptych of Cranfield as a merchant, as an administrator and as a minister. The first panel, occupying nearly half the book, painted Cranfield in his role as merchant and speculator. M. Prestwich, op. cit., put more emphasis on administration, politics and the gains of office. The details in chapter 8 here have been drawn from this.

E. A. Abbott, *Bacon and Essex* (London 1877) gave a penetrating analysis of feuds and declining morality at the court; but Sir John Neale's studies of Elizabethan Parliaments and his lecture 'The Elizabethan Political Scene' *PBA* (1948), reprinted in his *Essays In Elizabethan History* (London 1958) have stimulated recent work on clientage, faction and corruption. It will be apparent that the present chapter owes much to the work of these two scholars. *The Letters of John Chamberlain*, ed. N. M. McClure (Philadelphia 1939), extremely entertaining and largely accurate, best gives the flavour of the period from the point of view of London and the Court. Geoffrey Goodman, *The Court of King James The First*, ed. J. S. Brewer (London 1839) is another lively source, especially illuminating both because of Bishop Goodman's friendship with Cranfield and also for the appendix of letters in vol II.

9. CONSTITUTIONAL IDEAS AND PARLIAMENTARY DEVELOPMENTS IN ENGLAND 1603–1625

M. A. Judson, *The Crisis of the Constitution* (New Brunswick 1949), and J. W. Gough, *Fundamental Law in English Constitutional History* (Oxford 1955) give the best accounts of Jacobean constitutional theory, although J. W. Allen's *English Political Thought 1603–1644* (London 1938) is also useful. G. L. Mosse argues, unconvincingly, in *The Struggle for Sovereignty in England* (East Lansing 1950) that there was a fundamental ideological breach between Crown and Commons as early as 1610. F. D. Wormuth provides an interesting discussion of *The Royal Prerogative 1603–49* (Ithaca 1939).

S. R. Gardiner covers James's reign in the first five volumes of his massive *History of England* (London 1883), and his account of parliamentary history—though inevitably out of date on some points—is still well worth reading. Wallace Notestein's *The House of Commons 1604–10* (New Haven 1971) is a detailed narrative which makes little attempt to place James's first Parliament in perspective. T. L. Moir, *The Addled Parliament of 1614* (Oxford 1958) and

Robert Zaller, *The Parliament of 1621* (Berkeley 1971) are much shorter and more analytical studies. Robert E. Ruigh has written a scholarly account of *The Parliament of 1624* (Cambridge, Mass. 1971), though, in his concentration on foreign policy, he neglects important domestic legislation.

Notestein's brilliant British Academy lecture *The Winning of the Initiative by the House of Commons* (London 1924) shows how opposition leaders came to dominate the House by the 1620s; but W. M. Mitchell's argument, in *The Rise of the Revolutionary Party in the English House of Commons 1603–1629* (New York 1957)—that there was an organised opposition 'party' in the Lower House by the 1620s—is not convincing. P. Zagorin makes some interesting comments on Jacobean parliamentary history in *The Court and the Country* (London 1969). J. R. Tanner, *Constitutional Documents of the Reign of James I* (Cambridge 1930), prints many of the most important parliamentary documents of the reign.

D. H. Willson gives the best account of the proposed union with Scotland in 'King James I and Anglo-Scottish Unity', *Conflict in Stuart England*, ed. W. A. Aiken and B. D. Henning (London 1960), and C. H. Firth discusses the rise of opposition to the Crown in the Upper House in *The House of Lords during the Civil War* (London 1910), which covers the period 1603–60. D. H. Willson has written a detailed account of *The Privy Councillors in the House of Commons 1603–29* (Minneapolis 1940), and Menna Prestwich provides an excellent study of the disruptive role of court faction in Jacobean Parliaments in her book on *Cranfield* (Oxford 1966). E. R. Foster analyses 'The Procedure of the House of Commons against Patents and Monopolies, 1621–1624', in *Conflict in Stuart England* (op. cit.), and Clayton Roberts discusses Jacobean impeachment proceedings in *The Growth of Representative Government in Stuart England* (Cambridge 1966).

10. THE CROWN AND THE COURTS IN ENGLAND 1603–1625

A selection of articles and monographs, varying in quality, is given in the notes to this paper. The surface has only been scratched and there is a need for many studies of courts and aspects of law. The situation is not however quite so dismal as might be supposed from a reading of the disappointing second edition by M. F. Keeler of the *Bibliography of British History: Stuart Period, 1603–1714* (Oxford 1970).

A good survey of some aspects is provided by E. W. Ives, 'The Law and the Lawyers', in *Shakespeare in his own Age*, ed. Allardyce Nicoll (Cambridge 1965), pp. 73–86. Institutions, as they existed at the end of James's reign, are described by G. E. Aylmer, *The King's Servants* (London 1961), pp. 44–57. W. S. Holdsworth, *History of English Law*, notably vols I and IV–VI, remains inescapable. The inadequacies of this work are evident, but Holdsworth cannot be held responsible for authors who cite him as an authority. Among single-volume histories of English law there is little to match the sense of historical discipline found in T. F. T. Plucknett, *A Concise History of the Common Law* (London 1956). Margaret A. Judson, *The Crisis of the Constitution* (New Brunswick 1949), is perceptive. Some themes are pursued in W. J. Jones, *Politics and the Bench* (London 1). .). Intelligent commentary on this period can be found in the following works: J. P. Dawson, *A History of Lay Judges* (Cambridge, Mass. 1960) and *The Oracles of the Law* (Ann Arbor 1968); J. P. Kenyon, *The Stuart Constitution* (Cambridge 1966).

II. THE ENGLISH LOCAL COMMUNITY AND LOCAL GOVERNMENT 1603–1625

There is no general account of local government in this period but the best descriptions of the framework are in *The Tudor Constitution*, ed. G. R. Elton (Cambridge 1960) and A. G. R. Smith, *The Government of Elizabethan England* (London 1967). The early chapters of E. A. L. Moir, *The Justice of the Peace* (London 1969) give a useful description of the development of the office of J.P. but have very little information about James's reign. Studies of individual counties are not numerous, partly because of the loss of records, and those which have been produced are concerned with a longer period than the one examined here. The most illuminating and important is J. Hurstfield, 'County Government c.1530–c.1660' in the *VCH Wiltshire*, v (London 1957), a many-sided analysis which can be read with pleasure. Unfortunately W. B. Willcox, *Gloucestershire: A Study in Local Government 1590–1640* (New Haven 1940) is much less impressive, partly because the author tackled too much in the space available. T. G. Barnes, *Somerset 1625–1640* (London 1961) includes a number of helpful insights into the Jacobean period. The best way to appreciate the problems of local government however is to examine the quarter sessional records, which have been published in many counties: the most convenient guide is F. G. Emmison and I. Gray, *County Records* (Historical Association, Helps series no. 62, 1961).

Detail about particular aspects of local government can be found in several general works. One of the most useful is L. O. J. Boynton, *The Elizabethan Militia, 1558–1638* (London 1967) which includes an invaluable chapter on James's reign. Although now very old and in need of revision, E. M. Leonard, *The Early History of English Poor Relief* (reprinted London 1965) remains the standard work; one of its strengths is the use Miss Leonard made of local records. Alehouse regulation and Sunday observance can be studied in the diverting collection of scholarly essays, *Englishmen at Rest and Play*, ed. R. L. Lennard (Oxford 1931). M. G. Davies, *The Enforcement of English Apprenticeship 1563–1642* (Cambridge, Mass. 1956) is mainly concerned with the central courts but has much to say about local apprenticeship problems. J. H. Gleason, *The Justices of the Peace in England 1558–1640* (Oxford 1969) is a curious book which amplifies a good deal of what was already known about the social composition of the county benches and includes useful lists. There is much more originality in works on various towns, the product of the increased interest recently in urban history. The following include a good deal about town government: W. T. MacCaffrey, *Exeter, 1540–1640* (Cambridge, Mass. 1958); J. W. F. Hill, *Tudor and Stuart Lincoln* (Cambridge 1956); G. C. F. Forster, 'York in the 17th Century', in *VCH City of York* (London 1961) and 'Hull in the 16th and 17th Centuries', in *VCH East Riding*, I, *City of Kingston upon Hull* (London 1969); R. Howell, *Newcastle-upon-Tyne and the Puritan Revolution* (Oxford 1967). Unfortunately there is little in print about the relations between central and local government but an important thesis, J. S. Cockburn, 'A History of English Assizes from 1558 to 1714' (Ph.D., Leeds, 1970), traces the influence of the assize judges on local affairs and is shortly to be published. County government in Stuart Yorkshire will be dealt with by G. C. F. Forster in a forthcoming book.

Notes and References

INTRODUCTION   *A. G. R. Smith*

1. For a good exposition of this picture see D. H. Willson, *King James VI & I* (1956), pp. 1–158.
2. The phrase is Professor Donaldson's in *Scotland James V – James VII* (Edinburgh 1965), where it forms the title of the large section of the book devoted to the reign of James VI & I.
3. Quoted by C. V. Wedgwood, 'Anglo-Scottish relations, 1603–40', *TRHS*, 4th ser. XXXII (1950), 31.
4. S. G. E. Lythe, *The Economy of Scotland 1550–1625* (Edinburgh 1960), p. 16.
5. Quoted by Donaldson, op. cit., p. 212.
6. L. Stone, *The Crisis of the Aristocracy* (Oxford 1965), p. 247.
7. K. Thomas, *Religion and the Decline of Magic* (1971), pp. 192–3; W. B. Rye, *England as seen by Foreigners in the days of Elizabeth and James I* (1865), p. 151.
8. Willson, op. cit., p. 337; Donaldson, op. cit., p. 186.
9. R. Ashton (ed.), *James I by his Contemporaries* (1969), p. 10.
10. D. H. Willson, 'James I and his Literary Assistants', *HLQ*, VIII (1944), 57.
11. This has recently been forcibly emphasised by Conrad Russell, *The Crisis of Parliaments* (1971), pp. 268–9.
12. *CJ*, I, 142.
13. G. Davies, 'The character of James VI & I', *HLQ*, V (1941–2), 63.
14. David Hume, *The History of Great Britain, the reigns of James I and Charles I* (Pelican edn, 1970), p. 216.
15. Willson, *James VI & I*, pp. 378, 425.
16. R. Zaller, *The Parliament of 1621* (Berkeley 1971); Robert E. Ruigh, *The Parliament of 1624* (Cambridge, Mass. 1971). See also below, pages 160, 175–6.
17. *EHR*, LXII (1957), 119.
18. I. Macalpine, R. Hunter and C. Rimington, 'Porphyria in the Royal Houses of Stuart, Hanover and Prussia', *BMJ* (6 Jan. 1968), pp. 10–11; I. Macalpine and R. Hunter, *George III and the Mad Business* (1969), pp. 201–9.
19. James was still certainly capable of making shrewd judgements at the very end of his life. Note especially his warning to Charles and Buckingham in 1624 about their dealings with Parliament.
20. Russell, op. cit., p. 257.
21. P. Laslett, *The World we have Lost* (1965), p. 9.
22. Boris Ford (ed.), *From Donne to Marvel* (Pelican, 1960 edn), p. 27.
23. The Millenary Petition is printed in J. R. Tanner, *Constitutional Documents of the Reign of James I* (Cambridge 1930), pp. 57–60.
24. P. Collinson, *The Elizabethan Puritan Movement* (1967), p. 452, stresses the moderation of the Petition.

25. For what follows see Mark H. Curtis, 'The Hampton Court Conference and its Aftermath', *History* (Feb. 1961).

26. The Canons of 1604 are printed in E. Cardwell, *Synodalia*, I (1842), 245–329. For a useful commentary on them see P. McGrath, *Papists and Puritans under Elizabeth I* (1967), pp. 357–60.

27. S. B. Babbage, *Puritanism and Richard Bancroft* (1962), p. 217.

28. Collinson, op. cit., pp. 460–61.

29. The best account of developments in the Church of England in the early seventeenth century is by N. R. N. Tyacke, 'Arminianism in England in Religion and Politics, 1604 to 1640' (Oxford University D.Phil. thesis, 1968). There is a good brief sketch in Russell, op. cit., pp. 210–17, and suggestive comments in W. Lamont, *Godly Rule, Politics and Religion 1603–1660* (1969).

30. Lamont, op. cit., p. 64.

31. H. R. Trevor-Roper, *Archbishop Laud* (2nd edn, 1965), pp. 56–7.

32. Collinson, op. cit., p. 461.

33. C. Hill, *Economic Problems of the Church* (Oxford 1956), pp. 14–15, 32–5, 150.

34. Lamont, op. cit., p. 56; Tyacke, op. cit., p. 264.

35. Willson, *James VI & I*, pp. 273, 364.

36. C. H. Carter, *The Secret Diplomacy of the Habsburgs 1598–1625* (New York 1964); 'Gondomar: Ambassador to James I', *HJ*, VII (1964), pp. 189–208.

37. For the strength of anti-Spanish feeling see G. Davies, 'English Political Sermons, 1603–40', *HLQ*, III (1939–40), 1–22; Louis B. Wright, 'Propaganda against James I's "Appeasement" of Spain', ibid., VI (1942–3), 149–72.

38. Maurice Lee, Jr, *James I and Henry IV, An Essay in English Foreign Policy, 1603–10* (Urbana 1970).

39. W. E. Minchinton (ed.), *The Growth of English Overseas Trade in the Seventeenth and Eighteenth Centuries* (1969), p. 8.

40. J. P. Cooper, 'The Fall of the Stuart Monarchy', *New CMH*, IV (Cambridge 1970), 534.

41. B. E. Supple, *Commercial Crisis and Change in England 1600–1642* (Cambridge 1959), p. 4.

42. J. U. Nef, 'The progress of Technology and the growth of Large-Scale industry in Great Britain, 1540–1640', *EcHR*, V (1934–5), 3–24; 'Prices and Industrial Capitalism in France and England, 1540–1640', *EcHR*, VII (1936–7), 155–85; *The Rise of the British Coal Industry*, 2 vols (1932); *War and Human Progress* (Cambridge, Mass. 1950).

43. For evidence against Nef's thesis, see D. C. Coleman, 'Industrial Growth and Industrial Revolutions', *Economica*, new ser. XXIII (1956), 1–22; L. A. Clarkson, *The Pre-Industrial Economy in England 1500–1750* (1971), pp. 99, 106–7, 115–16; F. J. Fisher, 'Tawney's Century', in *Essays in the Economic and Social History of Tudor and Stuart England*, ed. F. J. Fisher (Cambridge 1961), p. 6; P. J. Bowden, 'Agricultural Prices, Farm Profits and Rents', in *The Agrarian History of England and Wales*, IV, ed. J. Thirsk (Cambridge 1967), 607–9.

44. S. G. E. Lythe, op. cit., p. 1.

45. Ibid., pp. 15–23; T. C. Smout, *A History of the Scottish People 1560–1830* (1969), pp. 153–4; W. G. Hoskins, 'Harvest Fluctuations and English Economic History, 1480–1619', *AgricHR*, XII (1964), 28–46; 'Harvest Fluctuations and English Economic History, 1620–1759', *AgricHR*, XVI (1968), 15–31.

46. Ibid., pp. 18–19; Clarkson, op. cit., p. 235.

47. Smout, op. cit., p. 148; Lythe, op. cit., pp. 29–30.

48. Ibid., p. 16.

49. Bowden, op. cit., pp. 593, 690, 694–5; E. Kerridge, 'The Movement of Rent, 1540–1640', *EcHR*, 2nd ser. VI (1953–4), 16–34.

50. W. G. Hoskins, 'The Rebuilding of Rural England, 1570–1640', *Past and Present*, No. 4 (1953), 44–59; John Summerson, *Architecture in Britain 1530 to 1830* (1953), pp. 46–59.

51. A. Everitt, 'Farm Labourers', *The Agrarian History of England and Wales*, IV, ed. J. Thirsk, p. 398.

52. S. Pollard and D. W. Crossley, *The Wealth of Britain* (1968), pp. 83, 134; C. Wilson, *England's Apprenticeship 1603–1763* (1965), pp. 117–18; W. K. Jordan, *Philanthropy in England* (1959), p. 63; Bowden, op. cit., p. 605.

53. Pollard and Crossley, op. cit., p. 84; Fisher, op. cit., pp. 3–5; Wilson, op. cit., p. 236; Jordan, op. cit., p. 63; Everitt, op. cit., pp. 399, 438.

54. Ibid., pp. 435–6; R. B. Outhwaite, *Inflation in Tudor and Early Stuart England* (1969), p. 10; Bowden, op. cit., pp. 599, 601, 865.

55. J. Pound, *Poverty and Vagrancy in Tudor England* (1971), pp. 93–4.

I.   SCOTTISH POLITICS 1567–1625   *Jennifer M. Brown*

1. *Basilikon Doron of King James VI*, ed. J. Craigie, I (Scottish Text Society, 1944), 83.

2. W. C. Dickinson, *Scotland from the earliest times to 1603* (2nd edn, Edinburgh 1965), p. 354.

3. *CSP Scot*, VI, 523.

4. G. Donaldson, *Scotland: James V–VII* (Edinburgh 1965), pp. 61–2.

5. This is made very clear by the picture of the English aristocracy given in L. Stone, *The Crisis of the Aristocracy* (Oxford 1965), in the section entitled 'Power', pp. 199–270.

6. This phrase is used as a subtitle by Maurice Lee, *John Maitland of Thirlstane and the Foundation of the Stewart Despotism in Scotland* (Princeton 1959).

7. *Basilikon Doron*, I, 87.

8. *CSP Scot*, XII, 117; it should be stressed that James was making a joke, if a grim one, about the management of his finances, and not a general statement of policy.

9. *Basilikon Doron*, I, 117.

10. Ibid., I, 87.

11. *CSP Scot*, VI, 521.

12. D. H. Willson, *King James VI and I* (1966), p. 111.

13. *The Warrender Papers*, ed. A. I. Cameron, II (Scottish History Society, 1932), 299–301.

14. For details of Bothwell's career, see Donaldson, *James V–VII*, pp. 190–2.

15. The origins and use of the general band on the borders are discussed by T. I. Rae, *The Administration of the Scottish Frontier, 1513–1603* (Edinburgh 1966), pp. 116–19.

16. *Basilikon Doron*, I, 79, 71.

17. *RPC*, IX, 24–33; this gives both the bond by the chiefs of the Western Isles promising obedience to the king, and the Statutes of Iona.

18. *The Lag Charters, 1400–1720*, ed. A. L. Murray (Scottish Record Society, 1958), pp. 55–6.

19. *APS*, III, 624–5.

20. *Basilikon Doron*, I, 89. There is not space in this chapter to discuss this important subject fully. It is most effectively dealt with by G. Donaldson, *James V–VII*, pp. 222–6. Also J. R. Lander, 'Bonds, coercion and fear: Henry VII and the peerage', in *Florilegium Historiale: Essays presented to Wallace K. Ferguson* (Toronto 1971), argues convincingly that attempts by the Crown to strengthen royal justice should be seen as a policy of supplementing magnate justice rather than mounting 'a full frontal attack'; and it is probable that it was the former that James had in mind.

21. *RPC*, VI, 56–9.

22. *The Scots Peerage*, ed. J. Balfour Paul, IV (Edinburgh 1907), 305–14.

23. Sir William Purves, *Revenue of the Scottish Crown, 1681*, ed. D. Murray Rose (Edinburgh 1897), pp. xxxvii–xxxviii. I am indebted to Dr G. G. Simpson of the University of Aberdeen for drawing my attention to this letter. The text given here is a translation of the Scots original, which has an even stronger flavour of violent fury; indeed parts of it almost defy understanding.

24. Stone, *Crisis of the Aristocracy*, pp. 99–101.

25. I. B. Cowan, 'The Five Articles of Perth' in *Reformation and Revolution*, ed. D. Shaw (Edinburgh 1967), pp. 176–7. David Calderwood, *The History of the Kirk of Scotland* (Wodrow Society, 1842–9), VII, 488–501, gives an account of the passing of the Five Articles through Parliament and the voting list; he emphasises the amount of manipulation, the use of proxies and the widespread hostility to the Articles, though it must be remembered that he was hardly objective in his approach.

26. Willson, *James VI and I*, pp. 234–5.

27. Translated from Wotton's letter in Italian in Willson, *James VI and I*, pp. 136–7.

28. *Basilikon Doron*, I, 89.

29. Brian Manning, 'The Nobles, the People and the Constitution', *Past and Present*, IX (1956), 50. Manning is referring to England, and he therefore includes Parliament and the common law; but without these, his statement applies equally to Scotland, and makes a very valid point about the place of the monarchy.

30. Scottish R.O. Dalguise MS., GD 38/1/85b.

31. Quoted by D. H. Willson, 'Relations between Scotland and England in the Early Seventeenth Century', in *Scottish Colloquium Proceedings*, I (University of Guelph 1968), 16.

32. *The Political Works of James I*, ed. C. H. McIlwain (New York 1965), p. 294.

33. W. Taylor, 'The King's Mails, 1603–25', *SHR*, XLII (1963), 143–7.

34. Calderwood, *History*, VII, 250.

35. McIlwain, *Political Works of James I*, p. 291.

2.   THE SCOTTISH CHURCH 1567–1625   *Gordon Donaldson*

1. Hallam, quoted by P. Hume Brown, *History of Scotland*, II (Cambridge 1912), 224.

2. David Calderwood, *History of the Kirk of Scotland* (Wodrow Society, 1842–8), V, 439–40.

3. Gordon Donaldson, *The Scottish Reformation* (Cambridge 1960), p. 227.

4. This oath is printed, with the English Oath of Supremacy on the facing page, in W. Croft Dickinson and Gordon Donaldson, *Source Book of Scottish History*, III (Edinburgh 1954), 12–13.

5. Calderwood, III, 164.

6. *Wodrow Soc. Miscellany*, I (1844), 289–90.

7. Calderwood, III, 538, 542.

8. Ibid., V, 440.

9. Ibid., 531.

10. Ibid., 131.

11. Ibid., IV, 165.

12. John Knox, *History of the Reformation in Scotland* (ed. W. Croft Dickinson, 1949), II, 29.

13. Calderwood, IV, 499–501.

14. *CSP Scot*, X (1936), No. 441.

15. Hume Brown, op. cit., p. 205.

16. Calderwood, III, 717–18.

17. James Melville, *Autobiography and Diary* (Wodrow Society, 1842), p. 271.

18. Calderwood, V, 439–40.

19. Ibid., VI, 597.

20. The fullest examination of ecclesiastical administration in this period is unprinted (Walter Roland Foster, 'Ecclesiastical Administration in Scotland, 1600–1638', Edinburgh Ph.D. Thesis, 1963).

21. Archibald Johnston of Wariston, *Diary*, II (Scottish History Society, 1919), 23.

22. D. Harris Willson, *King James VI and I* (1956), p. 101.

23. The first and third drafts are printed in *Scottish Liturgies of James VI* (Church Service Society, 1901), the second in *Scottish History Society Miscellany*, X (1965).

24. *Original Letters relating to the ecclesiastical affairs of Scotland* (Bannatyne Club, 1851) II, 524.

25. *RPC*, XIII (1896), 744.

26. John Row, *History of the Kirk of Scotland* (Wodrow Society, 1842), pp. 377–8.

3.   THE ECONOMY OF SCOTLAND UNDER JAMES VI AND I
S. G. E. Lythe

1. On which see P. Hume Brown, *Scotland in the Time of Queen Mary* (1904) and M. Bingham, *Scotland under Mary Stuart* (1971).

2. T. Pagan, *The Convention of the Royal Burghs of Scotland* (Glasgow 1926).

3. J. Davidson and A. Gray, *The Scottish Staple at Veere* (1909) and M. P. Rooseboom, *The Scottish Staple in the Netherlands* (The Hague 1910).

4. Lord Cooper, 'The Numbers and Distribution of the Population of Mediaeval Scotland', *SHR*, XXVI (1947), 2ff.

5. G. S. L. Tucker, 'English Pre-Industrial Population Trends', *EcHR*, XVI (1963), 205ff.

6. G. Donaldson, *Scottish Historical Documents* (Edinburgh 1970), p. 162.

7. A. Maxwell, *Old Dundee Prior to the Reformation* (Edinburgh and Dundee 1891), p. 198.

8. Several are quoted in P. Hume Brown, *Early Travellers in Scotland* (Edinburgh 1891).

9. I. A. Bowman 'Culross Colliery: A Sixteenth-Century Mine', *Industrial Archaeology* 7 (1970), 353.

10. Quoted in full in A. Cochrane, *Description of the Estate of Culross* (Edinburgh 1793), pp. 9–11.

11. *Extracts from the Burgh Records of Dunfermline*, ed. A. Shearer (Dunfermline 1951), p. 126.

12. The history of precious metal mining is S. Atkinson, *The Discoverie and Historie of the Gold Mynes in Scotland* (original edn 1619, reprinted Bannatyne Club 1825). See also W. R. Scott, *The Constitution and Finance of Joint Stock Companies to 1720* (Cambridge 1910), II.

13. H. M. Robertson, 'Sir Bevis Bulmer', *Journal of Economic and Business History*, IV (1931), 101ff.

14. *Records of the Convention of the Royal Burghs of Scotland*, ed. J. D. Marwick, II (Edinburgh 1870), 107.

15. *RPC*, VII, 278–9.

16. J. A. Fleming, *Flemish Influence in Britain* (Glasgow 1930), I, 339.

17. J. U. Nef, *The Rise of the British Coal Industry* (1932), I, 185.

18. Ibid, I, 84.

19. Rooseboom, *Scottish Staple*, Document 119.

20. These and all subsequent Baltic trade figures are calculated from *Tabellar over Skibsfart og Varetransport gennem Øresund 1497–1660*, ed. N. E. Bang (Copenhagen 1922). It is now generally agreed that whilst this record is reliable on the number of ships it generally understates the quantity of commodities carried.

21. PRO, Exchequer and King's Remembrancer, E. 190/24/4.

22. *RPC*, VIII, 568–9.

23. Many are listed in R. Chambers, *Domestic Annals of Scotland* (Edinburgh 1858), I, 507–14.

24. See for example the essays in P. H. Ramsey (ed.) *The Price Revolution in Sixteenth Century England* (1971).

25. E. Burns, *The Coinage of Scotland* (Edinburgh 1887), II, 348, 411.

26. Hopetoun Papers, quoted in R. W. Cochran Patrick, *Records of the Coinage of Scotland* (Edinburgh 1876), I, 106.

27. *The Compt Buik of David Wedderburne*, ed. A. H. Millar, Scottish History Society, XXVIII (1898), 46, 71, 72.

28. Melros Papers, quoted in P. Hume Brown, *Scotland before 1700 from Contemporary Records* (Edinburgh 1893), p. 283.

29. J. Dow, 'Scottish Trade with Sweden', *SHR*, XLVIII (1969), 64–79 and 124–50.

30. W. Lithgow, *The Totall Discourse of the Rare Adventures and Painefull Peregrinations of long nineteene yeares travayles* (1632), p. 422.

31. J. D. Marwick, *The River Clyde and the Clyde Burghs* (Glasgow 1909), p. 45.

32. *RPC*, IX, 551.

33. Derived from the Treasurer's Accounts printed in *Extracts from the Records of the Burgh of Edinburgh*, VI (1936), Appendix XV.

34. *CJ*, I, 359.

35. See for instances *RPC*, VI, 577 and VII, 80, 114.

36. PRO, E. 190/308/4.

37. PRO, E. 190/101/28.

38. A. Murray, 'The Customs Accounts of Dumfries and Kirkcudbright', *Trans. of the Dumfries and Galloway Nat. Hist. and Antiq. Society* XLII (1965), 125.

39. *The Household Books of Lord William Howard*, Surtees Society (1877).

40. I have examined this more fully in 'The Union of the Crowns in 1603 and the Debate on Economic Integration' in *Scottish Journal of Pol. Econ.*, v (1968), 219–28.

41. *RPC*, XII 107.

42. Illustrated in my *The Economy of Scotland in its European Setting 1550–1625* (Edinburgh 1960), pp. 188 and 230.

43. *The Port Books of Boston*, ed. R. W. K. Hinton (1956), pp. xlv, 42, 43.

4. JAMES VI AND I AND WITCHCRAFT   *Christina Larner*

I am indebted to Professor H. R. Trevor-Roper and Mrs R. Mitchison for reading this chapter in typescript and for making a number of valuable suggestions.

1. See e.g. M. Summers, *The Geography of Witchcraft* (1927), pp. 201–53; R. Trevor Davies, *Four Centuries of Witch Beliefs* (1947), pp. 5–12; G. Parrinder, *Witchcraft* (1958), p. 25.

2. John Knox, *History of the Reformation*, ed. Laing (Edinburgh 1848) II, 383.

3. *The Book of the Universall Kirk of Scotland*, Maitland Club (1839) I, 19.

4. *Autobiography of James Melvill*, Wodrow Society (1842), p. 58.

5. Knox, op. cit., II, 486.

6. David Calderwood, *History of the Kirk of Scotland*, Wodrow Society (1842–9) III, 736.

7. G. F. Black, *A Calendar of Cases of Witchcraft in Scotland* (New York 1938), pp. 21–3.

8. 9. Geo. II c. 5, 1736, *The Statutes at Large* (1764), VI, 206–7.

9. 16 Mary c. 73, 1563, *APS* II, 539.

10. F. Legge, 'Witchcraft in Scotland', in *Scottish Review* (1891) XVII, p. 261.

11. Robert Bruce, *Sermons in the Kirk of Edinburgh* (Edinburgh 1591), reprinted in Wodrow (1843), p. 348.

12. Ibid., p. 354.

13. Ibid., p. 359.

14. Calderwood, op. cit., V, 129.

15. See e.g. Charles Williams, *James I* (1934), p. 106; C. and H. Steeholm, *James I of England* (1938), pp. 141–2; D. Harris Willson, *King James VI and I* (1963 edn), pp. 26, 65; and W. McElwee, *The Wisest Fool in Christendom* (1958), p. 71.

16. For a fuller account see Christina Larner, 'Scottish Demonology in the Sixteenth and Seventeenth Centuries' (unpublished Edinburgh University Ph.D. thesis, 1962), pp. 101–10.

17. *Ane fruitfull meditation* (Edinburgh 1588).

18. See Helen Stafford, 'Notes on Scottish Witchcraft Cases 1590–1591', in *Essays in Honor of Conyers Read* (Chicago 1953), pp. 96–118.

19. See G. F. Black, op. cit., p. 24.

20. The rumours were said to have been started by Peder Munk, admiral of the Danish fleet on both voyages, who wanted to blame the storms on the wife of a Copenhagen baillie whom he had insulted. There was already a tradition of trials in Copenhagen over naval disasters. See Bering Liisberg, *Vesten for Sø og Østen for hav Trolddom i København og i Edinburgh 1590* (Copenhagen 1909), pp. 7–26, and Robert Bowes, English ambassador to Scotland, to Burghley, 23 July 1590, *CSP Scot*, X 365.

21. D. Harris Willson, *King James VI and I*, p. 92.

22. G. L. Kittredge, 'English Witchcraft and James I', in *Studies in the History of Religions* (New York 1912), p. 3.

23. *CSP Scot*, x, 510.

24. Ibid., x, 514.

25. Ibid., x, 522.

26. Ibid., x, 523–5.

27. *News from Scotland* (1591), reprinted in David Webster's *Collection of Rare and Curious Tracts on Witchcraft* (Edinburgh 1820), p. 32.

28. *Daemonologie* (Edinburgh 1597), p. 2.

29. Ibid., p. 46.

30. Ibid., p. 5.

31. *Daemonologie*, p. 7.

32. See C. L'Estrange Ewen, *Witch-hunting and Witch Trials* (1929), pp. 112f. and Alan MacFarlane, *Witchcraft in Tudor and Stuart England* (1970), p. 28.

33. See Henry N. Paul, *The Royal Play of Macbeth* (New York 1950).

34. See e.g. G. Parrinder, *Witchcraft*, p. 28.

35. *Nugae Antiquae*, ed. T. Park (1804), I, 366–7.

36. *Meditation on the Lord's Prayer* (1619), pp. 125–6.

37. Macfarlane, op. cit.

38. *Religion and the Decline of Magic* (1971).

39. For a fuller discussion of the anthropological contribution to witchcraft history see Christina Larner, 'English and Scotch Witches', in *New Edinburgh Review* (Feb. 1971).

5. THE ENGLISH CATHOLIC COMMUNITY 1603–1625
John Bossy

1. S. R. Gardiner, *History of England . . . 1603–42*, I (1883), 231 f.

2. Conrad Russell, *The Crisis of Parliaments: English History, 1509–1660* (1971), p. 266.

3. A. J. Loomie, 'Toleration and Diplomacy: the Religious Issue in Anglo-Spanish Relations, 1603–5', *Transactions of the American Philosophical Society*, new series LIII, part 6 (1963); C. H. Carter, *The Secret Diplomacy of the Habsburgs* (New York and London 1964), esp. pp. 44 f., 55; John Bossy, 'Henri IV, the Appellants and the Jesuits', *Recusant History*, VIII (1965), 80–122; A. F. Allison, 'Richard Smith, Richelieu and the French Marriage', ibid., VII (1964), 148–201.

4. C. H. McIlwain (ed.), *The Political Works of James I* (Cambridge, Mass. 1918), Introduction; T. H. Clancy, 'English Catholics and the Papal Deposing Power, 1570–1640', *Recusant History*, VI (1962), 205–27, VII (1963), 2–10, partly reproduced in his *Papist Pamphleteers: the Allen-Persons party and the Political Thought of the Counter-Reformation in England, 1572–1615* (Chicago 1964); Aveling, *Northern Catholics*, p. 247.

5. *A Theological Disputation concerning the Oath of Allegiance* (1613), dedicatory Epistle, p. (15). For Widdrington, see McIlwain, op. cit., pp. lxxiii–xxv; W. K. L. Webb, 'Thomas Preston *alias* Roger Widdrington', *Biographical Studies* (=*Recusant History*), II (1953), 216–68; D. M. Lunn, 'The Origins and Early Development of the Revived English Benedictine Congregation' (Cambridge University Ph.D. thesis, 1970), pp. 307 ff.

6. Clancy, art. cit., VI, 211f., or *Papist Pamphleteers*, p. 92; cf. McIlwain, op. cit., p. lxxiii, for Widdrington; Tierney-Dodd, *Church History*, IV, p.

cxlvii, for Blackwell; Jordan, *Development of Religious Toleration in England*, II, 499f., 505, 514.

7. Cf. my Introduction to A. O. Meyer, *England and the Catholic Church under Queen Elizabeth* (1967 reprint), pp. xxvii, xxx, and p. 419 of text; Meyer's view is followed in substance by Jordan, op. cit., pp. 492ff. Clancy, *Papist Pamphleteers*, p. 99, indicates an approach similar to that taken here.

8. Bossy, 'Henri IV, the Appellants and the Jesuits', pp. 87–91.

9. Tierney-Dodd, *Church History*, IV, pp. cxxxvi, clxxvi; *CSP Dom., 1611–18*, p. 28; R. Challoner, *Memoirs of Missionary Priests*, ed. J. H. Pollen (1924), pp. 293, 303f.; Clancy, 'English Catholics and the Papal Deposing Power', VII, 3, for a defence of the deposing power written by one of the secular clergy leaders, Matthew Kellison, in 1617.

10. As most recently argued by Francis Edwards, *Guy Fawkes: The Real Story of the Gunpowder Plot?* (1969); cf. eg. Aveling, *West Riding*, pp. 229f. Edwards does however bring out some neglected aspects of the plot, notably its connection with the progress of Anglo-Spanish relations.

11. Gardiner, *History of England*, i, 246, 273f.; H. R. Trevor-Roper, *The Gentry, 1540–1640* (*EcHR* Supplements, no. 1, s.d.), pp. 38f.; P. Caraman, *Henry Garnet and the Gunpowder Plot* (1964), pp. 302, 305.

12. Edwards, *Guy Fawkes*, pp. 63–5.

13. Loomie, 'Toleration and Diplomacy', pp. 31, 40–41; Bossy, 'Henri IV, the Appellants and the Jesuits', p. 104 and n. 130 (the person referred to should be, not the earl of Arundel, but Lord Arundell of Wardour); Lunn, 'Origins and Development of the English Benedictine Congregation', pp. 80, 85–99; Edwards, *Guy Fawkes*, p. 82. I am pleased to find the point of view taken here supported by Russell, *The Crisis of Parliaments*, p. 264.

14. Cf. Clancy, *Papist Pamphleteers*, pp. 94f., also 120ff., for Catholic difficulties in grasping the common-law framework within which much English political argument was conducted after 1600.

15. Tierney-Dodd, *Church History*, III, pp. clxxxi–iii (Brief *Venerunt nuper*, 1602); IV, p. cclxxx (erection of chapter, 1623); Hughes, *Rome and the Counter-Reformation in England*, pp. 312 ff.; *Letters of Thomas Fitzherbert, 1608–10* ed. L. Hicks, Catholic Record Society, XLI (1948), 4–43 passim; P. Guilday, *The English Catholic Refugees on the Continent* (1914), pp. 307ff. (Douai).

16. Meyer, *England and the Catholic Church*, p. 458; Hughes, *The Reformation in England*, III (1954), 395.

17. Tierney-Dodd, *Church History*, III, p. clxxxi.

18. Caraman, op. cit., (n. 11); for Blount, Bernard Basset, *The English Jesuits* (1967), pp. 156–89; for Fitzherbert, Catholic Record Society, xli, 1–3, and some comments in my 'Character of Elizabethan Catholicism', in T. Aston (ed.), *Crisis in Europe, 1560–1660* (1965), p. 245.

19. The Jesuit statistics from 1621 are in Foley, *Records of the English Province*, VII, part 1, table facing p. clxviii; Basset, *The English Jesuits*, p. 164; Aveling, *Northern Catholics*, pp. 235f.

20. Aveling, *Northern Catholics*, pp. 164f., 236f.; Caraman, *Henry Garnet*, p. 318; Basset, *English Jesuits*, pp. 168–74; *Camden Miscellany*, II (Camden Society, 1853), 21–64.

21. Examples in *Letters and Memorials of Robert Persons*, i, ed. L. Hicks, Catholic Record Society, XXXIX (1942), 98, 108, 321–40; Caraman, *Henry Garnet*, pp. 45f., 88, 103f., 216f.

22. *Letters of Robert Persons*, I, 322, 332; Caraman, *Henry Garnet*, pp. 104,

217; 'Modus vivendi hominum Societatis', in Foley, *Records of the English Province*, II, 3–6 (written in 1616, though the phrase quoted comes from a comment added in the 1640s).

23. Caraman, *Henry Garnet*, pp. 45f., 88, 172, 215ff.; Foley, *Records of the English Province*, IV, 333ff. (Somersets); II, 311, 316f., and VII, part 2, pp. clxiif. (financial records of the 'College of the Immaculate Conception' or Derbyshire district; with *VCH Leicestershire*, II, 67f., these references indicate that the large funds of this district came from the Vaux sisters); II, 396f. (Petres). Other benefactions went to build Jesuit establishments abroad: Basset, *English Jesuits*, pp. 160f.

24. Basset, *English Jesuits*, pp. 162–7; for the same concern among the Benedictines, Lunn, 'Origins and Development of the English Benedictine Congregation', p. 162.

25. Foley, *Records of the English Province*, VII, part 2, 1112; III, 257f.; cf. Aveling, *Northern Catholics*, p. 237.

26. Richard Sibbes, quoted in Christopher Hill, *Economic Problems of the Church from Archbishop Whitgift to the Long Parliament* (Oxford 1956), p. 245.

27. Most recently studied in D. M. Lunn, thesis cited above, n. 5, though this still leaves one rather in the dark about the operation of the Benedictine mission in England.

28. Jordan, *Development of Religious Toleration*, II, 54, 70f., uses the term 'missionary party' in a different and, I think, inappropriate sense.

29. Hughes, *Rome and the Counter-Reformation in England*, pp. 367, 411; Allison, 'Richard Smith, Richelieu and the French Marriage' (above, n. 3), pp. 156–7. The emergence of the issue from about 1600 may be traced in T. G. Law (ed.), *The Archpriest Controversy*, (2 vols, Camden Society, 1896, 1898), I, 54, 195; Caraman, *Henry Garnet*, p. 315; Catholic Record Society, XLI, 94, 100. I have tried to indicate some wider implications of the argument in my 'Postscript' to H. O. Evennett, *The Spirit of the Counter-Reformation* (Cambridge 1968), pp. 135–42.

30. View put forward in W. J. Trimble, *The Catholic Laity in Elizabethan England* (Cambridge, Mass. 1964), esp. chs. II & III; cf. the sharp comment of J. P. Kenyon, *The Stuart Constitution* (Cambridge 1966), p. 448, n. 6.

31. It would take too long to justify these figures here; they are my own calculations based on the evidence in B. Magee, *The English Recusants* (1938), pp. 83, 96ff.; for a local example which supports them, see the estimates for Yorkshire in Aveling, 'Some Aspects of Yorkshire Catholic Recusant History, 1558–1791', in G. J. Cuming (ed.), *Studies in Church History*, IV (Leiden 1967), 110, n. 1.

32. Aveling, *Northern Catholics*, pp. 235–43, and *West Riding*, p. 237; Jordan, *Development of Religious Toleration*, II, 493; Mathew, *The Jacobean Age*, pp. 11, 230.

33. Cf. Mathew, op. cit., p. 11.

34. Stone, *The Crisis of the Aristocracy*, pp. 729f., 741; Mathew, *The Jacobean Age*, pp. 238ff., 27f. (Arundells), 124f. (Howards); R. B. Manning, *Religion and Society in Elizabethan Sussex* (Leicester 1969), pp. 159ff. (Brownes); Keith Lindley, 'The Lay Catholics of England in the Reign of Charles I', *Journal of Ecclesiastical History*, XXII (1971), 201 (Paulets); F. H. Pugh, 'Monmouthshire Recusants in the Reigns of Elizabeth and James I', *South Wales and Monmouthshire Record Society Publications*, no. 4 (1957), 59–110, and R. Mathias, *Whitsun Riot* (1963).

35. Stone, Crisis of the Aristocracy, p. 242; Penry Williams, 'The Northern Borderland under the Early Stuarts', in H. E. Bell and R. L. Ollard (eds), Historical Essays, 1600–1750, presented to David Ogg (1963), pp. 11f.; Joan Wake, The Brudenells of Deene (2 edn, 1954), pp. 101ff.; W. H. B. Court, The Rise of the Midland Industries, 1600–1838 (1953 edn), p. 90; Catholic Record Society, XXII (1921), 156f.

36. Catholic Record Society, LVI (1964), 1–20; Margaret Blundell, Cavalier: Letters of William Blundell to his Friends, 1620–1698 (1933); for Blundell's father, head of the family during James's reign, T. E. Gibson (ed.), Crosby Records (Chetham Society, 1887), pp. 45ff.

37. A. C. Southern (ed.), An Elizabethan Recusant House (London/Glasgow 1954); J. Morris (ed.), Troubles of our Catholic Forefathers, III (1877), 467f.; Wm. Palmes [S.J.], Life of Mrs Dorothy Lawson (ed. G. B. Richardson, Newcastle upon Tyne 1851).

38. Southern, op. cit., pp. 35, 47f.; Palmes, op. cit., pp. 38, 40, 42f.

39. Claire Cross, The Royal Supremacy in the Elizabethan Church (1969), pp. 112f.; Aveling, 'Some Aspects of Yorkshire Catholic Recusant History', (op. cit., n. 31), p. 105.

40. A. L. Rowse, The England of Elizabeth (1950), pp. 450, 454; J. E. Neale, Elizabeth I and her Parliaments, 1584–1601 (1957); Trimble, The Catholic Laity in Elizabethan England, pp. 151f.; Tierney-Dodd, Church History, IV, pp. ccxxvii–xxxiii.

41. Keith Thomas, Religion and the Decline of Magic (1971), pp. 74, 182, 187, 202, 488–9, 492; note the long series of references to Jesuit reports of exorcism, etc., p. 489, n. 1.

42. Foley, Records of the English Province, VII, part 2, 1109; another story, ibid., p. 1143, of a Protestant servant converted while teaching a poor Catholic woman to read her prayer-book.

43. E.g. the account of the Lancashire career of the Benedictine Ambrose Barlow, in Challoner, Memoirs of Missionary Priests, pp. 392ff.; though Barlow also had a reputation as an exorcist.

44. Stone, Crisis of the Aristocracy, p. 731, who probably exaggerates the prevalence of an attitude which may only have become general later on; Mathew, The Jacobean Age, pp. 231f.

45. Helen C. White, English Devotional Literature (Prose), 1600–1640 (Madison, Wisconsin 1931), pp. 64–8, 75ff., 89–115, 131–52; Louis L. Martz, The Poetry of Meditation (New Haven/London 1962 edn).

46. The First Book of the Christian Exercise, appertaining to Resolution (1st edn Rouen 1582), p. 6; cf. my 'Character of Elizabethan Catholicism', Crisis in Europe, 1560–1660, pp. 230–2, 245f. The classic example of the reception of the 'Book of Resolution' in seventeenth-century England is in Matthew Sylvester (ed.), Reliquiae Baxterianae (1696), p. 3.

6. ENGLISH OVERSEAS TRADE IN THE REIGN OF JAMES I
Brian Dietz

I wish to thank my colleague Dr L. K. J. Glassey for reading this chapter in typescript and for making a number of valuable suggestions.

1. A register of laden ships entering the port of London in the year from Michaelmas 1599 reveals that 79 per cent of the total of 54,511 tons came from

France and countries to the north, 11 per cent from the Peninsula and the Mediterranean and 3 per cent from the Atlantic islands. PRO E190/11/1. See also L. R. Miller, 'New evidence on the shipping and imports of London, 1601–1602', in *Quarterly Journal of Economics*, XLI (1927).

2. For the Elizabethan background see especially F. J. Fisher, 'Commercial trends and policy in sixteenth-century England' in *EcHR* x (1940); L. Stone, 'Elizabethan overseas trade', ibid., 2nd ser. II (1949); G. D. Ramsay, *English Overseas Trade in the Centuries of Emergence* (1957); T. S. Willan, *Studies in Elizabethan Foreign Trade* (Manchester 1959) and *Early History of the Russia Company* (Manchester 1956); K. R. Andrews, *Elizabethan Privateering* (Cambridge 1964).

3. The uncertain relationship between harvest fluctuations and trade is discussed by B. E. Supple, *Commercial Crisis and Change in England 1600–1642* (Cambridge 1959), pp. 14–19.

4. Astrid Friis, *Alderman Cockayne's Project*, p. 145 *et seq.* The debates are discussed by R. Ashton and T. K. Rabb in *Past and Present*, nos 38 (Dec. 1967), 40 (Jul. 1968), 43 (May 1969).

5. W. B. Stephens, 'The West-Country Ports and the Struggle for the Newfoundland Fisheries in the Seventeenth Century', *Trans. Devon Assn for the Advancement of Science . . . Arts*, LXXXVIII (1956); G. T. Cell, *English enterprise in Newfoundland 1577–1660* (Toronto 1969), ch. VI.

6. Bertha Hall, 'The Trade of Newcastle upon Tyne and the North-East Coast, 1600–1640' (London M.A. thesis, 1934). The same trends were observable at Boston: see *The Port Books of Boston 1601–1640*, ed. R. W. K. Hinton (Lincoln Record Society, 1956).

7. 'England's Treasure by Foreign Trade' printed in *Early English Tracts on Commerce*, ed. J. R. McCulloch (1856).

8. *CJ*, I, 987.

9. The figure quoted in note 1 above may be compared with 2,201 tons of incoming ships at Exeter in the same year and 5,119 at Bristol in 1594–5. PRO E190/937/6; 1131/10.

10. On London see Millard, Fisher and Supple, as cited in the Bibliographical Note.

11. Friis, op. cit., p. 177.

12. E.g. Exeter, where most of the merchants also specialised. Cf. Stephens, *Seventeenth Century Exeter*, pp. 44–6.

13. Lionel Cranfield; see R. H. Tawney, *Business and Politics under James I* (1958), p. 67. Although T. K. Rabb's list of company members (see Bibliographical Note) shows that many merchants joined more than one trading organisation, evidence of their actual business suggests that they did tend to specialise. Cf. Friis, op. cit., pp. 177–8, 232–3.

14. Friis put most of the blame on the Cockayne fiasco, but Supple, J. D. Gould, 'The trade depression of the early 1620s', in *EcHR* 2nd ser. VII (1954–5) and R. W. K. Hinton (see Bibliographical Note) independently arrive at the conclusion that monetary factors were at the root of the crisis.

15. Friis, op. cit., pp. 231–3.

16. H. Taylor, 'Price Revolution or Price Revision? The English and Spanish Trade after 1604', *Renaissance and Modern History* XII (1968).

17. *Crisis and Change in the Venetian Economy in the Sixteenth and Seventeenth Centuries*, ed. B. Pullen (1968).

18. R. Davis, 'England and the Mediterranean, 1570–1670' in *Essays in the Economic and Social History of Tudor and Stuart England*, ed. F. J. Fisher

(Cambridge 1961); A. C. Wood, *History of the Levant Company* (Oxford 1935).

19. As well as his book cited in the Bibliographical Note, see K. N. Chaudhuri, 'The East India Company and the Export of Treasure in the early Seventeenth Century', in *EcHR* 2nd ser. XVI (1963–4).

20. Supple, op. cit., p. 198. This paragraph is largely based on Supple, ch. 9, but see also J. D. Gould, 'The Trade Crisis of the early 1620s and English Economic Thought', *Journal of Economic History*, XV (1955).

21. As collated and analysed by Millard.

22. Taylor, loc. cit. But compare the claim made in 1626 that England shipped bullion from Spain to half the value of commodity imports. Tawney, op. cit., pp. 28–9.

23. W. R. Scott, *The Constitution and Finance . . . Joint Stock Companies*, I, 184–5.

24. Rabb, op. cit., pp. 38 seq.; J. Parker, *Books to Build an Empire* (Amsterdam 1965), ch. XI.

25. Supple, op. cit., p. 9.

26. Ralph Davis, 'English Foreign Trade, 1660–1700', in *EcHR* 2nd ser. VI (1954).

27. In 1617 Trinity House, Deptford, made a survey of London's shipping in the previous year for a proposed tax assessment to combat the Barbary corsairs. From this data it can be calculated that 50 per cent of the total tonnage of 56,205 plied routes north of Cape Finisterre, 28 per cent south and west of the Cape, with 22 per cent employed in the East India trade. These proportions may be compared with shipping movements for 1599/1600 given above in note 1. I am grateful to Mr Geoffrey Harris for making available transcripts of the relevant documents in the Trinity House Deptford MSS Transactions, 1609–25.

7. COLONIAL DEVELOPMENTS IN THE REIGN OF JAMES I
Louis B. Wright

1. Cited from V. T. Harlow's edition of *The Discovery of the Large, Rich, and Beautiful Empire of Guiana* (1928), p. 72, by Louis B. Wright, *The Colonial Search for a Southern Eden* (University of Alabama, 1953), p. 15.

2. Samuel Purchas, *Hakluytus Posthumus, or Purchas His Pilgrims* (Glasgow 1906), XVI 385.

3. From John Smith, *A Map of Virginia* (1612). This passage is reprinted in *The Elizabethans' America*, edited by Louis B. Wright (1965), p. 183.

8. ENGLISH POLITICS AND ADMINISTRATION 1603–1625
Menna Prestwich

1. J. E. Neale, *Elizabeth I and her Parliaments 1584–1601* (1957), p. 212; W. Notestein, 'The Winning of the Initiative by the House of Commons', in *PBA*, XI (1924), 175.

2. 'Harrington's Interpretation Of His Age', in ibid., XXVII (1941), 161.

3. *Society and Puritanism in Pre-Revolutionary England* (1964), p. 134; *Intellectual Origins of the English Revolution* (Oxford 1965), pp. 2, 287, 34–5.

4. *Angevin Kingship* (1955), pp. 1–2.

5. Art. cit., p. 25.

6. *EcHR*, XI (1941); ibid., XVIII (1948); ibid., Supplement 1, 'The Gentry 1540–1640' (1953).

7. *The Crisis of the Aristocracy 1558–1641* (Oxford 1965), pp. 6, 13.

8. *Business And Politics Under James I: Lionel Cranfield as Merchant and Minister* (1958).

9. John Hacket, *Scrinia Reserata, A Memorial of John Williams* (1692), I, 104.

10. *LJ.*, III, 344.

11. Sir George Carew, *A Relation of the State of France with the Characters of Henri IV, and the Principal Persons of that Court* (1609), 1749 edn, p. 484.

12. Ibid., p. 436.

13. Geoffrey Goodman, *The Court of King James The First*, ed. J. S. Brewer (1839), I, 322.

14. *Fragmenta Regalia* (1641), cited J. E. Neale, 'The Elizabethan Political Scene' in *Essays in Elizabethan History* (1958), pp. 79–80.

15. Op. cit., I, 39.

16. Goodman, op. cit., I, 174.

17. HMC *Salisbury MSS*, XVII, 76.

18. A. G. R. Smith, 'The secretariats of the Cecils, circa 1580–1612', *EHR*, LXXXIII (1968).

19. Report of Sir Robert Pye in *EHR*, XIII, 721–2, 729; D. Mathew, *The Jacobean Age* (1938), Appendix, pp. 323, 330–1.

20. *The Journal of Sir Roger Wilbraham, Camden Misc.*, X (1902), 114; L. Stone, 'The Building of Hatfield House', in *Archaeological Journal*, CXII (1956), 128.

21. Goodman, op. cit., I, 204.

22. J. Spedding, *The Works of Francis Bacon* (1857–74), IV, 278.

23. J. Hurstfield, *The Queen's Wards* (1958), pp. 297–325; J. E. C. Hill, *The Century of Revolution* (Edinburgh 1961), p. 39; L. Stone, 'The Fruits of Office: The Case of Robert Cecil, First Earl of Salisbury, 1596–1612', in *Essays in The Economic and Social History of Tudor and Stuart England*, ed. F. J. Fisher (Cambridge 1961), p. 115.

24. L. Stone, ibid., p. 112.

25. W. R. Scott, *The Constitution And Finance Of English, Scottish and Irish Joint-Stock Companies to 1720* (Cambridge 1912), I, 23–4, 96–7, 134–6.

26. HMC *Salisbury MSS*, XVII, 220 (10 Aug. 1604).

27. Ibid., XVII, 630–1 (1605).

28. Ibid., XVI, 394.

29. HMC *Cranfield Papers 1551–1612*, I, 146 (18 Aug. 1607).

30. *Fortescue Papers*, ed. S. R. Gardiner (Camden Soc., 1871). Gardiner, in contrast to recent favourable verdicts on Salisbury's administration, deplored the redundancy, p. 90, note 2.

31. Scott, op. cit., I, 139; Spedding, op. cit., VII, 86–7. Professor Hurstfield, on the other hand, speaks of 'the tremendous drive behind Salisbury's scheme to increase the revenue through impositions' in *History*, 56 (1971), 238.

32. HMC *Salisbury MSS*, XVIII, 164; L. Stone, art. cit., 'The Fruits of Office', p. 100; M. Prestwich, op. cit., p. 35.

33. *Parliamentary Debates in 1610*, ed. S. R. Gardiner (Camden Society, 1852), Appendix D, pp. 163–79.

34. *The Letters of John Chamberlain*, ed. N. E. McClure (Philadelphia 1939), I, 358 (17 Jun. 1612).

35. Ibid., I, 533 (26 May 1614).

36. *The Court And Times Of James The First* (1848), I, 336.

37. Hacket, op. cit., I, 148.

38. J. Rushworth, *Historical Collections* (1721), I, 456; Hacket, op. cit., I, 39; *The Autobiography of Sir Simonds D'Ewes*, ed. J. O. Halliwell (1845), I, 166.

39. Spedding, op. cit., V, 187 (1615); for a full discussion of the Cockayne project, see B. E. Supple, *Commercial Crisis and Change in England 1600–1642* (Cambridge 1959); for details of Cranfield's proposals, see M. Prestwich, op. cit., ch. IV.

40. Spedding, op. cit., V, 275; M. Prestwich, op. cit., p. 204.

41. *Fortescue Papers*, op. cit., pp. 90–1 (12 Oct. 1619).

42. Spedding, op. cit., VII, 110, 116 (23 Jul., 7 Oct. 1620); M. Prestwich, op. cit., p. 250.

43. S. R. Gardiner, *History of England 1603–42* (1883), III 98.

44. Hacket, op. cit., I, 39.

45. Goodman, op. cit., II, 216–17 (4 Dec. 1621).

46. Rushworth, op. cit., I, 339.

47. *Ben Jonson*, ed. C. H. Herford and Percy and Evelyn Simpson (Oxford 1925–52), I, 192

48. Neale, op. cit., p. 69.

49. *Debates in the House of Commons 1621*, ed. Notestein, Relf and Simpson (New Haven 1935), V, 517–18, 526–7.

50. M. Prestwich, op. cit., p. 371. Professor Tawney, *Business and Politics*, pp. 221–2 was more optimistic that the Crown had reached solvency in so far as annual expense was concerned, but he also wavered, since he conceded that the surplus shown on the account of 1624 might be fictitious and that 'a diminished deficit would be nearer the truth'.

51. Hacket, op. cit., I, 225.

9. CONSTITUTIONAL IDEAS AND PARLIAMENTARY DEVELOPMENTS IN ENGLAND 1603–1625
Alan G. R. Smith

I wish to thank my colleagues, Mr P. J. Parish, Mr G. B. A. M. Finlayson and Dr B. Dietz for reading this chapter in typescript and for making valuable suggestions.

1. *The House of Commons 1604–10* (New Haven 1971), pp. 504–5.

2. *The Parliament of 1621* (Berkeley 1971). Robert E. Ruigh is also sympathetic to James in *The Parliament of 1624* (Cambridge, Mass. 1971).

3. *The Crisis of the Constitution* (New Brunswick 1949).

4. *The Struggle for Sovereignty in England* (East Lansing 1950).

5. C. H. McIlwain (ed.), *The Political Works of James I* (Cambridge, Mass. 1918), pp. 307–8.

6. J. R. Tanner (ed.), *Constitutional Documents of the Reign of James I* (Cambridge 1930), pp. 260–61.

7. J. W. Gough, *Fundamental Law in English Constitutional History* (Oxford 1955), pp. 31–2.

8. S. R. Gardiner (ed.), *Parliamentary Debates in 1610*, Camden Society Publications, LXXXI (1862), 24.

9. Tanner, p. 261.

10. Gough, pp. 37, 41.

11. *CJ*, I, 254.

12. Tanner, p. 341.

13. J. Spedding, *The Letters and the Life of Francis Bacon*, IV (1868), 177.

14. Tanner, pp. 25, 278.

15. *LJ*, III, 250.

16. Tanner, pp. 28, 78, 276, 278.

17. *CJ*, I, 143, 314, 315.

18. E. R. Foster (ed.), *Proceedings in Parliament 1610*, II (New Haven 1966), 344.

19. Judson, pp. 229–30.

20. *CJ*, I, 158.

21. *Calendar of State Papers Venetian 1603–07* (1900), p. 479.

22. *CJ*, I, 511.

23. Frances Relf (ed.), *Notes of the Debates in the House of Lords 1621–8*, (1929), pp. 5–7.

24. D. H. Willson, *The Privy Councillors in the House of Commons 1604–29* (Minneapolis 1940), passim. For the events of 1614 see T. L. Moir, *The Addled Parliament of 1614* (Oxford 1958).

25. M. Prestwich, *Cranfield, Politics and Profits under the Early Stuarts* (Oxford 1966), pp. 135ff., 286ff., 423ff.

26. Tanner, p. 222.

27. W. Notestein, *The Winning of the Initiative by the House of Commons* (British Academy Raleigh Lecture in History, 1924), passim; *The House of Commons 1604–10*, pp. 435ff.

28. Foster, I, 279.

29. W. M. Mitchell, *The Rise of the Revolutionary Party in the English House of Commons 1603–29* (New York 1957), p. 53.

30. *CJ*, I, 431.

31. Tanner, pp. 289, 286.

32. 21 Jac. I c.33. *Statutes of the Realm*, IV (1819), 1247–62.

33. E. R. Foster, 'The Procedure of the House of Commons against Patents and Monopolies, 1621–1624', *Conflict in Stuart England*, ed. W. A. Aiken and B. D. Henning (1960), p. 75.

34. 21 Jac. I c.3. *Statutes of the Realm*, IV, 1212–14.

35. For the revival of impeachment see C. Roberts, *The Growth of Responsible Government in Stuart England* (Cambridge 1966), ch. 1.

36. HMC *Mar and Kellie, Supplementary* (1930), p. 200. Robert E. Ruigh stresses the conflict between Charles and Buckingham on the one hand and the king on the other over foreign policy in 1624. *The Parliament of 1624*, passim.

37. *APC 1621–23*, p. 110.

38. Edward Hyde, earl of Clarendon, *The History of the Rebellion and Civil Wars in England*, ed. W. Dunn Macray, I (1888), 28.

39. F. D. Wormuth, *The Royal Prerogative 1603–49* (Ithaca 1939), p. 93.

10. THE CROWN AND THE COURTS IN ENGLAND 1603–1625
W. J. Jones

1. J. Hawarde, *Les Reportes del Cases in Camera Stellata*, ed. W. P. Baildon (1894), pp. 176–7; T. F. T. Plucknett, *A Concise History of the Common Law* (1956), pp. 50, 487.

2. D. E. C. Yale, Introduction to E. Hake, *EPIEKEIA* (New Haven 1953), p. xvi.

3. H. Hulme, 'Charles I and the Constitution', in *Conflict in Stuart England*, ed. W. A. Aiken and B. D. Henning (1960), pp. 89, 93.

4. Christopher Hill, *Intellectual Origins of the English Revolution* (Oxford 1965), p. 246.

5. Gardiner commented that 'the natural tendency of the judges was to put forward on every occasion the authority of the sovereign.' S. R. Gardiner, *History of England*, I (1887), 335; R. W. K. Hinton, 'The Decline of Parliamentary Government under Elizabeth I and the Early Stuarts', *CHJ* (1957), p. 129; 'English Constitutional Theories from Sir John Fortescue to Sir John Eliot', *EHR* (1960), pp. 421, 422.

6. J. P. Kenyon, *The Stuart Constitution* (Cambridge 1966), p. 8.

7. Elizabeth R. Foster, *Proceedings in Parliament, 1610* (New Haven 1966), I, xvi.

8. HMC *Hastings*, IV, 256, 263.

9. P. Williams, *The Council in the Marches of Wales under Elizabeth I* (Cardiff 1958); 'The Activity of the Council in the Marches under the Early Stuarts', *WHR* (1961), pp. 133–60; 'The Attack on the Council in the Marches, 1603–1642', *THSC* (1961); R. R. Reid, *The King's Council of the North* (1921); F. W. Brooks, *The Council in the North* (1963); G. T. Lapsley, *The County Palatine of Durham* (Cambridge, Mass. 1900); R. A. Marchant, *The Church under the Law* (Cambridge 1969); see also P. Tyler, Introduction to R. G. Usher, *The Rise and Fall of the High Commission* (Oxford 1968).

10. T. G. Barnes, 'Star Chamber Mythology', *AJLH* (1961), pp. 1–11; 'Due Process and Slow Process in the Late Elizabethan–Early Stuart Star Chamber', *AJLH* (1962), pp. 221–49, 315–46.

11. W. J. Jones, *The Elizabethan Court of Chancery* (Oxford 1967).

12. Marjorie Blatcher, 'Touching the Writ of Latitat: an Act "of no great moment"', in *Elizabethan Government and Society*, ed. S. T. Bindoff, Joel Hurstfield and C. H. Williams (1961), pp. 188–212; Plucknett, p. 130.

13. H. E. Bell, *An Introduction to the History and Records of the Court of Wards and Liveries* (Cambridge 1953); Joel Hurstfield, *The Queen's Wards* (1958).

14. *The Life and Letters of Sir Henry Wotton*, ed. L. P. Smith (Oxford 1907), II, 490.

15. Add. MSS, 14822, f.14; W. S. Holdsworth, *History of English Law*, I (1956), 423–4; 'The Rights and Jurisdiction of the County Palatine of Chester', ed. J. B. Yates, *Chetham Misc.* (1856), p. 28; Jones, pp. 120–21, 159.

16. T. Powell, *The Attourney's Academy* (1623), subtitle.

17. Sir E. Coke, Preface, *The Fourth Part of the Institutes of the Lawes of England* (1669).

18. W. B. J. Allsebrook, 'The Court of Requests in the Reign of Elizabeth' (London University M.A. thesis, 1937), pp. 156–7.

19. Reid, pp. 316–19; Brooks, pp. 26–9; *APC 1613–14*, pp. 219–21.

20. J. P. Dawson, *The Oracles of the Law* (Ann Arbor 1968), p. 48.

21. Powell, p. 168.

22. Involvement with the Crown has often been interpreted as a weakness but such an approach pays too much attention to the notion of independence assumed by later generations. The performance and position of the judges would certainly raise questions during the reigns of James I's son and grandsons; it may have been the wrong kind of strength, but it certainly was not weakness.

23. *The Political Works of James I*, ed. C. H. McIlwain (New York 1918), pp. 334–5. On this occasion—it was 1616—James allowed his own sense of

grievance to appear: 'none of you but will confess you have a King of reasonable understanding, and willing to reform.'

24. J. P. Cooper, 'The Fall of the Stuart Monarchy', in *New CMH*, IV, ed. J. P. Cooper (Cambridge 1970), p. 539; Kenyon, pp. 103, 106.

25. Hawarde, p. 255.

26. Cf. Dawson, pp. 68–73.

27. This experiment, inaugurated before Coke's appointment to the bench, ended early in the reign of Charles I.

28. Williams, *Council in the Marches of Wales*, pp. 224–5; 'Attack on the Council', pp. 3–6; 'Activity of the Council', pp. 138–9; H. A. Lloyd, *The Gentry of South-West Wales, 1540–1640* (Cardiff 1968) pp. 167–73; Reid, pp. 316–19; HMC *Salisbury*, XVII, 466.

29. J. R. Tanner, *Constitutional Documents of the Reign of James I* (Cambridge 1930), p. 182; *State Trials*, II, 134.

30. HEH El. 2010.

31. 1 Brownl., 44, 46; 2 Brownl., 1–3, 27–8, 38–9; Marchant, p. 113.

32. Win., 78, 103; 2 Brownl., 7; Edith G. Henderson, *Foundations of English Administrative Law* (Cambridge, Mass. 1963), pp. 121, 122.

33. Coke, *Fourth Institute*, pp. 135–8; Holdsworth, I, 550–8; 1 Brownl., 42; 2 Brownl., 16–17, 26–7, 30; W. J. Jones, 'Ellesmere and Politics, 1603–1617', *Early Stuart Studies*, ed. H. S. Reinmuth (Minneapolis 1970), pp. 24–5; J. Campbell, *The Lives of the Chief Justices of England* (1849), p. 360; Allsebrook, pp. 70–1, 113, 152–9; Jones, *Chancery*, pp. 82, 382; Coke, *Fourth Institute*, pp. 97–8.

35. Tyler, p. xxiii; 2 Brownl., 14–16, 18–20, 37.

36. 2 Brownl., 18–20.

37. Tanner, pp. 146–8, 186–7.

38. Coke, *Fourth Institute*, p. 136; *Political Works of James I*, pp. 312–13; HEH El, 2008, 2010; Kenyon, pp. 73–5.

39. Tanner, pp. 162–3.

40. Tyler, p. xxxiii; HEH El, 1988, 2013.

41. *The Egerton Papers*, ed. J. P. Collier (Camden Society 1840), pp. 446–8.

42. The point is made by Cooper, p. 535.

43. Hawarde, p. 54.

44. W. J. Jones, *Politics and the Bench* (1971), pp. 80–3.

45. Jessie L. Stoddart, 'Constitutional Crisis and the House of Lords, 1621–1629', (University of California, Berkeley, Ph.D. thesis, 1966).

46. E. W. Ives, 'The Law and the Lawyers', in *Shakespeare in his Own Age*, ed. Allardyce Nicoll (Cambridge 1965), p. 73.

47. Dawson, pp. 72–3. Plucknett, p. 281.

48. T. L. Moir, *The Addled Parliament of 1614* (Oxford 1958), p. 95.

49. Cited D. Veale, *The Popular Movement for Law Reform, 1640–1660* (Oxford 1970), p. 1.

II. THE ENGLISH LOCAL COMMUNITY AND LOCAL GOVERNMENT 1603–1625   *G. C. F. Forster*

1. A. M. Everitt, 'Social mobility in early modern England', *Past and Present*, No. 33, p. 59.

2. R. H. Tawney in his Introduction to D. Brunton and D. H. Pennington, *Members of the Long Parliament* (1954), p. xvi.

3. See Bibliographical Note for general surveys.

4. J. C. Sainty, *Lieutenants of Counties, 1585–1642* (*BIHR*, Supplement no. 8, 1970), pp. 2–9, 11–40.

5. *The Earl of Hertford's Lieutenancy Papers, 1603–1612*, ed. W. P. D. Murphy, Wiltshire Record Society, XXIII, 5, 10.

6. *The Montagu Musters Book, A.D. 1602–1623*, ed. J. Wake, Northamptonshire Record Society, VII, pp. xiii–lxii; L. O. J. Boynton, *The Elizabethan Militia, 1558–1638* (1967), chs 2 and 7.

7. For what follows I have drawn extensively on Boynton, *The Elizabethan Militia*, ch. 7.

8. *Montagu Musters Book*, pp. 3–53; *Hertford's Lieutenancy Papers*, pp. 7–9, 13–14.

9. *Hertford's Lieutenancy Papers*, p. 11; *Montagu Musters Book*, pp. 53–194; J. Hurstfield, 'County Government c.1530–c.1660' in *VCH Wiltshire*, V, 84–8.

10. *Hertford's Lieutenancy Papers*, pp. 11–13.

11. E.g. PRO, State Papers Domestic, James I, L, no. 97.

12. Boynton, *Elizabethan Militia*, ch. 8.

13. Hurstfield, *VCH Wiltshire*, V, 93. Grand larceny involved the theft of goods valued at more than 12d.

14. 'Undersettlers', sometimes called 'inmates', were squatters or undesirable dwellers in crowded tenement properties. See G. C. F. Forster, 'York in the 17th Century', *VCH York*, passim, and 'Hull in the 16th and 17th Centuries', *VCH East Riding*, I, *City of Kingston upon Hull*, passim; J. W. F. Hill, *Tudor and Stuart Lincoln* (Cambridge 1956), p. 134.

15. *North Riding Quarter Sessions Records*, I and II, ed. J. C. Atkinson, North Riding Record Society, passim; S. S. Tollit, 'The First House of Correction for the County of Lancaster', *Transactions of the Historic Society of Lancashire and Cheshire*, CV, pp. 69–78.

16. W. K. Jordan, *Philanthropy in England 1480–1660* (1959), pp. 126–7, 130–2, 244–5; Forster, *VCH York*, pp. 171–2 and *VCH Hull*, p. 163; Hurstfield, *VCH Wilts*, V, 94 seq.; E. M. Leonard, *The Early History of English Poor Relief* (reprinted 1965), pp. 138, 167, 213, 223, 243.

17. M. W. Beresford, 'The Common Informer, the Penal Statutes and Economic Regulation', *EcHR*, 2nd ser. X, 10, 222, 224–7.

18. G. D. Ramsay, *The Wiltshire Woollen Industry* (Oxford 1943) pp. 61–2; Forster, *VCH York*, p. 166; H. Heaton, *The Yorkshire Woollen and Worsted Industries* (Oxford 1920) passim; M. G. Davies, *The Enforcement of English Apprenticeship 1563–1642* (Cambridge, Mass. 1956), pp. 83–4, 138 seqq., 195, 276.

19. R. K. Kelsall, *Wage Regulation under the Statute of Artificers* (1938), pp. 1–59; Ramsay, *Wilts Woollen Industry*, p. 62.

20. North Riding Record Office, Sessions Minutes and Orders, III, fols. 276 seqq.

21. *Englishmen at Rest and Play*, ed. R. L. Lennard (Oxford 1931), pp. 162 seqq.

22. A. H. A. Hamilton, *Quarter Sessions from Queen Elizabeth to Queen Anne* (1878), pp. 67 seqq.

23. HMC *Salisbury*, XX, 127, 153–4, 175, 226, 244, 250; Leonard, *English Poor Relief*, pp. 144 seqq., 185.

24. See *APC* for the period 1620–5, passim; Ramsay, *Wilts Woollen Industry*, pp. 76, seqq., Leonard, *English Poor Relief*, pp. 144 seqq., 185 seqq.,

243; B. E. Supple, *Commercial Crisis and Change in England 1600–1642* (Cambridge 1959), pp. 64–72.

25. Hurstfield, *VCH Wiltshire*, v, 97–9, 104.

26. *APC 1616–17*, pp. 255–6, 281–2, 301, 355; *Official Papers of Sir Nathaniel Bacon*, ed. H. W. Saunders, Camden Society, 3rd ser. XXVI, 26–7.

27. Hurstfield, *VCH Wiltshire*, v, 103–4.

28. *Diary of Lady Margaret Hoby*, ed. D. M. Meads (1930), pp. 3, 33–4, 36–7, 269–72; C. H. D. Howard, *Sir John Yorke of Nidderdale* (1939), passim; H. Aveling, *Northern Catholics* (1966), pp. 202 seqq. The episodes are treated in greater detail in my *County Government in Stuart Yorkshire* (forthcoming).

29. T. G. Barnes, *Somerset 1625–1640* (1961), p. 285.

30. R. R. Reid, *The King's Council in the North* (1921), pp. 382 seqq.; C. V. Wedgwood, *Thomas Wentworth* (1961), pp. 30 seqq.; A. F. Upton, *Sir Arthur Ingram* (1961), pp. 164 seqq.

31. Reid, *Council in the North*, pp. 327 seqq; R. Howell, *Newcastle upon Tyne and the Puritan Revolution* (Oxford 1967), p. 28; W. T. MacCaffrey, *Exeter 1540–1640* (Cambridge, Mass. 1958), pp. 218 seqq.; Forster, *VCH York*, pp. 197–8.

32. *North Country Diaries*, ser. 2, Surtees Society, CXXIV, 6.

33. P. H. Williams, 'The Northern Borderland under the Early Stuarts', in *Historical Essays 1600–1750*, ed. H. E. Bell and R. L. Ollard (1963), pp. 1–17.

34. Hurstfield, *VCH Wiltshire*, v, 106.

35. J. S. Cockburn, 'A History of English Assizes from 1558 to 1714' (Ph.D. thesis, Leeds, 1970), pp. 346 seqq.

36. *APC 1613–14*, pp. 265–7; ibid., *1621–3*, pp. 291–2, 358, 411–12.

37. Hamilton, *Quarter Sessions*, pp. 78 seqq.; *Sir Nathaniel Bacon's Papers*, p. 24; Barnes, *Somerset 1625–1640*, p. 88.

38. J. Hawarde, *Les Reportes del Cases in Camera Stellata*, ed. W. P. Baildon (1894), pp. 367–8; Cockburn, op. cit., pp. 321 seqq.

39. *Constitutional Documents of the Reign of James I, 1603–1625*, ed. J. R. Tanner (Cambridge 1961), pp. 19–21.

Notes on Contributors

JOHN BOSSY, Lecturer in History, University of Belfast; graduate of Cambridge. He has written articles on early modern English and European Catholicism and has edited *The Spirit of the Counter Reformation* by H. E. Evennett (1968).

JENNIFER M. BROWN, Lecturer in Scottish History, University of Glasgow; graduate of Glasgow. She is preparing a study of the Scottish nobility from the fifteenth to the seventeenth centuries.

BRIAN DIETZ, Lecturer in History, University of Glasgow; graduate of London. His main interest is early modern English trade and he has edited a London Record Society Publication, *The Port and Trade of Early Elizabethan London* (1972).

GORDON DONALDSON, Professor of Scottish History and Palaeography, University of Edinburgh; graduate of Edinburgh and London. Author of *The Making of the Scottish Prayer Book of 1637* (1954); *The Scottish Reformation* (1960); *Scotland—James V to James VII* (1965) and of many other books and articles.

GORDON C. F. FORSTER, Senior Lecturer in Modern History, University of Leeds; graduate of Leeds. He has written extensively on English local history in the early modern period and has a forthcoming book, *County Government in Stuart Yorkshire*.

WILLIAM J. JONES, Professor of History, University of Alberta; graduate of London. Author of the *Elizabethan Court of Chancery* (1967); *Politics and the Bench* (1971) and of articles on sixteenth and seventeenth century English legal history.

CHRISTINA LARNER, Lecturer in Sociology, University of Glasgow; graduate of Edinburgh. Author of articles on English and Scottish witchcraft and an unpublished Edinburgh University Ph.D. thesis, 'Scottish Demonology in the Sixteenth and Seventeenth Centuries'.

S. G. E. LYTHE, Professor of Economic History, University of Strathclyde; graduate of Cambridge. Author of *Life and Labour in Dundee from the Reformation to the Civil War* (1958); *The Economy of Scotland in its European Setting 1550–1625* (1960); and of articles on Scottish economic history.

MENNA PRESTWICH, Fellow of St Hilda's College and Lecturer in Modern History in the University of Oxford; graduate of Oxford. Author of *Cranfield: Politics and Profits under the Early Stuarts* (1966) and of articles on early modern English and European history.

ALAN G. R. SMITH, Lecturer in History, University of Glasgow; graduate of Glasgow and London. Author of *The Government of Elizabethan England* (1967); *Science and Society in the Sixteenth and Seventeenth Centuries* (1972);

and joint editor (with J. Hurstfield) of *Elizabethan People: State and Society* (1972).

LOUIS B. WRIGHT, Director, Folger Shakespeare Library, Washington D.C., 1948–68; graduate of Wofford College and of the University of North Carolina. His numerous books include *Middle Class Culture in Elizabethan England* (1935); *The Cultural Life of the American Colonies* (1957); *The Dream of Prosperity in Colonial America* (1965); *The History of the Thirteen Colonies* (1967).

Index